# DATE DUE

|  |  |  |  |
|---|---|---|---|
|  |  |  |  |
|  |  |  |  |
|  |  |  |  |
|  |  |  |  |
|  |  |  |  |
|  |  |  |  |
|  |  |  |  |
|  |  |  |  |
|  |  |  |  |
|  |  |  |  |
|  |  |  |  |
|  |  |  |  |
|  |  |  |  |
|  |  |  |  |
|  |  |  |  |
|  |  |  |  |
|  |  |  |  |
|  |  |  |  |
|  |  |  |  |

DEMCO 38-296

# TELEVISION UNDER THE TORIES

# TELEVISION UNDER THE TORIES

## Broadcasting Policy: 1979–1997

Peter Goodwin

 Publishing

First published in 1998 by the
British Film Institute
21 Stephen St, London W1P 2LN

The British Film Institute is the UK national agency with responsibility for encouraging
the arts of film and television and conserving them in the national interest.

British Library Cataloguing-in-Publication Data
A catalogue record for this book is available from the British Library

ISBN 0–85170–613 4 (hbk)
    0–85170–614 2 (pbk)

Cover design: Swerlybird Art & Design
Cover image: *Spitting Image*, 1990 (Central Broadcasting).

Set in Minion by Fakenham Photosetting Limited, Fakenham, Norfolk
Printed in Great Britain by St Edmundsbury Press, Bury St Edmunds

# Contents

# Acknowledgments

This book was originally conceived of as an account of the 1991 ITV franchise race. That task was both more speedily and ably performed by Andrew Davidson's *Under the Hammer* (Davidson, 1992). So my book changed in scope and tone. My thanks to Tana Wollen and Richard Paterson for originally commissioning it, and to Richard for patiently and good-humouredly nudging it through its transformation and eventual realisation. My thanks, too, to the BFI for a very generous research grant. My apologies to them all, for my unforgivable slowness in repaying their faith.

Charlie Brown, Jonathan Davis, Tom O'Malley, Colin Sparks and Jane Ure Smith read and commented on an earlier draft. My thanks to all of them – they have greatly improved my earlier efforts – and my apologies for not taking on board all of their thoughtful comments.

Most of the research for this book was done at the library of the Independent Television Commission (ITC). The ITC performs an invaluable public service by providing an excellent open-access library on the matters of its concern – a policy which should put the BBC, OFTEL and the Radio Authority to shame. The staff of the ITC library are not only knowledgeable, they are also unfailingly helpful. My thanks to them for their inestimable help, and my apologies for my inordinate demands.

Conventionally, books are dedicated. I happily take advantage of that convention by dedicating this one to my parents, John and Irene Goodwin.

# 1 Forces for Change?

Television as a mass medium was born (in the USA and Britain) in the 40s. By the early 60s it had spread to virtually all industrialised countries. And by the 1970s it had long been seen throughout the industrialised and industrialising world – whether for good or bad – as the established mass medium *par excellence.*

We may usefully term this whole long period – from the 40s right through to the second half of the 70s – the 'first wave' of television. For all the changes in organisation and developments in programming that took place in those thirty or so years, essentially the new mass medium of television functioned in the same fashion throughout. As Jay Blumler neatly puts it:

> Based on a single delivery system (broadcast air waves), television consisted of a small number of channels, programmed by a comparatively small number of competitors for viewers' attention. The main sources of finance, lines of industry organisation, and patterns of audience patronage were relatively stable. (Blumler, 1991, p. 194)

There were, of course, major national differences between how that handful of channels was managed. In the USA television, from its birth, had been in private hands, albeit subject to a substantial degree of state regulation supposedly in the public interest. In most of Europe the channels had been in state or (as the industry often preferred to see itself) 'public' ownership. In a few industrialised countries (most notably Britain) there was, on the face of it, a mixture of the two systems – some of the handful of channels being publicly owned, others in private ownership but subject to substantial state regulation. This question of national differences in organisation was by no means unimportant. But, that said, Blumler's neat summary retains its essential truth. Television's first wave was characterised by a few terrestrial channels, with secure and stable sources of revenue, and a high degree of state regulation – broadcasting, free to air, a generalised range of programming to a mass audience.

Beginning, roughly, from the end of the 70s, this established and relatively stable pattern of organisation that had characterised television's first wave was thrown open to challenge:

> 'A gale of creative destruction' [Blumler takes the term from the economist Joseph Schumpeter (1942)] has been unleashed on electronic media systems throughout the advanced industrial world. An extraordinary mix of technological, organisational, financial, and political factors has disrupted the familiar patterns of such [broadcasting] systems and forced their architects to re-examine and redeploy their resources. (Blumler, 1991, p. 194)

Two decades after the challenge to television's first wave began, the process of re-examination and reorganisation has not yet reached a final conclusion. But, already, by the second half of the 80s and early 90s, it had given rise to a spate of books and articles on 'The new television marketplace' or 'The broadcasting revolution'. In one sense this book follows along that path. But it takes advantage of the fact that it is written a few years after much previous discussion. Many earlier commentators were describing changes which were only just beginning. During the last few years we have seen many of the new developments translate into practice. Two decades into television's second wave is surely more than enough time to begin to make a considered assessment of the process – and begin to assess later achievements against earlier plans. This book is a contribution to that assessment. Its direct focus is narrow, in two ways.

First, it is about one country – the United Kingdom (or Britain, as I shall often colloquially, if not entirely accurately, call it).

Second, it is about how, during this period, a particular national government (the Conservative administrations of Margaret Thatcher and John Major, 1979–1997) attempted to influence the processes of change in television. This is, then, a book about *government policy* on television in a period of upheaval in the industry. It is *not* about how the various players in the industry responded to that upheaval, although, of course, those industrial players are never far from the centre of our story.

For most readers in the UK this specific focus will not need much justification. We, after all, have to live with the consequences. For readers outside the UK (and more internationally minded readers within it) a little more justification is required. Four things, I suggest, make the UK experience of more than mere parochial interest.

First, the UK may not be the USA or Japan, but it is still, on a world scale, a comparatively large and comparatively highly industrialised country, and one that possesses a rather 'mature' television system. If the widespread developments in television that I have just identified have any reality, one would surely expect them to be operating here.

Second, because we live in a world in which nation states, with their own particularities, remain important in policy formulation, global tendencies must still work themselves out in a national framework. Particularly when it comes to government policy, and particularly when it comes to television, it is dangerous to neglect the concrete national case study for the neat abstract global generalisation.

Third, in the wake of worldwide political, economic and social changes of the last two decades, the UK Conservative government – particularly under Margaret Thatcher – has been widely viewed as something of an international pioneer. So, for anyone generally interested in television policy, the activities of this pioneer in the field of television should have particular importance.

Lastly, from the birth of the medium, UK television and its organisation have carried special international significance. Rightly or wrongly, the 'BBC model' was much imitated outside the UK during television's first wave. It still continues to be looked on for inspiration: for example, in Eastern Europe (Jakubowicz, 1993, p. 23). To the extent that the UK broadcasting model has been internationally imitated, so, to the same degree, how the original of that model has fared in the face

2

of the global challenges of the 80s and 90s is also a matter worthy of international concern.

What was this 'extraordinary mix of technological, organisational, financial, and political factors' that threatened to up-end the stable system of television's first wave? There were a number of different sets of factors, which often interacted, and, even more often, were claimed to interact. They are, however, logically distinct. It is worthwhile starting by disentangling these different forces at work in the challenge to the traditional structures of television. And, having disentangled them, it is worth subjecting each to some preliminary critical scrutiny.

Four general pressures for change in television can be distinguished – the economic, the social and cultural, the technological and the political.

Television's first wave had coincided with what many economists have called the 'Great Boom'. From the 40s to the early 70s the economies of the industrialised world were characterised by high employment, relatively constant economic growth and with it the growth of mass consumption, and a high degree of state intervention and public spending. With those features went a 'welfare consensus'.

In the 70s this post-war economic and social order broke down. 'The "oil crisis" of winter 1973–4 and an international crash in the summer of 1974 brought the golden years to an abrupt and painful end.' (Armstrong et al., 1984, p. 309) That did not, however, mean a return to the 30s – a return to chronic slump and stagnation; the two decades since the mid-70s have witnessed some important bursts of economic growth. But it did mean that, in Eric Hobsbawm's words, 'the history of the twenty years after 1973 is that of a world which lost its bearings and slid into instability and crisis' (Hobsbawm, 1994, p. 403). The reasons why the Great Boom came to an end, and the nature of the new economic order which succeeded it have been, and continue to be, the subject of enormous debate. This is not the place to even begin to go into that discussion. But, amid the contending analyses, one feature of the decades after 1973 stands out:

> The central fact about the Crisis Decades is not that capitalism no longer worked as well as it had done in the Golden Age, but that its operations had become uncontrollable. Nobody knew what to do about the vagaries of the world economy or possessed instruments to manage them. The major instrument for doing so in the Golden Age, government policy, nationally or internationally co-ordinated, no longer worked. The crisis decades were the era when the state lost its economic powers. (Hobsbawm, 1994, p. 408)

If state intervention no longer delivered the goods, or at least no longer delivered them with any certainty, then it is scarcely surprising that a system of television so bound up with the state intervention of the post-war boom should feel the consequences. However, the very nature of the television systems of the first wave meant that any such consequences were unlikely to occur simply through the unmediated workings of the world economy. The gale of a more internationally competitive global economic order could – and did – blow away shipyards and machine-tool factories simply by the strength of its own force, regardless of what governments might try to do.

But television was different. Its own domestic 'markets' were protected by the technical limitations of terrestrial broadcasting and by the cultural limitations of national difference. So the traditional television systems could be more easily

3

shielded from the economic storm. The fact that there might be cheaper programming produced elsewhere would not produce an automatic effect on systems which catered for domestic tastes. Brazilian *telenovellas* might be cheaper to produce than *Coronation Street*, and they were certainly much cheaper to acquire, but they wouldn't get you sixteen million British viewers. And even if they could, the 'customers' of television were almost wholly private households, who had much less ability to evade national regulation than business consumers. The dominant technology of terrestrial distribution was peculiarly susceptible to national regulation. In order for those national television systems to be opened up to the general economic storm, other factors for change would have to make the initial breach. Then, and only then, could the forces of the world economy begin to do whatever direct work they were capable of.

One such initial impulse for change might be social and cultural changes occurring within the domestic market. If the culture of the domestic audiences moved away from the culture supplied by the television systems of the first wave, then that might generate a pressure for change from within, which in turn could open up those national systems to further economic challenge. Such a scenario needs to be taken seriously. Much discussion about society and culture in the industrialised world in the 80s and 90s has focused on the increasing fragmentation of mass culture, a growing awareness of 'difference' between genders, ethnic groups, sexual orientations and generations and the growth of more individualised lifestyles. Alongside, and not necessarily in contradiction with this, many other commentators have claimed to perceive a growing globalisation of culture. If either, or both, developments occurred sufficiently strongly, then they might indeed generate an audience revolt against traditional television systems. Those systems of television's first wave were, after all, established and perfected precisely to cater for *mass* audiences and for *national* audiences. If those mass audiences fragmented, or those national audiences globalised, then here surely was a force for the initial breach.

But there are a number of problems with this line of thinking. First, the claim of mass audience fragmentation is often considerably overdone. Reviewing some very interesting audience research from the USA in the late 70s and early 80s, W. Russell Neuman concludes:

> Within the mass of mass society there is a vital diversity of interests and tastes that are frustrated by the process of aggregation and homogenization practised by the major media industries ... But in pursuing the matter of different cultural and informational motivations, perceptions, and worldviews one finds reason to pause. The elements of adventure, humour, violence, sex and pathos have been consistently present in primordial myths, nineteenth-century novels, and modern media fare (perhaps in roughly equal proportions). (Neuman, 1991, p. 127)

The television channels of the first wave had often been peculiarly adept at providing that mix of elements. So long as they continued to provide that mix, sufficiently updated and of a satisfactory 'quality', the handful of general television programme channels have since shown considerable ability to retain the lion's share of the audience, against their particularist niche challengers. If this was true in the USA, it has been even more true in Europe.

Second, whatever fragmentation of culture was occurring, it might to some

4

degree be accommodated within the traditional handful of channels under state control or substantial state regulation. Indeed, as we shall see in Chapters 2 and 3, such an attempt was made in Britain. The Annan Committee on the future of broadcasting in the late 70s specifically and prominently identified some important new cultural demands among the changing UK television audience, and proposed to allocate the fourth available UK terrestrial channel to meet them. The proposal was put into effect, in modified form, in the early 80s, with the establishment of Channel Four. Both for the new channel itself, and in its impact on the rest of the channels, this attempt to address new and more diverse audience demands, within the framework of a limited number of highly regulated terrestrial channels, was not without success.

Third, if the claims about the fragmentation of the mass audience can be overdone, so too can be the claims about the globalisation of the national audience. In the 80s there was much debate in Europe, in both policy and academic circles, about the prospect of 'Wall-to-wall Dallas' (Collins, 1990, pp. 151–2). Most commentators saw this as a threat to viewers' interests; a minority saw it as a positive development. But whether seen as threat or benefit, both approaches claimed to discern a real growth in the taste for 'international' (in practice, American) television programming among viewers. But despite the changes that have taken place in the structures of television over the past decade – changes which might have been expected to reinforce this globalisation tendency – all the evidence of the last two decades shows that, at least in Europe, domestic television audiences have retained a stubborn preference for domestically produced programmes. A handful of American programmes still achieve massive international primetime success. But today no one talks about 'Wall-to-wall *X Files*' or 'Wall-to-wall *Baywatch*', for the good reason that such programmes are the exception rather than the rule. Save for made-for-cinema feature films, primetime viewing in most large European countries in the second half of the 90s continues to be captured by domestically made programming. This, it needs to be stressed, implies no normative judgment – popular domestic programmes could be of both a lower as well as a higher intellectual level than *Dallas*. But it does suggest that a tendency to more globalised television consumption simply did not exist as a decisive pressure on the television industry. In that respect television stands in stark contrast to cinema, where the audience has indeed moved decisively away from the national, and towards the distorted global culture of Hollywood, whatever national governments have tried to do to stop it.

Lastly, even if television viewers were dissatisfied, they could not, under the television systems of the first wave, vote with their feet. For technical reasons, terrestrial television broadcasting had only a slight overspill across national frontiers. In contrast, terrestrial *radio* broadcasting has displayed rather more transnational overspill, and offshore pirates or 'official' foreign commercial radio broadcasters have sometimes been able to capitalise significantly on the dissatisfaction of domestic audiences. Paddy Scannell and David Cardiff argue that Radio Luxembourg did this in Britain in the 30s (Scannell and Cardiff, 1991, pp. 228–32, 295–8, 376). Eli Noam argues that radio pirates were an important early factor in the changes of European broadcasting in the 80s (Noam, 1991, p. 5). But, in television, so long as terrestrial broadcasting remained technically the only possibility, pirates had no such opportunity.

So, discontented television audiences would have to stick with what they were given – or act politically to change it. In Britain, at least, there has been little evidence of such mass political demands in the television field. One result of this is that the UK debate on television policy, which this book chronicles, has been, despite the vigour of some of its protagonists, largely confined to élite circles. 'How to organise television' was never even a marginal feature of British election campaigns in the 70s, 80s or 90s. Viewers' desires figured prominently as objects of discussion in the élite debate, but primarily in terms of real or supposed expectations, rather than as conscious articulators of immediate political demands.

There were undoubtedly some significant changes in the culture of television audiences from the mid-70s onwards. They influenced both public policy and existing broadcasters, and, once the old systems were changed, they have no doubt had other effects. But, for a combination of the reasons given above, these changes were not directly decisive in the initial challenge to the old established television systems, and, as we shall see, this was particularly so in Britain. So, perhaps in contrast to some other spheres of economic and social change of the last two decades – for example, health and education (where opting out of the public system has long been a real possibility for the rich) or telecommunications (where business customers were important) – in television the consumer was not the first mover. As Kenneth Dyson and Peter Humphreys observed in 1990 in their international survey of changing communications markets and policies: 'compared with telecommunications, broadcasting policy has been less demand driven' (Dyson and Humphreys, 1991, p. 13).

On the face of it, technological change has played a far more important part in the 'broadcasting revolution' than changes in consumer preferences. Three different supposed technological changes have been widely seen from the mid-70s as playing a central role in the challenge to the old broadcasting systems. Two of these were new technologies of distribution for television – cable and direct broadcasting by satellite. The third was the technical 'convergence' of broadcasting, telecommunications and computing, and the digital 'revolution' which underpinned it. Each of these three technological developments, and its possible effects, needs distinguishing. And each warrants some preliminary close critical examination.

Cable and direct broadcasting by satellite each produced the same result. They effectively abolished, or at the very least substantially alleviated, the 'spectrum scarcity' of terrestrial television. Whereas terrestrial television had been technically limited to delivering only a handful of channels (although rarely as few as national regulators cared to allocate), cable and satellite could each provide dozens.

There were, however, two important differences between cable and satellite. Direct broadcasting by satellite was a genuine technological innovation of the 70s. Before then it was, quite simply, not technologically possible (telecommunication satellites were a development of the 60s, dish sizes small enough to enable practical DBS a development of the 70s). Furthermore, as well as eliminating (or qualitatively diminishing) spectrum scarcity, direct broadcasting by satellite allowed television broadcasting to significantly spill over across national frontiers. The old threat of the offshore radio stations would now be extended to television. Television audiences, too, could now vote with their feet.

Cable did not have this additional feature. Whether buried in the ground or carried above it, cable's very tangible physical presence in the locality rendered it totally subject to national regulation. Also, there must be severe doubts as to whether cable television can even be seen as a *technological* development of the 70s. Technologically, it has been possible to carry television and sound broadcasting over wire ever since, or even before, they could be transmitted over the airwaves. And indeed in many countries, for various reasons, significant chunks of the audience have long had their programmes so delivered. It was regulatory or economic reasons, rather than technological limitations, which prevented important extra programme services being delivered by wire.

The distinction is sometimes made between the technology of 'narrowband' (few channels) and 'broadband' (dozens of channels) cable. But it is not a technological divide located in the 70s. Even narrowband cable could have supplied extra channels (with additional wiring) had regulators permitted it and entrepreneurs felt it worthwhile to finance it. Of the two broadband technologies, coaxial cable predated the 'cable revolution' of the 70s, while fibre optics (as a practical technology) postdated it. Cable, as a provider of significant extra programme services, rather than as a humble re-broadcaster of the handful provided by terrestrial television, mushroomed in the USA in the second half of the 70s as a result of regulatory decisions and economic calculations. But for the rest of the industrialised world this American regulatory and commercial development was generally perceived as a technological one. Outside the USA, in the late 70s, as a result of the American example earlier in the decade, broadband cable effectively came to be seen as major new technology, with potentially revolutionary consequences for the existing organisation of television, regardless of whether or not its technology was in fact new.

In contrast to cable, the convergence of broadcasting, telecommunications and computing – based on the 'digital revolution' – was a genuinely new technological development. It was, however, more of a development in theory than in practice, until right at the end of the period we are discussing. To date, for the average television viewer, little or no convergence has actually gone on. In so far as convergence was a factor in the challenge to the first wave of television that emerged from the 70s it was, like audience tastes, an indirect factor. The (often exaggerated) prospect of convergence meant that television was now increasingly seen as part of a rapidly expanding, and therefore commercially potentially lucrative, information technology sector. The new technology of convergence therefore worked its initial effects on television systems through the prism of industrial policy – through government desire to promote what was seen as an important newly developing industry (see Chapters 4 and 5). Unless, and until, the 'new' technologies of television delivered satellite television 'pirates', not subject to national regulation, towards which discontented audiences would gravitate, then 'new' technology alone was unlikely to directly make the first breach in the old television systems.

We are therefore left with one last factor as the decisive force in the challenge to the first-wave television systems – the political one. If national governments operating within the old 'welfare consensus' regulated the traditional television systems, so too might national governments – armed with a different agenda – choose to de-regulate or re-regulate those systems. That, and only that, would allow the other forces we have discussed to enter the breach and demonstrate their mettle.

From the late 70s onwards, this was precisely what happened. One consequence of the breakdown in the post-war economic order was a resurgence of free-market or 'neo-liberal' politics, most notably exemplified by Margaret Thatcher's UK election victory of 1979 and Ronald Reagan's US victory of 1980 (Green, 1987, pp. 1–2). Soon, political recipes – like market liberalism, deregulation and privatisation – which had been off the political agenda since before the Second World War, were politically centre-stage. This does not necessarily mean that there was some inexorable link between political neo-liberalism and the breakdown of the post-war boom. (Although the subsequent adoption by proclaimedly social democratic administrations of free-market policies might suggest there was at least some connection.) So we have a question mark here as to how much this was a purely political challenge to established structures and to what degree an inevitable political response to an economic one. This is one of the questions this book will seek to address so far as the limited field of UK television is concerned. But, either way, we are effectively dealing with a *political* phenomenon – a phenomenon of government policy.

The new neo-liberalism posed a challenge across the social and economic spectrum – from health to transport. The structures of television's first wave had been established in precisely the period of the dominance of state intervention and welfarism, against which the new neo-liberalism defined itself. So, for that reason alone, television was directly in the firing-line of the neo-liberal challenge. Being in the firing line is, however, rather different from being shot at. It tells you next to nothing about what part of your body will be targeted, how accurate the aim will be or how many bullets will be fired. The neo-liberals might well have a hostility to the old order, and some rough vision of the new, but in the real world there were various ways of getting there, and different paces at which to travel. Which road would be chosen, and at what pace it would be travelled, have been very definitely political, and not economic, matters both in general and in the specific field of television. This question of alternative strategies *within the neo-liberal camp* will form another important theme of our story.

In this worldwide revival of the fortunes of neo-liberal politics that has been so important an international feature of the last two decades, the British Conservative administration of 1979–97 has been widely seen to have a central place. It was the first 'New Right' administration to gain office in a major industrial country – Margaret Thatcher's election victory of May 1979 pipped Ronald Reagan to the post by a clear year and a half. It was seen by many domestic and foreign observers – both critics and supporters – as being particularly vigorous and far-thinking in its advancement of a neo-liberal programme. And, in its concrete achievements, there can be no dispute that in some areas – for example, the deregulation of telecommunications – the UK Conservative government pioneered an approach which others would later follow.

That said, the questions begin. From virtually the moment the Conservatives regained office in Britain in 1979, there began a vigorous debate on what has often been referred to as 'Thatcherism'. How coherent was it? How effectively did it promote the neo-liberal agenda? How much did it persist into the administration of John Major? How substantial were the real results of its policies? And were these results for good or ill?

This book attempts to illuminate some of those general questions in the specific field of television – a field which has been rather neglected in more general studies of the Thatcher phenomenon.

It seems wise, then, to make some preliminary observations about the debate on 'Thatcherism', and to suggest what bearing they might have on the UK Conservative governments' television policies between 1979 and 1997.

One of the most significant and influential studies of the politics of the British Conservative government after 1979 is Andrew Gamble's *The Free Economy and the Strong State*. Gamble builds upon the influential analysis of 'Thatcherism' developed in the 80s by the magazine *Marxism Today*, but in an altogether more nuanced way than some of that magazine's contributors. Gamble's argument is that Thatcherism can best be seen as:

> A political project developed by the Conservative leadership, which sort to reestablish the conditions – electoral, ideological, economic and political – for the Conservative Party to resume its leading role in British politics ... As a political project Thatcherism had three overriding political objectives – to restore the political fortunes of the Conservative Party, to revive market liberalism as the dominant public philosophy and to create the conditions for a free economy by limiting the scope of the state while restoring its authority and competence to act. It is because Thatcherism deliberately set out an alternative to the policy regime that had been established since the 1940s that it has attracted such attention. (Gamble, 1994, pp. 4–5)

Talk of Thatcherism as a *new and distinct political project* immediately raises two questions. First, *how* new was the project? Second, how much could it even be dignified by the term 'project'? In other words, to what extent was it the enacting of a single thought-out plan? Gamble identifies two poles of criticism of his approach which coincide with these questions. The first, he claims, 'objects to the use of the term on the grounds that Thatcherism is in principle no different from other forms of Conservatism'. The second 'is sceptical that the Thatcher government ever pursued clear and consistent ideological objectives' (Gamble, 1994, p. 2).

Gamble associates his second set of critics with the work of another leading commentator on the politics of the Thatcher era, Peter Riddell. Riddell is withering in his criticism of the approach to 'Thatcherism' propounded by *Marxism Today*, most clearly and subtly expressed in Gamble:

> Hindsight often provides the coherence and clarity denied to contemporaries. To talk, as the new Marxists do, of a coherent hegemonic project, or of the Thatcher project, is meaningless as well as absurd. ... The word 'project' conveys the impression of the *Blue Peter* television programme and papier-mâché models ... The new Marxists may be right to see the Thatcherism of the late 1980s as a deliberate attempt to replace the post-war social democratic consensus and to create an economic and political constituency

for capitalist values and aspirations. But that has been very much a second and third-term phenomenon. That was not what the Conservatives were about in opposition or in their first term, up to 1983. The radicalism of the late 1980s has developed on the basis of earlier political successes. Or, rather, many of the most important new policies have been the result of the failures of initial policies and in response to circumstances. (Riddell, 1991, pp. 4–5)

We can see that, amid his scorn for the notion of 'projects', Riddell makes one important concession to the position he criticises – 'The new Marxists may be right to see the Thatcherism of *the late 1980s* as a deliberate attempt to replace the post-war social democratic consensus and to create an economic and political constituency for capitalist values and aspirations' (my emphasis).

Gamble, in turn, makes two important concessions to critics like Riddell. First, he recognises that:

Thatcherism is sometimes represented as though in 1979 there existed a set of policy blueprints ready for immediate implementation. No actual policy process could ever work in that way. What distinguished the Thatcher government from its predecessors was not detailed policy plans but its strategic sense of its long-term objectives and its pragmatism concerning the means to achieve them. (Gamble, 1994, p. 6)

Second, an important part of Gamble's book (Chapter 4) is devoted to mapping out three different phases (1979–82, 1982–7 and 1987–90) of the Thatcher government, with the claim that the Thatcher administration 'became more radical as time went on' (p. 130).

So, in an important sense, in dealing with different approaches to Thatcherism, we do not have two diametrically opposed analyses, but rather a spectrum of possibilities, with the extremes ruled out on either side. The issue is not whether the politics of the Thatcher governments were totally planned in advance or merely pragmatic responses to events, but rather just *how* coherent they were, or even more importantly, how coherent they became. That is one of the central questions I will try to answer with regard to the post-1979 Conservative government's television policy. I will also explore to what extent that television policy was an extension of broader concerns on the part of the government, and to what extent specific to the particularities of television.

The concept of 'Thatcherism' raises three other issues, all of which also have a bearing on television policy. First, how much did 'Thatcherism' end with Margaret Thatcher's fall from office, and how much did it continue under John Major?

Second, how effective has 'Thatcherism' been in achieving its proclaimed goals? There has been an array of books which attempt to grapple with this problem of the extent of the real achievements of the Thatcher revolution. They span a wide range of different policy areas, across macroeconomic, industrial and social policy, and among them have been various attempts to make an assessment of post-1979 Conservative broadcasting policy. This book will endeavour to draw up a more detailed balance sheet of Tory achievements – set against proclaimed goals – in the specific sector of television. Most previous assessments have focused on the Thatcher years. This book gives equal weight to the six and a half years of John Major's premiership that followed, both as years of new and important policy initiatives and modification or shelving of old ones, and as years in which previous policy initiatives worked their way through into practice.

Lastly, I will attempt to make a more general assessment of post-1979 Tory television policy, adopting a point of view which is generally critical of the Tory project (whether new or old, coherent or not). One indisputable fact about the Tory years in the UK is that what started out as peculiarly Conservative Party nostrums have since – for good or ill – become the conventional wisdom of public policy, accepted both by Tony Blair's New Labour Party and by the great majority of 'independent' commentators and experts. This is true of television broadcasting, just as it is of local government, health care, public utilities or education. In the following chapters I will endeavour to trace the shifts in conventional wisdom on television over the past two decades and relate them to Tory policy. But conventional wisdom does not necessarily equate to truth. As I shall try to show, this is at least as much the case in television as it is in other spheres of public activity. Some more general political criticisms of the neo-liberal agenda may be reinforced by an analysis of how it has been applied to British television over the last two decades. If the evidence supports them, the fact that such criticisms sit uncomfortably with what has become the conventional wisdom about broadcasting should not stand in the way of making them.

We need to bear in mind throughout this account that Government policies are not made by governments alone. Governments have to get their initial ideas for policy from somewhere. And that somewhere more often than not means somewhere else. Even the most ideological administrations do not simply suck all their policies out of their own heads. And once they have got their initial policy ideas, even the most determined administrations do not proceed to implement them by simple diktat. They face obstacles and they consult. And – to a greater or lesser extent – they modify their policies in accord with those obstacles and the results of their consultations. They are also more or less vigorously lobbied by interested parties, and more or less vigorously opposed by their political opponents. These processes, too, have their effects.

So, in examining Tory policy on television we must take note of the other actors in the play, and their relative importance and effectiveness. Those other actors include civil servants, regulators, different elements within the industry and other related industries, political think-tanks, the press and the political opposition. We will try and assess their respective impact.

# 2  UK Television 1979

When Margaret Thatcher won the general election of May 1979 her new administration inherited responsibility for a solidly established national television system with a very considerable international reputation. 'Those of us who have discussed the matter abroad,' commented the Annan Committee on *The Future of Broadcasting* in 1977, 'or with those who have lived in other countries and can make comparisons, are struck by how often we meet with the response: "The British have the the the best broadcasting in the world" ' (Annan, 1977, p. 28).

Similar views have been much repeated in subsequent years. No doubt they contain, and always have contained, both a good deal of parochial smugness on the part of British observers and an equal dose of uninformed romanticism from commentators abroad. But they also reflect a considerable measure of truth. In 1979 Britain had one of the longest-established and strongest television systems in the world, one which had a number of distinctive and, often rightly, admired features. Britain, along with the USA and Germany, had been one of the three pre-war pioneers of television, with the BBC starting television broadcasting in 1936. The war interrupted this early beginning, but the BBC recommenced television broadcasting in 1946, ahead of any other European country.

This early post-war beginning was more than reflected in the growth of the new medium in Britain. By 1972, 93 per cent of British households had a television, and by 1979, the figure had risen to 97 per cent – virtually saturation point. Of those 1979 UK television households more than two-thirds had a colour set (GHS, 1996, p. 26). Television had become a universal medium in the UK earlier than in virtually any other European country. So, for example, in 1965 Britain was second only to Sweden in the European league table of television licences per thousand of population. With 249 per 1,000 it was significantly ahead of West Germany (193) and way ahead of either France (133) or Italy (116) (UNESCO, 1989, 10.29). So the incoming Thatcher government inherited one of the world's most mature television markets and one of its most experienced television audiences.

This maturity and experience was not simply due to an early start and rapid growth. It was also a product of some peculiar features of the organisation of television in Britain. From their early days, first radio and then television in the UK were part of a state monopoly run by a public corporation at arm's length from government – the BBC. Historically this model of organisation served as the major international alternative to the wholly commercial structures of broadcasting in the USA.

But Britain was also a pioneer in mixing state broadcasting with commercial.

The UK broke its state monopoly of television in 1955 with the birth of ITV. The only other European country to make a similar step at that time was Finland. The rest of the Continent had to wait for a generation or more for the state monopoly of television to end. In Italy commercial television began on a local pirate basis in the early 70s, and was legitimised by a decision of the Italian Constitutional Court in 1976. By 1979 national commercial networks in Italy were only just beginning to gel. In France commercial television was to start only in 1984, and in Germany in 1985. In most of the rest of Europe it came even later.

So, in 1979, the Thatcher administration inherited not merely a long-established television system but one which also had extensive experience of at least limited competition in television provision, which was then virtually unparalleled in Europe, and indeed in most of the rest of the world.

The introduction of commercial television to Britain in the early 50s was initially deeply controversial and largely driven by Thatcher's predecessors in the Conservative Party. But by 1979 both the existence of commercial television in Britain, and its coexistence with a public broadcaster, had long since ceased to be a matter of political debate between the major parties.

Commercial television in the UK rapidly had an impact on public broadcasting. The BBC responded to competition by developing a distinctly more popular touch, and thus succeeded in retaining a substantial section of the television audience. It also responded to its new competitor and to changes in British society by becoming politically more independent of the government of the day, and socially and culturally less deferential to the British Establishment (Scannell, 1996, p. 28).

If the public service side of British television rapidly became more 'independent' after 1955, the 'independent' side soon took on more public service characteristics. From the start British commercial television operated within a public service framework. The regional ITV companies were in theory simply contractors to supply programming (in return for the right to sell advertising) to a public body, with public service goals, first called the ITA (Independent Television Authority), and then renamed the IBA (Independent Broadcasting Authority) when it took over responsibility for the newly authorised commercial radio in 1972. In 1962 the Pilkington Committee on broadcasting had lambasted the early performance of ITV (Pilkington, 1962, pp. 51–68). It consequently recommended awarding the now available third television channel to the BBC and advocated changes to the governance of ITV which would bring commercial television more firmly within a public service framework. Pilkington's recommendations on the third channel were accepted by the (then Conservative) government and BBC 2 started broadcasting in 1964. The Committee's formal recommendations on the governance of ITV were not taken up. But their substance was. As the Annan Committee put it in 1977, 'the Pilkington Report transformed the face of ITV' (Annan, 1977, p. 146). The ITA and then the IBA obliged the contractors to cut back on some more nakedly commercial programme formulas and imposed upon them more stringent public service obligations.

Thus was born, by at least the end of the 60s, what the Annan Committee was to call the 'duopoly' in British television, and the Peacock Committee later to label the 'comfortable duopoly'. It was this – by 1979 firmly established – duopoly that Thatcher's government inherited. Any estimation of the changes that the

Conservatives were to try and make to British television in subsequent years must therefore start by outlining the key features of this television duopoly.

In 1979 British television consisted of three generalist channels, all broadcasting a full range of informational and entertainment programming. Two of these, BBC 1 and BBC 2, were national channels programmed, scheduled and transmitted by a single public corporation, the BBC. The third, ITV, was a national network, programmed and effectively scheduled by a federation of regional commercial television companies for transmission by a second public television authority, the IBA. In 1980 the audience shares of these channels were roughly as follows: 39 per cent to BBC 1, 12 per cent to BBC 2 and 49 per cent to ITV (AGB, 1996a, p. 46).

British television in 1979 was, in effect, exclusively terrestrial television. Years of public investment in terrestrial transmission infrastructure by both the BBC and ITA/IBA had ensured that by the end of the 70s nearly 100 per cent of the UK population were able to receive over the airwaves a television signal of acceptable (and, by international standards, high) quality.

While that terrestrial transmission system was being built, cable redistribution of first radio and then television had been a significant minority feature of British broadcasting, particularly in areas where terrestrial reception was, or had been, poor. At the beginning of the 80s some 2.5 million UK households – 14 per cent of the total – received their television via 'narrowband' cable with a capacity of perhaps half-a-dozen channels. What these households received over the wire was the same three television channels that the rest of the population received over the airwaves – albeit with better picture quality and perhaps cheaper receiving equipment. At most, British cable subscribers got an extra out-of-region ITV service – an add-on which was not of great significance given that the most popular of ITV programmes were overwhelmingly nationally networked.

The idea of using cable to provide *extra* television services (in addition to relaying the terrestrial ones) was not an entirely new one in British broadcasting policy. Between 1966 and 1968 Harold Wilson's Labour government authorised commercial experiments with a pay cable television service (consisting mainly of films) in Southwark, Westminster and Sheffield. And from 1972 Edward Heath's Conservative government authorised experiments with community cable services (relying heavily on voluntary personnel for programming) in a number of towns, including Bristol, Wellingborough, Sheffield and Greenwich. By 1976, all but Greenwich had been abandoned (Hollins, 1984, pp. 45–6). Given the 'failure' of these experiments, British cable, in 1979, still remained confined essentially to the relay of terrestrially broadcast services. As the terrestrial transmission system improved in quality, the attractions of cable relay became less, to the extent that by the end of the 70s the UK cable industry was in slow decline. In 1982 it was reported that subscribers had fallen by 140,000 over the past five years, and some of the leading companies traditionally involved in British cable were already pursuing withdrawal strategies (ITAP, 1982, p. 10).

With direct reception by satellite negligible (dishes were numbered in hundreds rather than thousands), British television in 1979 was to all intents and purposes confined to the BBC/ITV duopoly.

The BBC and ITV competed for audiences, but not for revenue. BBC television

14

carried no advertising and was funded wholly (apart from a small revenue from international programme sales) by the licence fee, of which the BBC was the sole recipient. ITV, in contrast, was funded entirely (again, apart from international programme sales) by the sale of airtime for advertising. Each regional ITV contractor was the monopoly seller of television advertising in its area (apart from London, where the region was split between a weekday and a weekend contractor). So, not only did the two major poles of the duopoly not compete for revenue, but within the commercial side there was little or no internal competition for revenue. One early proprietor of a regional ITV company had famously described an ITV franchise as 'a licence to print money' (Sendall, 1982, p. 150). That may have been an exaggeration, but the relatively secure monopoly funding of ITV had long been recognised by the government, which imposed a special tax – the 'levy' – on either ITV advertising revenues or profits.

Competition for audiences between the two sides of the duopoly was intense, but not unlimited. Both the BBC and ITV operated under public service constraints which ensured that they did not provide a schedule designed simply to maximise audience numbers, but instead broadcast a wider range of different types of informational and cultural programmes than would have been supplied by the demands of crude audience maximisation. The result was that in 1979 the three UK channels were widely perceived as providing a more varied diet of programming than the three US networks.[1]

The British television industry of 1979 was a vertically integrated one. On the BBC side of the duopoly this vertical integration was absolute. The BBC transmitted and scheduled its programmes and made virtually all of them in-house. On the ITV side things were somewhat more complicated. The IBA was the sole transmitter of ITV programmes and had some theoretical responsibility for their scheduling. In practice, the scheduling of regional programmes was done by the regional companies individually and the scheduling of network programmes by a committee of the ITV companies together with the IBA. ITV regional companies made virtually all of their regional programmes in-house. National news programming was made by ITN, collectively owned by all the ITV companies. Apart from news, originally commissioned network programmes for ITV were made, in the main, in-house by the 'big five' ITV companies. These did not compete for programme slots but carved up network provision between them. Virtually all other originally commissioned ITV programmes not made by the 'big five' were produced in-house by the other smaller regional companies. In 1979 there were only a handful of independent television production companies ('independent', that is, of the broadcasters). They contributed probably less than 1 per cent of the programme output of either BBC or ITV.

Vertically integrated, and with two separate, large and fairly secure streams of income, British television in 1979 was produced by a largely permanently employed workforce, predominantly concentrated in relatively big units. The BBC had about 23,000 employees in its Home Services, about 16,500 of whom worked in television,[2] and were heavily concentrated in London. The ITV companies had a total of 12,400 (plus another 1,300 in the IBA, and 575 in ITN) (Paulu, 1981, p. 128), more widely spread geographically, but concentrated in London and a handful of regional centres. Such employment structure provided fertile ground

15

for trade unionism. The old film and entertainment craft unions had early on established closed shops in much of ITV. And in the BBC, what had previously been a staff association, the ABS, was by 1979 rapidly transforming itself into a fully fledged trade union.

Alongside the growth of trade unionism, by 1979 the economic and institutional features of, and public constraints on, the television duopoly had also fostered a certain type of television 'professionalism'. This put 'programmes first', sometimes in the interests of audience maximisation but also from a public interest and cultural perspective. This 'professionalism' was not confined to the BBC; it also moulded the employee culture of the ITV companies. As late as 1986 research for the Peacock Committee reported that one of the ITV companies was 'sometimes described as more BBC than the BBC' (Nossiter, 1986, p. 21). In other words, it had the same public service culture as the BBC.

From the start, both BBC and ITV had been required to show a a large proportion of domestically produced (and therefore – with the exception of UK films – effectively originally commissioned) programming. Even before ITV went on the air the '86/14 rule' had been agreed by the regulators and the companies, whereby foreign-filmed programmes could only amount to 14 per cent of broadcast hours (Sendall, 1982, pp. 107–9). As the years went on, and as broadcasting hours increased, the rule came to be applied with an increasingly large number of loopholes. But the comparatively large size and affluence of the British television market helped to underpin the requirement that a substantial majority of programming, particularly at peak time, be domestically produced. A big advertising and licence fee base ensured that the broadcasters could afford to do what they were required to do. The economics and politics of the duopoly reinforced this. So by 1979 British television audiences were used to, and demanded, a large proportion of domestically produced material, with high production values, across the full range of programme genres (apart, perhaps, from feature films – a result more of the weakness of the British film industry than of British television).

These features of the duopoly provide the rational kernel of the international reputation of the British television system. Separate funding and an overall public service framework had secured diversity of programming, rather than the 'lowest common denominator' of commercially driven audience maximisation. Competition for audiences and one-remove control of public service, had contributed to a more popular and less deferential approach to television. Secure funding and public service obligations had produced a professional culture of, and an audience taste for, high-budget, sometimes controversial, domestically produced programming.

So, the television duopoly that Margaret Thatcher inherited was in many respects a particularly healthy one. But it was not without its domestic critics. Far from it.

## Challenges to the system

The decade before 1979, which had witnessed the consolidation of the classic British television duopoly, had also seen a vigorous critical debate about the state and future of British television. This debate received official recognition in the report of the Annan Committee on *The Future of Broadcasting*, published in 1977.

The debate was a complex one, which we can scarcely do justice to here. But some of its key features – and some of its key absences – need highlighting in order to properly understand Tory policy in the years that followed. Commenting on the decade and a half that had elapsed between the report of the Pilkington Committee in 1962 and its own in 1977, the Annan Committee observed:

> The most striking change in broadcasting was brought about by the change during this period [1962–77] in the culture of our country. The ideals of middle-class culture, so felicitously expressed by Matthew Arnold a century ago, which had created a continuum of taste and opinion, always susceptible to change and able to absorb the *avant-garde* within its own urban, liberal, flexible principles, found it ever more difficult to accommodate the new expressions of life in the sixties. The new vision of life reflected divisions within society, divisions between classes, generations and sexes, between north and south, between the provinces and London, between pragmatists and ideologues.... At once inflationary in the expectations of what political power could achieve and deflationary towards those in power who failed to give effect towards those expectations, the new mood expressed itself in a rhetoric of self-conscious unrest, in exploration rather than explanation, in the politics of perpetual crisis and strain, in innovation rather than adjustment, in the potentialities rather than in the probabilities of the future. (Annan, 1977, p. 14)

As the Annan Committee itself noted, this change in mood coincided with expanded recruitment in broadcasting. So its impact was felt within the duopoly. Established conventions of programme form and content were often successfully challenged by programme-makers. But the change in mood also issued a challenge to the structures of the duopoly. As Annan put it: 'The shift heightened the tensions between the Broadcasting Authorities themselves and the younger producers, but even more dramatically between the Broadcasting Authorities and the Government' (p. 15).

From Pilkington through to the end of the 70s the established position of the television duopoly was brought into question. 'It has been put to us', reported the Annan Committee:

> that broadcasting should be 'opened up'. At present, so it is argued, the broadcasters have become an overmighty subject, an unelected elite, more interested in preserving their own organisation intact than in enriching the nation's culture. Dedicated to the outworn concepts of balance and impartiality, how can the broadcasters reflect the multitude of opinions in our pluralist society? (p. 16)

Annan maintained that 'people of all political persuasions began to object that many programmes were biased or obnoxious' (p. 15). Such a formulation may have been a suitably diplomatic one for an official committee of inquiry to make, but it was hardly an accurate account of the predominant flavour of critical debate on the structures of broadcasting in the 70s. True, there had been one significant contribution to the broadcasting debate of the 60s and 70s which clearly stood on the right – the concern with so-called 'taste and decency' articulated by Mary Whitehouse's National Viewers' and Listeners' Association. (Although even here, as one notable left-wing contributor to the 70s debate, Nicholas Garnham, noted at the time, 'Much of the force behind the Whitehouse movement comes not so much from disgust with programmes as from a justifiable dislike of the arrogance of broadcasters' (Garnham, 1978, p. 45).

But the main thrust of criticism came – at least vaguely – from the left. It reflected the growth since the early 60s of trade union militancy, a shift in political mood to the left, new visions of gender and ethnic oppression, more forceful social and cultural liberalism and suspicion of a class- or Establishment-based state. All of these causes were seen in the 60s and 70s as the ideological terrain of the left. In broadcasting terms they entailed a critique of the television duopoly as representative of narrow Establishment interests, and the search for more bottom-up, democratically accountable and pluralist structures.

In a 1973 British Film Institute monograph on the *Structures of Television*, Nicholas Garnham argued that rather than the 'comforting, mythic view of British broadcasting':

> What we in fact have is a system in which two powerful institutions responsible not to the public but to the real, though hidden, pressures of the power elite, government, big business and the cultural establishment, manipulate the public in the interest of that power elite and socialise the individual broadcaster so that he collaborates in this process almost unconsciously. (Garnham, 1978, p. 16)

Garnham's view was symptomatic. Many of the 70s critics of the broadcasting duopoly might have cast their criticism in more liberal and pluralist language. However, in the specific circumstances of the 70s, these were but extra dimensions of the same universe of criticism. Much of it issued from the broadcasting trade unions and the new, and still (in Britain, at least) distinctly left-flavoured academic disciplines of media, film and cultural studies. More liberal- and pluralist-minded critics, including a significant number of television producers, engaged with their more ideological colleagues, not as opponents but as co-thinkers in the same terrain of debate. So, for example, proponents of independent production felt it natural to seek legitimation for their ideas in trade union circles. A handful of consciously free-market programme-makers were active in the discussion, but any overall free-market position was notable by its absence from the broadcasting debate of the 70s.

The 70s critique of the existing broadcasting set-up targeted all the institutions of the duopoly – including a single monolithic and unaccountable BBC – but became increasingly focused on demands about the future organisation of the fourth national terrestrial channel. Technically, such a channel had been available since the beginning of the 60s. By the end of the 70s most British television sets had a fourth button to switch it straight on. It was how the fourth channel was to be organised that excited twenty years of controversy.

The Annan Committee on *The Future of Broadcasting* was set up in this climate. A proposal for the establishment of a committee on the future of broadcasting had first been mooted at the end of the 1964–70 Labour government, and Lord Annan had been appointed to chair it. The committee was opposed as unnecessary by the Conservatives in opposition, and when the Tories gained office in 1970 they scrapped it. But Labour resurrected the committee when they, in turn, regained office in 1974.

18

A committee of inquiry into broadcasting had long been a unifying demand among the critics of the duopoly. However, when it reported in 1977 the Annan Committee disappointed many of them. The Committee was on the whole praising and protective of the existing structures of the television duopoly. But, in the main questions it addressed, it took the – predominantly leftish – 70s critics very seriously. And on the central issue of the fourth channel, it made important recommendations in their favour.

'We do not believe', the Annan Committee asserted early on in its report, 'that the present structure of broadcasting, which was devised to meet the needs of the 1960s, will be adequate to meet the demands of the 1980s.' It added, more specifically, that 'the present duopoly, under which all programmes broadcast are the responsibility of the BBC or the IBA, has already shown signs of becoming a strait-jacket and inhibiting the development of new services' (Annan, 1977, p. 29). These general assertions were very much in tune with the approach of the 70s critics. But when it came to examining many of their more specific themes for reform, the Committee was, after sympathetic consideration, ultimately unresponsive.

So, for example, the Committee considered but then rejected the proposal for an over-arching Executive Broadcasting Commission responsible for broadcasting as a whole. 'However pure and valiant the Commission might be in its early days, it would in the end become – what the Authorities are accused of being – a self-serving and self-perpetuating power group within the system' (p. 37). The Committee welcomed the fact that it had been forced to think through the role of the existing broadcasting authorities, but concluded that

> the Authorities are themselves accountable to Parliament for their decisions and the services they provide, and Parliament itself is accountable to the electorate. This pragmatic solution to a complex problem has stood the test of fifty years operation, and we consider should be maintained in its essentials. (p. 39)

Relations between government, Parliament and the broadcasting authorities did not, in the Committee's view, require much adjustment.

The Annan Committee considered at length whether the BBC should be broken up, but (with a dissenting minority proposing a split between radio and television) rejected the idea. 'The sheer size of the BBC's resources ... enables the BBC to produce programmes which in range and volume are probably unmatched' (p. 116). Similar praise was showered on the output of ITV. 'In our view,' asserted the Committee, 'there is no doubt that Independent Television, while remaining popular, has improved in quality during the last 12 years' (p. 148). In the lively and professional presentation of news, 'the commercial sector has by common consent surpassed the BBC' (p. 149).

In short, while the Annan Committee systematically addressed many of the issues raised by the 70s critics, and claimed that it too wanted to end the duopoly, most of its conclusions advocated a maintenance of the duopoly's central institutional and financial framework. The Committee did maintain that there was a need to make the broadcasting organisations 'more responsive to the opinions of their audience' (p. 39), but its specific institutional proposals on this score were modest – the most notable and enduring being that a statutory Broadcasting Complaints Commission should be set up (pp. 57–60).

On only one major issue did the Annan Committee come down decisively in favour of the 70s critics and advance some significant way towards its own stated ambition of ending the broadcasting duopoly. This was, however, the issue that had become the centrepiece of the previous decade's debates – the shape of the future fourth television channel.

There had been debate about what form the fourth channel should take ever since the Pilkington Committee (for a comprehensive survey of that debate, see Lambert, 1982, pp. 5–83). Put crudely, there were two sides to the argument. One side, broadly supported by the ITV companies and the IBA, argued that the fourth channel should become a second commercial station, run by the ITV companies – one or other form of 'ITV 2'. The opposing side, broadly supported by what we have called the 70s critics, argued for a new third force in television. This was variously conceived of as an educational channel, a locally oriented one or – an increasingly favoured option – a channel organised as an independent and pluralist publisher of programmes from a variety of previously under-represented sources. By the time the Annan Committee began its deliberations, the battle lines had in practice become slightly softened, because most advocates of 'ITV 2' envisaged some element of independent and complementary scheduling, a certain educational element and a significant supply of programming from sources additional to the ITV companies. The advertising industry added an extra complexity to the debate – eager that, on the one hand, the new channel should be commercial, but equally keen, on the other, that it should introduce competition into the sale of television advertising, and therefore should not be wholly controlled by the ITV companies. But that there remained a fundamental divide between the two basic positions – 'ITV 2' and a new independent third force in television – was still passionately felt among active participants in the broadcasting debate.

The most notable of the 'third force' schemes for the new channel was the proposed establishment of a National Television Foundation. This was first advanced by former BBC producer and then media academic, Anthony Smith, in 1972 (see Appendix II to Smith, 1976, pp. 287–96), vigorously advocated by him in the following years, and eliciting considerable support among the trade union, academic and producer critics of the duopoly. The National Television Foundation, argued Smith:

> would supplement existing broadcasting by broadening the input by allowing anyone to bring a project to it, whether an independent programme maker with a finely worked out plan, or a firm, organisation or individual with merely a well argued complaint that some issue was failing to get across to the public. The Foundation would then play a kind of impresario role, merely allocating resources to some but fitting producers, writers, technicians to others who arrived only with an idea, a grievance, a cause. (quoted in Annan, 1977, p. 234)

Among the many proposals made to the Committee, it was Smith's approach to the fourth channel which found most favour with Annan and his colleagues:

A great opportunity would be missed if the fourth channel were seen solely in terms of extending the *present* range of programmes ... We see the fourth channel as a challenge to broadcasters. Surely they will not be incapable of creating programmes of a different and intriguing kind. So we do not see the fourth channel merely as an addition to the plurality of outlets, but as a force for plurality in a deeper sense. Not only could it be a nursery for new forms and new methods of presenting ideas, it could also open the door to a new kind of broadcast publishing. (p. 235)

Such a vision, the Committee concluded, required a new authority. To leave the new channel in the hands of the IBA would be to ensure that it was dominated by ITV. So Annan and his colleagues recommended the establishment of an Open Broadcasting Authority (OBA). The OBA would not be required to provide either a balanced evening's schedule or to take responsibility for its programmes in the same way as the BBC or IBA. Instead, 'the OBA should operate as a publisher and its obligations should be limited to those placed on any other publisher'.

The programmes broadcast by the OBA would, the Committee anticipated, fall into three general categories: educational programmes; programmes made by individual ITV companies 'who have ideas for varying their programmes'; and, 'above all, there would be programmes from a variety of independent producers. We attach particular importance to this third category as a force for diversity and new ideas' (pp. 236–7).

The Committee proposed a mixture of funding sources for the OBA: sponsorship, public subscription, the Arts Council, CBI and TUC, educational bodies and, last but by no means least, advertising – organised in large blocks rather than the smaller spots in programme breaks traditionally practised by ITV (pp. 237–8).

So, on what was seen at the time as the crucial issue of the fourth channel, the Annan Committee had decided in favour of the 70s critics. On most other issues it had disappointed them. But it is testament to their influence on the climate of broadcasting debate in the second half of the 70s that, even where it rebuffed them, the critics largely set the agenda of the Annan Committee, the issues it addressed at length and the tone it often adopted in its report.

The climate of broadcasting debate in the 70s is indicated not only by the subjects that the Annan Committee chose to address but also by those it chose *not* to address. Four issues, all of them subsequently important in the broadcasting debate of the Thatcher and Major years, were effectively absent from the central deliberations of the Committee.

First was the question of the economic efficiency – and thus the cost to the consumer – of television services. Annan summarily dismissed the few representations his committee received on this score with the following remark: 'As far as we could judge, the BBC's use of resources, particularly television studios, was sophisticated and efficient' (p. 102).

Second was any notion of the inherent virtues of *market* competition. 'The new system [i.e. ITV alongside the BBC] has been successful because it introduced *regulated* competition into what was until then a monopoly,' emphasised Annan. 'We want to ensure that any new broadcasting system includes competition, not just for audiences but for variety and excellence' (pp. 29–30). But there Annan stopped. Its discussion of new possibilities for television, and its critique of the duopoly, was always framed in terms of public service, programme quality and diversity, and the audience, *not* the market.

Third was any conception of broadcasting as a national industry to be fostered for industrial purposes. How new developments in broadcasting might promote the international position of UK programming or UK equipment manufacturers was simply not a criterion which the Annan Report addressed in either its general deliberations or in formulating its recommendations.

And fourth was any substantial attention to the implications of the new technologies of television distribution via satellite or cable. The Annan Report devoted fewer than two of its 500 pages to satellite broadcasting, and fewer than a dozen to cable. And what it said in those few pages was distinctly low key. 'What future remains for cable television in the United Kingdom?' asked the report:

> We do not contemplate it providing yet another service comparable to BBC 1 or 2 or ITV, nor as an amplification to the fourth channel. There comes a time when there will be insufficient professional talent to provide further services of a traditional kind ... That is why we argue that cable television should develop as a local community service. A national cable network, and how it might operate, could be safely put off to the next century. (pp. 221–2)

On satellite television, Annan's timescale was similarly laid-back:

> We guess that countries in Western Europe, which have a heavy investment in conventional broadcasting and are relatively small geographically, will not give a high priority to providing broadcasting satellite services. But we cannot rule out the possibility that there will be a move to launch a service in the next 15 years. (p. 385)

In its neglect of these four issues, the Annan Committee was being neither eccentric nor perverse. It was, rather, reflecting the predominant strands of debate on television in Britain during the 70s. In this debate the issues of economic efficiency, the free market, broadcasting as a national industry on a world stage and the new technologies of distribution[3] were, in practice, marginal.

## Tory policy before 1979

The Conservative Party was not a major contributor to the long debate about television which preceded the Annan Report. Both in office and opposition the party had opposed the setting up of a committee of inquiry on the general future of broadcasting. It was, Tory Shadow Home Secretary, William Whitelaw, explained later, 'unnecessary and possibly even dangerous to subject our system of broadcasting to regular root and branch reviews which occupy many people's scarce time and may well lead only to a prolonged period of uncertainty' (HoC Debates, 23 May 1977, cols. 1028–9).

Such an attitude suggests that the Conservative front bench in the 70s had little or no desire to challenge the basic structures of the television duopoly. The party was certainly under no significant political or intellectual pressure to reform broadcasting in the direction of the market. In the 60s the Institute of Economic

Affairs (IEA), the longest-established of the free-market think-tanks which were to prove influential on Conservative thinking in the 80s, had published two pamphlets on the organisation of television (Altman et al., 1962; Caine, 1968). These called for, among other things, the use of terrestrial channels for pay-TV, the abolition of the licence fee and for advertising on the BBC. But such ideas showed no sign of gaining any significant support in the Conservative Party during the 70s, and it was 1982 before the IEA returned again to the subject of television.

Before Annan reported, the Conservative Party put forward no distinctive – and certainly no distinctively free-market – position on the fourth channel. Indeed, one of the very few contributions to the fourth channel debate to come from within the ranks of the Conservative Party in the early 70s suggested, as its first criterion for the new channel, that 'considerations of programming rather than financial gain [should] predominate' (Dyas, 1973, p. 7). Few Tories in 1977 would have openly dissented from that approach.

The publication of the Annan Report prompted the Conservative front bench to clarify its position both on the general structure of television and on the future shape of the fourth channel. Despite his original opposition to the establishment of the Annan Committee, William Whitelaw was effusive in his praise of its report. Making the Conservative front bench's official first response to the report in May 1977, Whitelaw began by emphasising his agreement with Annan's support for the status quo. Whitelaw spelt out at some length his support for the existing broadcasting authorities; his opposition to splitting up the BBC; his support for the licence fee and opposition to advertising on the BBC; and his belief that the IBA's control of the ITV companies was fair and satisfactory. He also agreed with Annan on the desirability of establishing a Broadcasting Complaints Commission – a 'very modest ... extension of bureaucracy' to give the viewing public 'a thoroughly reasonable right' was how he described it. But other than that, Whitelaw was opposed to the introduction of any new bodies into broadcasting regulation. For this reason, he opposed Annan's proposal for a Public Inquiry Board, which would, he maintained, simply involve 'more bureaucracy and cost' (HoC Debates, 23 May 1977, cols. 1029–35).

In short, in the general part of his response to the Annan Report, Whitelaw went out of his way to make absolutely clear his support for the central institutions of the television duopoly.

Turning to the subject of the fourth channel, Whitelaw drew a sharp distinction between what he saw as the spirit of the Annan proposals, which he supported, and their institutional embodiment in an OBA, which he opposed:

> Despite my basic dislike of new bodies ... I certainly appreciate the Committee's purpose. It wanted to ensure, as I understand it, that when the fourth channel was introduced it would provide programmes of different sorts, that minority interests would be catered for, and that independent producers would have greater opportunities. The thinking behind the proposal for the Open Broadcasting Authority was, therefore, both original and imaginative.

But, in Whitelaw's view, Annan's plan for an OBA suffered from a 'fatal flaw' – money. The Committee's proposals for financing the OBA, 'simply do not stand up to examination ... Some of the tentative suggestions might provide some money, although surely not enough. Others strain the imagination too far' (HoC Debates, 23 May 1977, col. 1035).

Whitelaw therefore proposed that the fourth channel should be given to the IBA and ITV companies, '*but on conditions that would meet the Committee's main purpose*' (my emphasis). The Shadow Home Secretary did not specify what such conditions might be, but he did single out as worthy of support proposals made by the ITV companies to Annan for an independent programme board for the fourth channel which might allocate time to a television foundation. If such a scheme were instituted, Whitelaw said, 'I would not feel so obsessed as the Committee did about this ogre of duopoly' (HoC Debates, 23 May 1977, cols. 1037–8).

Whitelaw's doubts about the financial viability of the proposed OBA were not confined to the Conservative Party. Similar misgivings clearly existed both within the Cabinet and in the Home Office, and it was to be over a year before Jim Callaghan's government issued its definitive response to Annan. The July 1978 White Paper, *Broadcasting*, did finally come down in favour of a new OBA to run the fourth channel, substantially along the lines proposed by Annan. But in its remaining months in office, the Labour government took no further steps to implement its plans. The door was left wide open for the incoming administration to determine how the fourth channel was to be established.

## Notes

1. For a contemporary example of such a perception, from an American author, see Paulu (1981) pp. 395–400.
2. This and all other figures given on employment in television should be treated with caution. The BBC did not separate radio and television employment in its published figures until 1982. For many years it confused authorised establishment with numbers actually employed. ITV figures are scattered in individual company reports, which may use different criteria for deciding whether someone is on staff or a freelance, have different year-end dates and may or may not include subsidiaries. Figures for independent production, independent facilities or cable and satellite broadcasters have never been systematically collated. In the early years information on these is non-existent; in later years, the figures are based on estimates from occasional, more or less representative, surveys. There is the increasingly significant additional problem of estimating freelance employment. And finally, where does television employment begin or end? A producer or camera operator is clearly 'employed in television' – except when he or she happens to be working on a feature film, an advertisement or a corporate video. Opinions may differ about whether an advertising salesperson, a subscription management worker or someone digging up the road for a cable company 'works in television'. And the very same security woman at the very same door, who once found herself on the books of the BBC (and therefore 'obviously' in the broadcasting industry), may now find herself on the books of Group 4 (and therefore equally 'obviously' in the private security industry).
3. Not that the 70s critics were unfamiliar with the possibilities of new technology. See, for example, the concluding chapter, 'Alternative Technology, Alternative Uses?', of Raymond Williams's widely read *Television: Technology and Cultural Form* (Williams, 1974, pp. 135–52).

# 3 Channel Four and More

## Establishing the fourth channel

The most important and immediate issue of television policy that faced the new Conservative government in 1979 was clearly the question that had dominated debate on the subject for most of the previous decade – the fourth channel. The new administration moved on the issue immediately. Just twelve days after the election, the Thatcher government's first Queen's speech announced: 'A Bill will be introduced to extend the life of the Independent Broadcasting Authority, which will be given responsibility – subject to strict safeguards – for the fourth television channel' (HoC Debates, 15 May 1979, col. 51).

The Tories had stuck firmly to their rejection of the OBA. But, beyond that, the 'strict safeguards' indicated considerable openness. The safeguards were presumably to ensure that, despite being run by the IBA, the new channel would provide the different kinds of programming that had been urged by Annan and welcomed by Whitelaw in 1977. In opposition the Tories had only spelt out that the fourth channel would need 'a separate programme planning board on which the main ITV companies would not have a majority' (HoC Debates, 26 July 1978, col. 1563). Beyond that barest of bones all other aspects of organisation of the new channel still needed filling in. How that was done would determine whether the new channel ended up as an ITV 2 dominated by the 'big five' ITV companies, or whether it would, as Whitelaw had maintained since 1977, embody the pluralistic and innovative spirit of Annan in more practical organisational guise.

There was therefore a considerable amount still to play for, and the various parties to the pre-Annan debate – ITV companies, IBA, aspirant independent producers, etc. – renewed their lobbying.

In September 1979 Whitelaw took an important step in filling in the details of the organisation of the new channel in a speech to the Royal Television Society convention in Cambridge (reprinted in the *Listener*, 20 September 1979). The main funding of the fourth channel would be by spot advertising. This would not, however, be sold in competition with ITV:

> I know that many people in the advertising world would like to have another source from which they could purchase advertising time on television. Having looked at this with particular care, the conclusion I have reached is that competitive advertising on the two channels would inevitably result in a move towards single-minded concentration on maximising the audience for programmes, with adverse consequences for both of the commercial channels, and, before long, for the BBC as well.

So far as the more general organisation of the channel was concerned, the government would leave a good deal up to the IBA:

> Our whole tradition, whether in the BBC's charter or in legislation for the control of independent television (and most would agree that this is a tradition which has proved basically sound), has been to entrust a wide measure of discretion to the broadcasting authorities.

However, on three key questions, Whitelaw did go on to elaborate the parameters within which the government expected the IBA to operate.

First, the channel would be a distinctive service: 'There must be programmes appealing to and, we hope, stimulating tastes and interests not adequately provided for on the existing channels.'

Second, the 'three main sources' of programming on the new channel would be the network ITV companies (the 'big five'), the regional ITV companies (the smaller ten) and independent producers – but not necessarily in that order. There would be no quotas for programmes from the different types of supplier, but

> the fourth channel should not be dominated by the network companies. There will, therefore, be a substantial contribution from regional, as opposed to the network, ITV contractors and from independent producers. The independent producers have a most important role to play. . . .

These two commitments were still vague, and subject to varying interpretation from the different prospective players in the new channel. But together they firmed up Whitelaw's 1977 commitment that, although the Tories might intend the new channel to be ITV 2 in form, in substance it would embody much of the spirit of Annan's OBA – alternative programming, a significant part of which would come from alternative programme makers.

Whitelaw's third specification in the September RTS speech involved a shift of ground from previous Tory proposals. In their 1979 manifesto the Conservatives had promised a specifically Welsh-language fourth channel in Wales. Now, four months into government, Whitelaw proposed a 'single national programme service' with only limited Welsh-language programming. This retreat from previous commitments immediately provoked an outcry from Welsh-language campaigners. The outcry generated perhaps the only genuinely mass campaign on a television issue during the entire Thatcher and Major governments, that went beyond the ranks of the broadcasting industry and the political élite. This campaign culminated in the pledge by Plaid Cymru President, Gwynfor Evans, to fast until death, unless the government created a special Welsh-language fourth channel in Wales. Towards the end of the progress through Parliament of the 1980 Broadcasting Bill, the government bowed to the Welsh-language opposition, reversed its policy on the issue a second time, and agreed to establish a specifically Welsh-language fourth channel – S4C – in Wales (Tomos, 1982, pp. 47–53).

So far as the rest of the UK was concerned, the Home Secretary's 1979 RTS speech was greeted with approval by most of the various industry lobbyists. Whitelaw's proposals were more specific than they had been in 1977, but were still sufficiently vague to provide comfort both to the big ITV companies and to those

26

who wanted a more alternative and pluralist fourth channel. The speech did, however, effectively invite the IBA to fill in much of the missing detail. And by the late 70s the IBA was altogether more independent of the network ITV companies, and their desire to dominate an ITV 2, than it had been at the beginning of the decade (Lambert, 1982, p. 85).

The IBA published its detailed proposals for the fourth channel in November 1979 (IBA *Annual Report*, 1979/80, pp. 137–42). The proposals reflected both the Authority's recently found independence from the big ITV companies and the influence of Annan and the pre-Annan debate on its thinking about the fourth channel.

The IBA began by welcoming Whitelaw's approach, so far, to the fourth channel. It announced that the Authority intended to establish a company, with its own board, to run the new channel. The board would most likely consist of between twelve and fourteen people. These would include an 'independent' chairman and deputy chairman. Four members would come from the ITV companies, while five others 'would be able to speak on behalf of other potential suppliers of programmes, having the trust of independent producers, for example, or a special concern for the educational role of the channel' (p. 137).

The channel would, the IBA proposed, 'among other things, provide opportunities for a wider range of programme supply, since, for the first time a channel will be looking to independent producers for a significant part of its output'. The programme controller would make his decisions on merit, so there would be no quotas on sources of programme supply:

> However, with that prime qualification, a possible pattern at the start would be that between fifteen and thirty-five per cent of the output would come from independent producers, with between twenty-five and forty per cent from the major ITV contractors, a further ten to twenty per cent from the regional ITV contractors, up to fifteen per cent from ITN, and five to fourteen per cent from foreign sources. (p. 138)

On programme content, the IBA envisaged that the fourth channel would have its own distinctive character and be 'complementary' to ITV:

> Programmes, while still intended to appeal to as many viewers as their individual terms of reference allow, can address themselves to particular interests or concerns and adopt new approaches far more freely than at present. Our wish is that the Fourth Channel will take particular advantage of this freedom, and that enterprise and experiments will flourish. It must provide opportunities for talents which have not been fully used, for needs to be served that have not yet been defined, and for the evolution of ideas which, for whatever reason – personal, structural, institutional – have yet to be revealed.

Such a service would not, however, be confined to small audiences. The fourth channel would not be a totally 'minority service':

> Rather we would see the present 'mix' on ITV's single channel continuing, while the Fourth Channel roughly reversed that 'mix', with about two-thirds of its programmes addressing sections of the audience who want something particular or want something different. In the remaining one-third there would be programmes intended to appeal to larger audiences, though often in a style different from that of some popular programmes now seen. (p .138)

Lastly, the IBA's proposals addressed the financing of the new channel in more detail than Whitelaw had yet done:

> The annual budget for the Fourth Channel would be determined by the Authority, after consultation with the Channel's board. Initially our forecasts suggest that it could be in the order of £60–80m, in 1979 terms. The sum required would be raised from the ITV programme contractors, as a Fourth Channel subscription.' (p. 138)

In return, advertising space on the fourth channel would be sold by the ITV companies in their own regions. So the new channel would, in effect, be funded by a levy, set by the IBA, on the continued ITV monopoly of television advertising sales. 'Nevertheless,' the IBA added:

> we should not wish to see the Fourth Channel as a permanent pensioner of ITV1 ... we would hope to see the Fourth Channel in due course adding between a fifth and a quarter, in real terms, to the total advertising revenue now earned by the programme contractors. (p. 140)

Altogether more detailed than Whitelaw's RTS speech, the IBA's proposals for the fourth channel were susceptible to less varied interpretation by interested parties, and were therefore the object of more criticism from those parties (Lambert, 1982, p. 104). Partisans of independent production felt they would bestow too much power and programming supply in the hands of the ITV companies; while the ITV 'big five' feared that they themselves would be left with too little, and that too many concessions had been made to what the ITV companies saw as the vague and uncommercial notions of the 70s critics.

But despite the conflicting criticisms – or more likely because they balanced each other out – the IBA's November 1979 proposals formed the basis on which the fourth channel was to be established. The legislation that provided for this was the 1980 Broadcasting Act. In keeping with Whitelaw's September 1979 RTS pronouncements, the Act left considerable discretion in the hands of the IBA. It therefore enabled the Authority to put into effect virtually everything it had proposed in November 1979.

Three specific prescriptions of the 1980 Act are worth mentioning. First, the Act embodied in statute the 'alternative' nature of the fourth channel:

> It shall be the duty of the Authority [IBA] –
>
> (a) to ensure that the programmes contain a suitable proportion of matter calculated to appeal to tastes and interests not generally catered for by ITV;
> (b) ... to ensure that a suitable proportion of programmes are of an educational nature;
> (c) to encourage innovation and experiment in the form and content of programmes,
>
> and generally to give the Fourth Channel a distinctive character of its own. (*Broadcasting Act*, 1980, 3(1))

This was, so far as the British tradition of broadcasting regulation was concerned, a quite original – and quite specific – statutory prescription. For the first time a television channel was given a specific statutory remit to be 'different'. This

'Channel Four remit' was to become an important fact of the British broadcasting scene and the British broadcasting debate. Internationally it was also original, and was to take on an exemplary status in debates on broadcasting in a number of other countries.

Second, the 1980 Act required the IBA to ensure that 'a substantial proportion' of the programmes broadcast on the fourth channel should be supplied by bodies other than the ITV contractors – in other words, they should be supplied by independent producers. Of course, the expression 'substantial proportion' was vague in the extreme. Many prospective independents might have preferred a quota for independent production, and one rather higher than the 15–35 per cent of the IBA's proposals. It remained to be seen how the IBA, and the controllers of the fourth channel, would interpret their remit in terms of programme supply. But for the first time in Britain, a television channel was being established with a statutory requirement for some significant element of independent production.

Last, but possibly not least, the 1980 Act gave a powerful indication as to the name of the new channel. Throughout the Act it was referred to as 'the Fourth Channel'. Back in 1977 Whitelaw had effectively claimed to be fulfilling the spirit of Annan's OBA in the organisational form of 'ITV 2'. The 1980 Broadcasting Act, coming on top of the IBA's November 1979 proposals, ensured that the name 'ITV 2' was dead. The ground was now cleared for 'Channel Four'. At least so far as the 70s debate was concerned, the name was not unimportant. But would the new channel live up to that name and the intentions that Whitelaw had proclaimed both in opposition (in response to Annan) and in government (in his 1979 RTS speech)?

## Channel Four in Practice

Soon to be empowered by the 1980 Act, and, at the very least, not discouraged by the government, the IBA rapidly set about implementing their November 1979 proposals on the fourth channel. In February 1980 the various interested parties (particularly the ITV companies and prospective independents) were invited to submit nominations for consultants on the fourth channel, who would form the board of the Channel Four Company when it was formally incorporated in December 1980, a month after the Broadcasting Act had received royal assent. This shadow Channel Four board was constituted in the summer of 1980 along the lines that had been set out in the IBA's November 1979 proposals.

Three things about its composition are worth noting. First, its Chairman and Vice-Chairman, former Labour minister, Edmund Dell, and actor and film-maker, Richard Attenborough, were both clearly independent of the big ITV companies. Both were also supporters of the Labour Party (although both were soon to join the SDP). There does not appear to have been any significant government pressure to put their own party nominees in place. Second, the shadow board included long-time advocates of an 'alternative' fourth channel, most notably Anthony Smith. Third, although the ITV companies had the four representatives outlined in the IBA's November 1979 proposals, only one of these was a managing director of one of the 'Big 5' ITV companies (Lambert, 1982, p. 116).

29

So the IBA had not merely relegated ITV to a minority on the board of the new channel, it had also endeavoured to stop this minority acting as a cohesive block in the interests of the ITV network programme suppliers.

These decisions were all taken by the IBA – not the government. But they were at the very least acquiesced to by the government. All of them pointed in the direction of a fourth channel that would lean closer to the independent and alternative model, rather than to 'ITV 2'.

A further pointer in this direction was given in September 1980 when the shadow Channel Four board announced the appointment of Jeremy Isaacs as Chief Executive of the new channel. Isaacs – incidentally another Labour supporter – was a distinguished programme-maker and one-time independent producer. He had voiced opinions on the fourth channel since the early 70s, envisaging a channel under the auspices of the IBA, but which would 'widen the range of broadcasting' (Isaacs, 1989, pp. 200–2). In August 1979, in the keynote MacTaggart lecture at the Edinburgh Television Festival, he had argued for a fourth channel which extends choice available to viewers; which extends the range of ITV's programmes; which caters for substantial minorities presently neglected; which builds into its actuality programmes a complete spectrum of political attitude and opinion; ... which encourages worthwhile independent production' (p. 19). And in his letter of acceptance of the Channel Four position, Isaacs included the following in his list of priorities: 'To encourage innovation across the whole range of programmes; ... To make programmes of special appeal to particular audiences; ... To provide platforms for the widest range of opinion in utterance, discussion and debate ...' (p. 25).

All this looked like – admittedly qualified – good news for advocates of alternative programming for the fourth channel. But how much did Channel Four live up to Isaacs's – and Whitelaw's – declared intentions, and to the guarded hopes of the 70s critics?

Channel Four began broadcasting in November 1982. It faced an initial round of press criticism for its supposedly small audiences, esoteric programming, alleged offences to taste and decency and left-wing bias. But it weathered this, perhaps rather artificial, storm, to become an accepted, if periodically controversial, part of the British television scene.

In its first full year of broadcasting (1983) Channel Four took 4.4 per cent of the British television audiences. By 1988, the last year in which Isaacs was Chief Executive, the new channel's share had more than doubled to 8.9 per cent. That was enough to put Channel Four in the same league as BBC 2. Under Isaacs's successor, Michael Grade, Channel Four's ratings stagnated for a couple of years, but in the early 90s they forged ahead again, narrowly overtaking BBC 2. In 1992, the last year of the 'old' regime (before the 1990 Broadcasting Act had come into full force), they reached 10.1 per cent. And in 1993, the first year in which it sold its own advertising, Channel Four's share reached a high point of 11 per cent (Channel Four *Annual Report*, 1995, p. 40).

By the time that the channel was forced to sell its own advertising by the 1990 Broadcasting Act, it was already justifiably confident that it could pay for itself. For the year to March 1990 Channel Four recorded that the subscription to fund it constituted 13.1 per cent of terrestrial television net advertising revenue, but its share of commercial television audience was 17.1 per cent (Channel Four *Annual Report*, 1989/90, p. 44). The IBA's November 1979 hopes that the fourth channel would not, in the long term, be 'a pensioner of ITV 1' had been met in full.

In one respect, therefore, Whitelaw's response to Annan in opposition had been more than fulfilled by his party's actions in office. In audience and revenue terms the Tories had established a more than viable new channel. Whitelaw's financial and organisational model for the fourth channel had been vindicated – at least in conventional broadcasting terms.

There were two other tests for Whitelaw's 1977 policy. Did the new channel substantially increase the number and type of voices represented on British television? And did it significantly add to the source of programme supply?

In its formative years Channel Four introduced a variety of programming innovations, many of which would have found favour with the 70s critics. The channel pioneered the treatment of gay, black and feminist issues in factual programming, entertainment and drama; a rather less narrowly 'balanced' treatment of current affairs; television support for feature-film production, much of it of 'art' films; access programming; a wide variety of experimental approaches across all genres; and some new devices for scheduling – for example, 'themed' evenings. Many of these innovations became accepted parts of the rest of British television in the subsequent decade. (For an assessment of the first ten years of Channel Four programming, see Harvey, 1994, pp. 117–24.)

There were, of course, limits to this innovation. Some of these were apparent early on in the channel's career. One notable example was *The Friday Alternative*, a current affairs programme broadcast in the channel's first year, which attempted to offer a different news agenda from that of the conventional television news broadcasters, including ITN (Channel Four's main news provider). Isaacs later recalled: 'nothing prepared me for the sheer élan of *The Friday Alternative* on our first Friday on the air. It had spark, it had sparkle.' But the programme also had problems, in Isaacs's and other eyes. Most crucial of these, according to Isaacs, was that it 'appeared consistently if not exclusively to present only one alternative viewpoint, that of the left'. This rapidly got the programme into trouble with the IBA, and with the Channel Four board. After a year, despite Isaacs's willingness to continue it in modified form, *The Friday Alternative* was axed (Isaacs, 1989, pp. 82–5). This was particularly significant, given that much of the 70s' critique of the duopoly's lack of pluralism had effectively come from the left. But it is also worth noting that the decision to end *The Friday Alternative* came from the regulators and the board – not directly from the government. Isaacs recalled that Whitelaw, in particular, was generally supportive of the channel's programming against its early critics (pp. 66–7).

Other limits began to appear as the channel matured. A contrast was often made between Channel Four's early years under Isaacs and its later years under Michael Grade. Under Grade, it was suggested from many quarters, Channel Four's alternative remit became increasingly sacrificed to audience maximisation. Anthony Smith's verdict on the channel's tenth anniversary is particularly noteworthy:

It [Channel Four] has now convinced itself that post-1993 it is to be just another commercial enterprise . . . it has given up its interventions in the world of cinema. . . . It has given up its support of workshops and, as far as I can see, also every other manifestation of extreme experiment. . . . It has stopped pushing at its boundaries every week, every day as it is supposed to do. . . . Ten years on there is a new generation of programme-makers hammering on the door – it should be their channel. It should be open to them. Is it? Is it really? (*Impact*, October 1992, pp. 9–11)

Against that verdict should be set three other features of Channel Four in the late 80s and early 90s. It continued, periodically, to shock pro-Establishment observers. Grade personally was regularly prominent in defending such controversial behaviour by the channel and the liberal thinking that went with it. And if Channel Four's programming appeared less challenging in its later years, that was to a considerable degree because many of its pioneering innovations had become the established currency of other channels. Even for iconoclasts, imitation is the sincerest form of flattery.

However Smith's critique of the channel, ten years on, raises a deeper issue. In 1977 Annan had reported the widespread feeling among the 70s critics that broadcasting should be 'opened up'. The Committee advocated an OBA to run the fourth channel for precisely that reason. Whitelaw claimed to fulfil the aim with a different structure. Over the range of programming issues we have described, Channel Four succeeded in this. But, a decade on, the channel was scheduled and supplied with programmes made almost exclusively by a layer of television professionals. They may well have had a wider range of horizons and they may well have come from a wider range of backgrounds than the previous generation of television professionals. But television professionals they remained nevertheless. In that respect, as Channel Four settled into a successful maturity, there were real limits to the extent to which it had 'opened up' the medium.

This question of a reconstitution of television professionalism is to some degree bound up with the other criterion of Channel Four's success – its diversification of the sources of programme supply. Throughout the 70s debate and the lobbying over the constitution of Channel Four, much of the argument had centred quite crudely on how much of the new channel should be programmed by ITV, and how much of it should be supplied by independent producers. The IBA's 1979 proposals had, remember, suggested an initial proportion of 15–35 per cent of programming from independents, and 35–60 per cent from ITV. In other words, while a significant share of programmes would, for the first time in Britain, be made by independent producers, the lion's share would come from the ITV companies. From the start, Channel Four in practice reversed this share-out. In 1983, of the total programme hours which Channel Four transmitted, 29 per cent was supplied by independent producers and only 25 per cent by ITV. In money terms the balance was even more favourable to independent producers – in 1983 the channel spent £19.1 million on commissions from independents, but only £7.9 million on commissions from ITV. The same balance continued in later years (Channel Four *Annual Report*, 1986/7, p. 8).

So, in terms of supply, ITV was, from the start, very much the junior partner in Channel Four. The independents' proportion of total programme hours did not decisively break through the 35 per cent upper estimate of the November 1979 IBA proposals. However, this was only because, from its early days, and even more once the channel increased its daily hours of transmission, the proportion of broadcast transmission time taken up by acquired (mainly foreign) programming was far higher than the IBA had originally envisaged (in 1983 purchased programming constituted 37 per cent of Channel Four hours; in 1995, including repeats, the figure was just over 50 per cent (Channel Four *Annual Report*, 1986/7, p. 8; 1995, p. 29).

With this balance of programming supply, Channel Four effectively brought into being a substantial new sector in the British television industry – the independent production sector. What, in the 70s debates, had largely been aspirant independent producers, became, with the establishment of Channel Four, real – if generally somewhat precarious – ones. In 1984/5, for example, Channel Four made payments to 313 independent production companies, the vast majority of which had simply not existed before the creation of the channel.

Already fired by the 70s debates, and now with real economic interests to protect and promote, independent producers were vociferous in advancing their cause. An Independent Programme Producers' Association (IPPA), specifically geared towards the fourth channel, had been formed in the summer of 1980 (Lambert, 1982, p. 123). At first almost exclusively financed by Channel Four commissions, the new independent production sector soon began to extend its aspirations to the other terrestrial channels. In the mid-80s independent producers found the ear of the Peacock Committee and mounted an extremely successful campaign for a 25 per cent independent production quota on BBC and ITV. It took time for that quota to have an effect, however, and for most of the 80s the independent production sector remained largely dependent on Channel Four. But by the mid-90s independent producers had found their place in the rest of UK television. A major survey of independent producers in 1995 showed Channel Four providing only 15 per cent of independent producers' income, behind the BBC (33 per cent) and ITV (20 per cent) (Price Waterhouse, 1995, p. 6). Channel Four had been absolutely decisive in creating, virtually from scratch, the independent production sector, but, scarcely a dozen years on, that independent production sector had clearly outgrown its Channel Four origins.

In the debates of the 70s the case for independent production of programming had gone hand in hand with the case for alternative programme content. The establishment of Channel Four seemed to confirm the essential link between the two arguments. The independent production sector was, after all, brought into existence by a channel whose specific remit was to be alternative. It was therefore quite natural that the output of the new sector at first bore an alternative stamp. But as the independent production sector has grown beyond Channel Four, the equation of independent production with alternative content can no longer be taken for granted. Today – for good or evil – the bulk of the turnover of the sector is taken by primarily commercially motivated companies, producing programming mainly for the two old pillars of the duopoly. Whether that programming is fundamentally more innovative because of its independent origins would be a hard case to prove.

In his memoirs published in 1989, Whitelaw observed of the creation of Channel Four that there is no political decision that I made in my political career that has had more impact on the daily life of families in Britain ... Initially I kept quiet when I heard voluble criticism of Channel 4, sometimes from my own colleagues. But steadily my confidence in its future success grew, and today I feel very pleased about its achievements. (Whitelaw, 1989, pp. 220–1)

The governmental architect of Channel Four had good reason to be proud of his achievement. In creating Channel Four, the government had speedily brought into reality the goal that Whitelaw had outlined in opposition in 1977 – a channel embodying the spirit of Annan but on a firmer financial footing and with a more pragmatic structure. And, so far as most observers were to judge over the following decade, it worked. The new channel secured a more than respectable audience, became financially secure enough to eventually loosen its ties with ITV, was genuinely and influentially innovatory in programming and succeeded in bringing into existence what had been a widely accepted goal of the 70s critics – a serious independent production sector.

This last achievement had a further spin-off in terms of subsequent Tory broadcasting policy. There were two quite different arguments for independent production. One was that independent production allowed new and alternative voices into television. This was the argument that had dominated the 70s debate, and it was a line of thinking whose roots lay very much on the left. But there was a second justification for independent production – that it helped introduce economic competition into television production, and so exerted a downward pressure on broadcasting costs, in particular by weakening the trade union organisation in the industry which had flourished in the large, vertically integrated organisations of the duopoly (for a critical assessment of this line of thought, see Sparks, 1994). This second argument was only to gain widespread currency with the publication of the Peacock Report in 1986. As Channel Four was established, it was the first argument which was dominant. However, partisans of independent production did make some rather opportunistic use of the second argument after 1979 in order to win support in the new Tory administration (see Lambert, 1982, p. 89; Isaacs, 1989, pp. 107–8). And Isaacs recalls Margaret Thatcher appealing to him in the summer of 1982, before the channel began transmission, to 'stand up for free enterprise' (p. 107). But in general, at the time Channel Four was created, this second argument was not the main one used to justify the place of independent production on the new channel.

How much the Tories, between 1977 and 1982, were conscious of the long-term advantages which independent production created for a more free-market policy remains uncertain. But conscious or not, Whitelaw's creation of Channel Four, alongside its more obvious achievements, did have the longer-term merit, from a Conservative point of view, of channelling an originally left-wing aspiration for independent production into a reality which was to give an important extra lever to the free-market right.

# ITV and the BBC in the Early Thatcher Years

In its creation of Channel Four, the first Thatcher administration was, perhaps surprisingly, successfully innovatory. But, so far as the rest of the terrestrial television system was concerned, the Tory government between 1979 and 1983 was, by and large, distinctly conservative – with a small 'c'. In legislative terms, it left the core of the television duopoly almost completely alone. And, in its use of the other instruments of influence at its disposal, the first term of the Tory administration after 1979 was, in general, both cautious in voice and modest in effect.

The Annan Report had recommended the extension of the life of the IBA to 1996. This, Whitelaw did in the 1980 Broadcasting Act. It would, he later explained, 'provide much-needed stability to television broadcasting, which had been damaged by uncertainty over the future of both major services' (Whitelaw, 1989, p. 219).

When the Tories gained office in 1979 the existing ITV franchises were scheduled to run out at the end of 1981. In February 1979 the IBA had published for consultation its plans for granting new ones. So, three months before the general election of 1979, the Authority had already publicly set in train the process of ITV franchise renewal, and also of awarding a new commercial breakfast licence. This process proceeded undisturbed by the change in administration.

In January 1980 the IBA advertised the old ITV and new breakfast franchises, invited applications by May and summoned applicants for interview in November and December. It announced the results of its deliberations shortly after Christmas 1980. Those results meant that three of the fifteen regional ITV franchises changed hands (two going to newcomers, one as a result of a forced amalgamation) and that the new commercial breakfast franchise was awarded to the apparently distinctively up-market, news and current affairs-oriented TV-am. The new franchises were allocated on the basis of programme promises and the 'beauty contest' of interview, without any requirement that the IBA explain its decisions, or any consideration of money. At the time, the opaqueness, and possible injustice, of this process was widely criticised in the press. And IBA Chairman Lord Thomson subsequently famously observed that 'there must be a better way' to allocate franchises (Potter, 1990, chs. 21–3, pp. 308–61).

However, at the time there were few suggestions as to what that 'better way' might be. A handful of contemporary commentators (for example, John Junor in the *Sunday Express* [4 January 1981] and an editorial in the *Spectator* [3 January 1981] ) suggested that franchises should go to the highest bidder. But these were minority – and soon to be forgotten – voices. Proposals for an ITV franchise auction received no public support from the government at the time. The new ITV franchisees were left, largely uncriticised, by the government to run their course.

In the early 80s this course involved rapidly rising advertising revenues. 'As advertising revenues grew', wrote one observer at the end of the decade, '– and for most of the 1980s they grew at 11 per cent per annum above the rate of inflation – the problem [for the ITV companies] ceased to be one of having enough money to make programmes and became one of how to spend it' (Davis, 1991, p. 41).

With this increase in revenue came a small but steady growth in the numbers employed by the ITV companies over the first half of the decade.

Three other aspects of ITV during those years are also worth noting. First, the ITV companies broadened their share ownership, thus becoming more susceptible to the demands of the stock exchange. Second, several ITV companies diversified into other business (Davis, 1991, pp. 41–2). However, as events were to turn out later in the 80s, such diversification was not, on the whole, very successful. Lastly, this period coincided with the expansion of commercial television in Europe. In this, the ITV companies played no part. Perhaps they were inhibited in doing so precisely because of their long-established and secure domestic revenues and their place in a highly regulated broadcasting framework. But whatever the reason, this, and other aspects of ITV performance drew no sustained government criticism in the early 80s. In practice, the new Tory government, before the Peacock Report, effectively let ITV get on with its business, governed by a framework determined long before the Thatcher administration had taken office.

On the BBC side of the duopoly the picture was much the same. In opposition Thatcher herself had been perceived by BBC executives as unenthusiastic towards the Corporation. Ian Trethowan, Director-General of the BBC at the time, recalled a meeting between Thatcher and a number of BBC editors in 1978: 'The lady arrived with all guns firing, she showed scant interest in, let alone tolerance of, the editors' problems, and berated them on their failings over a wide area, particularly their coverage of Northern Ireland' (Trethowan, 1984, p. 181). After 1979 there continued to be periodic outbursts from both government front and back benches about the BBC's coverage of Northern Ireland. And in 1982 there was a similar outburst over the Corporation's supposedly 'unpatriotic' approach to the Falklands War.

However, these occasional incidents of political hostility to BBC programming did not translate into any plans for changes in the institutional framework of the Corporation. Government spokesmen regularly uttered ritual praise of the BBC's important role in national life and the need to maintain its independence; the government dropped the previous Labour administration's proposal to set up 'service boards' which would have provided an instrument for closer government supervision of the BBC; the Home Secretary firmly refused to consider advertising on the BBC (HoC Debates, 20 February 1980, col. 192); and the government renewed the Corporation's Charter, virtually unchanged, for fifteen years from 1981.

The only significant legislative change the early Thatcher government made to the BBC was to include the establishment of a statutory Broadcasting Complaints Commission (BCC) (for all broadcasting) in the 1980 Broadcasting Act. And this was not a specifically Tory innovation. It had been recommended by Annan, and its establishment received cross-party support.

The only area, in those early years, in which the government did begin to chart a new course for the BBC was in its appointments to the Corporation's Board of Governors. From the start of the new administration, the Tories used their power of appointment to shift the balance of the Board, ensuring that it would be less bi-partisan, more sympathetic to the government and more interventionist within the Corporation. One notable appointee in this respect was William Rees-Mogg, former *Times* editor and Conservative supporter, who was Vice-Chairman of the Governors between 1981 and 1986 (O'Malley, 1994, pp. 136–41). However, the effects of this shift in composition of the Governors would only bring substantial results after 1985. Whatever may have been the intentions behind their selection, the Tory government's first two appointees as Chairman of the BBC Governors – George Howard (1980 to 1983) and Stuart Young (1983 to 1986) – both turned out to be strongly supportive of the Corporation's traditions against its critics.

So, with the exception of Channel Four (and it was a very important exception), Thatcher's first administration largely left British terrestrial television alone. In part, that may have been because of other political and legislative priorities. But surely an important factor was William Whitelaw's occupancy during this period of the office of Home Secretary, the Cabinet Minister responsible for broadcasting. As both his pronouncements at the time and his memoirs indicate, Whitelaw was an unreconstructed supporter of the duopoly. 'The organisation of the BBC and the IBA ensures broadcasting standards which are the envy of many other countries,' he pointedly declared in 1989, when both institutions had become very much the targets for reform in government circles (Whitelaw, 1989, p. 217).

This did not, however, mean that, with the exception of Channel Four, the Tories stood still on television before 1983. There were also new technologies of television distribution coming up for political attention – satellite and cable.

# 4 New Technologies, New Approaches: 1. Satellite

In 1977 the Annan Report had effectively relegated the new technologies of distribution – cable and satellite – to the margins of British television policy. In sharp contrast, the new Conservative government moved quickly to produce substantial reports on both satellite and cable television: a Home Office study on *Direct Broadcasting by Satellite* was published in May 1981; *Cable Systems* by the Cabinet Office's Information Technology Advisory Panel (ITAP) followed in March 1982; and an inquiry chaired by Lord Hunt on *Cable Expansion and Broadcasting Policy* reported in October 1982. The government rapidly formulated strategies based on those reports, implementing them even before it finally established a full, revised legal framework for the new broadcasting technologies with the 1984 Cable and Broadcasting Act.

The change in government in 1979 was not the decisive factor in this shift of emphasis. Just as any new government, regardless of its political colour, would have had to grapple with the inherited business of the terrestrial channels – old and new – which we have described in the last chapter, so any new government elected in 1979 would have had to consider seriously how it proposed to handle these two new distribution technologies.

The 1977 World Radio Administrative Conference (WRAC) had allocated to Britain five DBS television channels. As a result, any UK administration in the early 80s would have to confront the practical problem of what – if anything – it would do with these. An added spur to British government action was the prospect of the impact of spill-over from other countries' DBS channels on the UK's broadcasting ecology. And on cable, Jim Callaghan's Labour government had already parted company with Annan. Whereas Annan had wanted to confine cable to local or community service, and not authorise it to provide pay-TV, Labour's slim 1978 White Paper on *Broadcasting* maintained that 'in principle there seems to be no reason why both pay-television and community services should not develop side by side . . . there are possibilities which can be explored in the context of pilot pay-TV schemes' (Home Office, 1978, pp. 61, 63).

But although there was nothing distinctively Conservative – let alone Thatcherite – in the *amount* of attention given to cable and satellite in the few years after 1979, the *way* in which the Tories approached both technologies did have some very novel and ideologically distinctive features which were to prove of major importance in the development of British television policy in the 80s and 90s. This new thinking was particularly apparent in the case of cable. It was less clear in the Tories' early satellite policy, which was in many respects more in keeping with the pre-1979 broadcasting consensus. But even here there was, as we shall see, one crucial new element which marked a 'Thatcherite' break from that previous consensus.

However, because of their considerable differences in approach it will be useful to look at early 80s' Conservative policies on satellite and cable separately. In this chapter we will document how satellite policy was formulated in those early years, how it then worked out in practice, and how the government responded to this. In the next chapter we will do the same for cable.

## Satellite in theory

The new government moved on satellite first. On 13 March 1980, William Whitelaw announced to Parliament that he was setting up a Home Office study into DBS:

> Direct broadcasting by satellite, which could offer the United Kingdom up to five additional television channels, could mark a major development in our broadcasting arrangements and raise many complex issues. The United Kingdom has no plans for direct broadcasting by satellite at present, but I believe it is important to keep the present possibilities offered by technical developments in broadcasting under review. I have therefore decided to initiate a study of the implications of establishing a United Kingdom direct broadcasting satellite service by about 1985, which would be the earliest practicable date, or by about 1990.

This was carefully non-committal. But Whitelaw then went on to give clear indication as to the approach the study was to adopt. Alongside 'the technical, financial and resource implications for our broadcasting system and services', and 'likely developments in Europe', the study would also cover '*possible industrial benefits*' (Home Office, 1981 p. 3, or HoC Debates, 13/3/81, my emphasis). The study that Whitelaw had commissioned, *Direct Broadcasting by Satellite* (Home Office, 1981), appeared just over a year later.

One generally acute account of UK television policy has observed that 'the Home Office report on DBS when it emerged was not radical in tone. Indeed it was rather "wet" by Thatcherite standards; but the Home Office ... has a reputation for being soft on some issues' (Hood and O'Leary, 1990, p. 68). Such a verdict is, as we shall shortly see, in large part correct. But it underestimates just how innovatory was the attention the report gave – following Whitelaw's brief – to the supposed industrial opportunities presented by satellite. For good or ill, 'industrial opportunities' were quite marginal to the Pilkington or Annan reports. The 1981 DBS study saw 'industrial' considerations move to the centre of British television policy for the first time in the post-war period, and they have remained there – with some qualification in the second half of the 80s – ever since.

*Direct Broadcasting by Satellite* did not emerge with any firm recommendations for a specific strategy for the development of satellite television in the UK. Instead it set out a range of options. It is useful to look in some detail at those options, and the technological, economic and political assumptions on which they were based, and to set them against the record of how satellite television in Britain in fact turned out.

The technical framework with which the Home Office study began was the international allocation of DBS frequencies by the 1977 World Radio Administrative Conference. This had allocated each European country frequencies sufficient for a handful of satellite television channels receivable by its own population on a home dish of manageable size. Each country's satellite footprint was essentially national in scope, although right from the start the footprints were such that there was some significant overspill from one country to another. So, for example, one map included in the 1981 study (p. 11) had a substantial overspill from the French WRAC-allocated DBS satellite receivable in southern England on a 90cm dish (the size deemed suitable for home reception). There was a considerably bigger overspill with a larger dish. One of 2m (thought suitable only for community reception) would put most of the British population within the French, Irish, German and Nordic footprints (p. 13). On the technical level, the study concluded that 'the fact that footprints are designed essentially for national services and the possibility of interference from other services places limitations on the reception of overspill transmissions' (p. 12).

So DBS strategy, at least in the short run, was seen as a problem of the utilisation of a limited number (five) of UK-based and UK-directed satellite television channels. The threat – or opportunity – of UK-directed, directly home-received channels from satellites under other countries' jurisdictions was seen as marginal.

However, even from the perspective of 1981, the Home Office study added several significant riders to this viewpoint. In its opening technical chapters the study observed that 'developments in semiconductor technology offer the prospect of DBS receiving equipment of improved performance which could permit the use of a smaller antenna to achieve the standard of service'. These developments also implicitly opened up the technical possibility that dishes of a size suitable for home reception would be able to receive adequate reception from overseas-based satellites with a lower power than the 'national' DBS satellites (p. 12).

In a later chapter, when the study came to consider the 'overspill' issue in more detail, it remarked:

> Concern at the implications of overspill for broadcasting in the UK was reflected in many of the comments put to the study. The fear is that some European countries may decide to lease their satellite channels to commercial companies which would seek to provide popular programme services aimed at maximising audiences and profits, and that within the next few years these European super-stations as they are sometimes called might be receivable in the UK, might be in English or have a separate English-language sound channel, and might attract large numbers of UK viewers away from domestic services. (p. 76)

The Home Office report seemed to share the concern that, should this happen, it could put the whole of the UK's broadcasting ecology under threat. But the report went on:

> There are strongly varying opinions about whether such fears will be realised and if so, to what extent and when. It is not easy to make forecasts in this area, but many of the reports to date have failed to recognise the extent of the problems involved in the recep-

40

tion of foreign DBS transmissions and the comparatively limited plans for European DBS services to date. (p. 76)

The report concluded that overseas-based UK-directed satellite services – what it called commercial DBS 'super-stations' – would be 'unlikely to develop much before 1985 and possibly later' (p. 79). That prognosis was to prove correct. But again the Home Office study added a rider:

> Nevertheless the possibility that European DBS services will develop ... cannot be discounted. Some organisations which commented to the study considered that there was a real possibility of European DBS services of a kind which deliberately sought to attack UK audiences and advertising revenue. In general *they saw this possibility as strengthening the case for an early UK DBS service, and argued that unless a UK service was established at the same time as, or earlier than, attractive European services directed to UK audiences, a pattern could be established which would be difficult to break.* UK audiences might become accustomed to watching European services using equipment which was unsuitable for receiving UK DBS transmissions and might not be willing or able to spend more to receive any UK DBS services which were established subsequently. (p. 79, my emphasis)

With hindsight it is easy to see that it was precisely this possibility that turned out to be the case when Rupert Murdoch's UK-directed Sky service, transmitted from the Luxembourg-based Astra satellite, went on air in 1989, over a year ahead of the 'official' UK-based DBS service, BSB.

In 1981 the Home Office study made no firm recommendations about how fast (if at all) UK DBS services should be developed. It listed five options (p. 88), ranging in time from 'a full but early start ... perhaps in 1986' with two channels, to a later full or partial start, in 1990, to no DBS at all. But the report's assessment of the possible impact of overspill, and its timescale, made a powerful argument for the early start option.

Following the brief given by Whitelaw, *Direct Broadcasting by Satellite* devoted a separate chapter (Chapter 7) to what it called 'the industrial dimension' of the new broadcasting technology. It began:

> In the United Kingdom there is now an increasing awareness that there is likely to be a substantial world market in direct broadcasting satellites and the associated receiving equipment over the next decade and that it is an important element of what could be an even more valuable market for what is known as information technology, which the UK is well placed to develop. (p. 40)

The particular industries which the report singled out as 'likely to benefit most from the early introduction of a UK DBS service' were aerospace and electronics. Both industries were described as 'in the forefront of technological developments', and their future success as 'likely to be important to the health of the UK economy'. Both industries, the report continued, needed to compete successfully in international markets, and believed that their success would depend on the existence of a home market: 'Thus UK exports of satellites and receiving equipment and other receiving equipment could be strongly influenced by the decision on a UK DBS service and the date by which any service is introduced' (p. 41).

This was a second argument in favour of an early start. The report quoted estimates that in the coming fifteen years there would be an international market, outside the USA, Japan and the Eastern bloc, for over 100 large telecommunications satellites. A quarter of that might be the target of British manufacturers. But, 'without a UK DBS service, the industry believes that it would be unable to compete on satisfactory terms against other manufacturers who have already been able to develop and build satellites for their own domestic markets.' The UK aerospace industry therefore wanted a UK DBS start 'at the earliest possible date' (p. 41). The same message came from the manufacturers of broadcasting equipment and consumer electronics.

Among the other industries considered by *Direct Broadcasting by Satellite* one other that should be noted, in view of subsequent developments, was the film industry. Most comments to the study expected that DBS channels would rely heavily on feature films. And the report itself concluded: 'whatever the exact nature of any new DBS services, it seems likely that they would generate an increased demand for feature films.' The problem was that this increase in demand for film would be spread across film producers internationally: 'The UK industry is not particularly robust at the present time and could find it difficult to respond to competition, particularly from the USA.' So, the report tentatively observed, the case for either a quota or a levy on DBS programme services to encourage UK film production would 'need to be considered' (p. 46).

If the technical and industrial arguments pointed to an early start for UK DBS, what of the broadcasting arguments? And, regardless of whether UK DBS was to start earlier or later, what programmes would appear on it, by whom and under what sort of control?

Here, *Direct Broadcasting by Satellite* was particularly non-committal, but the specific framework within which it approached the questions tends to bear out the view that the Home Office study displayed the department's continued attachment to the parameters of public service broadcasting. Chapter 6 of the report discussed 'the broadcasting dimension' of DBS. The main feature of UK broadcasting policy to date, it explained, had been that 'broadcasting services should be provided only as public services and only by public authorities which have been specifically set up to act as trustees of the public interest in broadcasting' (pp. 33–4). The report continued:

> The services which our broadcasting system provides, particularly their quality and range, are appreciated at home and much admired abroad. It has been an aim of broadcasting policy, especially in relation to the use of additional broadcasting outlets, to improve programme standards and to widen choice of content and variety wherever possible. This may seem self-evident, but experience in other countries suggests that an increase in the number of broadcasting outlets does not in itself necessarily lead to better programme service or to wider variety. (p. 34)

Among the possible pitfalls the Home Office study pointed to were, first, that

> if competition for audiences were to become ... the dominant factor, while the choices of services might increase in terms of the *number* of programme services available, there is a risk that the *range* and *quality* of programmes across the various broadcasting outlets might be reduced.

Second:

> there is a risk too that a new DBS service, which for a considerable period would be likely to be viewed by a minority, could have the effect of siphoning programme material from, and thereby impoverishing, the existing services which are viewed by a majority of the public. (pp. 38–9)

The report's chapter on 'the broadcasting dimension' concluded that if 'the primary aim were to minimise the risks to existing broadcasting services and the new services which are to be introduced over the next few years [Channel Four and breakfast television]', then there should be no early start for UK DBS. But this strategy would in turn carry the risk of the UK 'opt[ing] out of a development which other industrialised countries ... are experimenting with, and one which could prove important'.

There was another option:

> If the primary aim were to provide new broadcasting opportunities which could be exploited, broadcasting considerations would point to a modest start with DBS services (perhaps one or two television channels only) ... This would enable us to build on the essential features of the existing system.

It would also be more flexible, allowing the addition of further DBS services at a later date in the light of experience (p. 40).

Though this was not directly spelt out, the thrust of the report's discussion of 'the broadcasting dimension' was therefore to reinforce the case, suggested by 'the industrial dimension' and by the likely eventual challenge from UK-directed European DBS services, for an early start with UK DBS. However, the report's treatment of broadcasting considerations also hinted that (although, again it did not specifically conclude this) the early start should be a modest one, and one whose programme services would be provided under the auspices of some sort of public authority and within some sort of public service framework.

This public authority could be either the BBC or the IBA (or both together), which would have the advantage of minimising the risk to existing services. Alternatively, a new specifically DBS authority could be set up, but, the report observed, 'it is questionable whether the establishment of a new authority would be justified if the IBA were able to take on these functions' (pp. 64–5).

However, the IBA – at the time preoccupied with the introduction of the fourth channel – was opposed to an early introduction of DBS. The IBA commented to the study that it 'did not believe there will be a broadcasting case for more channels until after 1990, by which time the expansion of the independent system which is now in the pipeline will have been completed' (p. 51).

Two specific proposals were made to the study for new DBS services. One was by the BBC for two DBS channels. One of these would be 'a subscription service which would include feature films, first runs of BBC special productions, opera, drama, music and extended coverage'. The second proposed channel would be used for 'retransmissions of the "best of BBC 1 and BBC 2" in a new form'. Granada's proposal was for a service consisting 'largely of recent feature films. ... Granada foresaw that, as such a service developed, it might include spectaculars, sporting and other events'. Although the company saw its proposal as being funded mainly by subscription it did not want either advertising or sponsorship ruled out (pp. 50–1).

So, for all its carefully phrased presentation of the different considerations, and its refusal to come down explicitly in favour of any of the options under discussion, the Home Office study made an implicit case for one of them. An early start for DBS was necessary so that UK industry could secure a slice of what was seen as an important developing international market. In order to minimise the risks to the UK's existing broadcasting, that start should be a modest one and come under the auspices of either the BBC or IBA. Given the BBC's apparent enthusiasm to run a DBS service and the IBA's opposition to early development, it followed that the BBC should be entrusted to make the early start. It was precisely this conclusion that William Whitelaw drew when he made his response to the report in the House of Commons on 4 March 1982:

> The Government now see a need for early decisions if the industrial opportunities which DBS offers this country are to be grasped in good time, in a situation in which there will be keen international competition. The Government have therefore decided, in principle, that this country should make an early start with DBS, with the aim of having a service in operation by 1986. Because of the importance of making an early start the Government have concluded that the best course would be to start with two channels initially, the number of channels could be increased ... as and when demand justified it.
>
> On the industrial side, various interests in the aerospace and related industries are ready to play their part in this challenging new venture and we shall be working closely with them and with the domestic electronics industry to ensure that the economic benefits are effectively realised for the United Kingdom.
>
> It is clear that DBS must develop in a way that is consistent with our existing broadcasting arrangements, especially as regards supervision and maintenance of proper programme standards. The BBC has already put forward proposals for two DBS channels. ... The IBA and commercial companies have also shown some interest in providing DBS services, but their plans are less well advanced. Additionally, more time will be needed to develop the right framework, which will be likely to involve legislation. In these circumstances the Government believe that the right course, if the necessary early agreements are to be reached between satellite providers and users, is to authorise a go-ahead with the BBC proposals.

Commercial television companies could come in later. In the meanwhile, the 'immediate requirement is for the BBC and the British aerospace industry to enter into discussions with a view to agreeing detailed proposals'. These discussions were already going on, and would continue over the next three years. They were to be profoundly influenced by one additional element in Whitelaw's announcement: 'the Government expect the capital cost of providing the satellite system to be met in the private sector' (HoC Debates, 4 March 1982).

Between 1982 and 1985 the BBC entered into a series of negotiations with potential British satellite providers, first on its own, and then in conjunction with the IBA and the ITV companies, in an effort to start a viable DBS service. Each stage of negotiation foundered, because the participants did not believe that they could make the commercial sums for the proposed service add up.

For eighteen months after Whitelaw's announcement the BBC alone negotiated with potential providers of the satellite hardware. In December 1983 the Corporation decided that it could proceed on its own no longer, and approached the government and the IBA to explore the possibilities of co-operation. In March 1984 the government proposed a joint DBS venture between the BBC, the ITV companies and other private investors. The institutional framework was put in place for a joint BBC/IBA satellite option in the 1984 Cable and Broadcasting Act, with the provision to establish a Satellite Broadcasting Board consisting of equal numbers from the IBA and the BBC Board of Governors. Provision was also made in the Act for the IBA to go it alone. This attempt to bring the IBA, BBC and other private companies together for a DBS venture resulted in a consortium known as the 'Club of 21'. But in June 1985 the 'Club of 21' finally announced that they too felt unable to proceed (O'Malley, 1994, pp. 141–5).

One of the major participants in these negotiations, the BBC's then Director-General, Alasdair Milne, has since given his own account of their frustrated course. Milne recalls that the BBC 'started down the DBS road with high hopes back in 1980'. It applied to run two DBS channels, because

> we were keen to get involved in this technology, as we had always been throughout our history, not least because it must surely, one day replace the transmitters that cover and sometimes despoil our countryside and become the new method of sending television and radio signals to everybody in the country. We also saw DBS as a new way of delivering quite different programme opportunities to an audience that would make its selection on a new pattern, and we thought we could achieve that as well as anyone else. Moreover we thought that in time this new service might earn the BBC some additional money. (Milne, 1989, p. 109)

Soon after the March 1982 announcement, Milne explains:

> the Government had stipulated that the satellite must be British-made, and to that end a consortium of GEC, British Aerospace and BT was formed calling itself UNISAT. Very early on in our negotiations the price of the satellite became a matter of dispute between us. (p. 112)

The attitude of the government to such difficulties is suggested by Milne's account of a meeting with Kenneth Baker, then the Minister of Information Technology at the DTI, in July 1982:

> He [Baker] wanted DBS to go ahead soon as part of the 'information technology-led industrial revolution'. But the Government intended to have no financial involvement, and he made that very clear. It was essentially an arm-twisting session to urge the project on. Speed, he said, was of the essence. (p. 113)

A further major difficulty, in Milne's view, was then added when it appeared that the government would impose an additional requirement on the new DBS service, that it be broadcast on the new C-MAC system rather than the UK's traditional PAL technology (p. 113).

By August 1983, according to Milne, plans had not advanced and the BBC Governors were considering (but had not yet decided) to approach the IBA and the ITV companies for their co-operation. In the following two or three months,

Milne recalls that 'the situation developed at great speed', thanks largely to apparent interest from Thorn/EMI in forming a partnership. However, in December of that year, Thorn/EMI revealed that they did not want to enter a partnership, because 'they felt it was too high a risk'. After that setback, the BBC moved into negotiations first with the ITV companies and then, at the government's insistence, with the ITV companies plus other private companies in the 'Club of 21'. These joint negotiations, too, eventually concluded that 'DBS as planned was not a viable business' (pp. 115–17). The Club finally threw in the towel in 1985.

There are no equivalent reflections from the inside about how the government viewed these ultimately frustrated attempts to establish a UK DBS service involving the BBC. We can only record its public comments at the time, which display a profound lack of awareness that the plans for a industry-boosting early start for DBS (and cable) in the UK were foundering. For example, in February 1984 Kenneth Baker told the House of Commons:

> One of the reasons why we are so keen on cable and DBS is that at present we have a lead in both these technologies. If cable systems can be operated in the United Kingdom in the next 12 months, and if the satellite can be launched successfully, we shall have satellite television in this country in 1987–88 and have a lead on any other European country. That will give us a technological lead in the manufacture of sets and equipment. That is why we are pushing ahead so strongly. (HoC Debates, 29 February, 1984, col. 253)

In fact, by 1984, there was very little evidence of any government push to overcome the major obstacles that were already apparent.

Milne makes the following verdict on the BBC's three years of negotiations over involvement in DBS, which he describes as being, ultimately, 'one of the chief failures in my time as Director-General of the BBC' (Milne, 1989, p. 118):

> Both the Governors and Management were rightly worried about the possible financial damage to the heartland of the BBC operations. Nobody had any experience of this type of venture; judgements about satellite and programme costs were obviously important, but decisions about the manufacture, delivery and sales of receivers were critical. At times we thought we could persuade the Department of Trade and Industry to go in for a pump-priming exercise to get the making of the sets started. They were after all doing such things within the rest of the economy. But the Government's philosophy was clear and undeviating. They had made the opportunities possible within the international agreements. It was up to the BBC, or anyone else, to pick up the baton and run with it, or not. They would not put one penny of public money towards this kind of venture which they saw as purely commercial ... This was a new medium that would be financed by consumer participation or not at all. They did not like the thought that it might fail, but they were not to be harried into a change of policy by the prospect of failure. (p. 117)

It is difficult not to accept the overall thrust of Milne's verdict. In March 1982 the government had decided on an early – 1986 – start on DBS for industrial reasons, so as to make the UK a world leader in the market for satellite and associated business. Government prescription of a British satellite system was entirely in keeping with that strategy. Also, in the same month, the government had quite reasonably decided on the BBC as the initial DBS service provider, on the grounds that the

Corporation was the organisation most advanced in its plans for such a service. But having willed the industrial end, the government, quite explicitly, ruled out the means – some injection of public funding – with the eventual result that, after more than three years, the prospect of BBC involvement in starting a UK DBS service finally foundered for good. The results of this failure were threefold:

First, the BBC, from 1985 until the 90s, withdrew from its ambition to be directly involved in any DBS service. In January 1988 the BBC explained its new approach to the House of Commons Home Affairs Select Committee. The Corporation's new strategy on DBS had two central strands. On the one hand, 'the BBC does not wish, over a foreseeable planning and funding period, to compete to manage any of the new services or to compete with them for advertising and subscription income.' On the other hand:

> new channels may offer the BBC valuable commercial opportunities for the onward sale of programmes, skills and resources. If so, the BBC seeks the freedom to exploit its existing resources and generate as much income as possible for reinvestment in programmes. (HoC Home Affairs Committee, 1988 II, p. 25).

The government's 1982 DBS strategy had been based primarily on industrial priorities, but the central involvement of the BBC in providing the proposed DBS service ensured that public service provision would have some significant place in deliberations on the use of the new technology. After 1985, with the BBC's withdrawal, policy towards satellite broadcasting in the UK was effectively focused exclusively on commercial considerations – any use of the new delivery system for public service purposes was relegated to the margins of debate.

Second, with the subsequent advertisement of a DBS franchise by the IBA and its award to British Satellite Broadcasting, one major part of the government's original industrial approach on DBS collapsed. In May 1987, soon after it had won the franchise, BSB awarded the contract for provision of two DBS satellites to the American company, Hughes Aircraft. As one commentator put it soon after, 'in the buyer's market which existed in the mid-80s, Hughes was able to put together the best finance and launch date package' (Goodfriend, 1988, pp. 167–8). Back in 1982, the opportunities offered to the *UK* aerospace industry were one of the key reasons for an early UK DBS start. After 1987 DBS was to proceed without those supposed opportunities being fulfilled.

A third consequence of three years of frustrated negotiation plans was that the 'early start', which the government in 1982 had claimed to consider so important, was no longer viable. That early start was, as we have seen, originally scheduled to be in 1986. When BSB was finally awarded a DBS franchise at the end of that year it expected its launch to take place no earlier than 1989. That brought it perilously near the time when, as the Home Office report had predicted, it would face – and perhaps lose out to – competition from UK-directed European-based commercial DBS services. As we shall shortly see, this was precisely what happened.

Soon after the collapse of the 'Club of 21' in 1985 the government asked the IBA to look into the possibility of awarding a DBS franchise in its own right. The IBA found considerable commercial interest, the government authorised the Authority to go ahead and in April 1986 the IBA advertised a franchise for three DBS channels (IBA, 1985/6, p. 6).

By the closing date in August the IBA had received five applications for the full three channels, together with two for single channel services. 'The number and quality of applications', commented the IBA, 'were high – reassuringly so in view of the difficulties that had been encountered by earlier attempts, involving the BBC, to proceed with a UK DBS project' (IBA Annual Report, 1986/7, p. 7). The membership of the competing consortia indicates the range of commercial interest that existed at the time in satellite television for a UK audience. Unsuccessful participants included Rupert Murdoch's News International, London ITV licensee, LWT, and future London ITV franchise-winner, Carlton Communications.

In December 1986 the IBA announced that it had awarded the franchise to British Satellite Broadcasting (BSB). The winning consortium also had a star-studded cast. BSB was composed of the increasingly media-oriented conglomerate, Pearson (the owner of the *Financial Times*); ITV franchisees, Granada and Anglia; successful electrical hardware supplier, Amstrad; and Richard Branson's Virgin.

BSB promised one channel of 'fast-moving fun entertainment' with 'plays, series, soap operas from the UK, US, Australia, Canada and elsewhere'; a channel devoted to what 'is actually happening in the world as the viewer switches on', with eight to ten hours a day provided by ITN; and a third channel that would be split between subscription movies in the evening and early morning and a Disney channel during the day.

This was a high-cost and self-consciously 'quality' approach to satellite broadcasting. According to the then Chairman of the IBA, Lord Thomson, two factors won BSB the franchise: 'We looked at the degree to which applicants were willing to devote resources to programming.' A second factor was BSB's dual-track plan for revenue – both advertising and subscription (*Broadcast*, 5 May 1990, pp. 20–1).

Right from the start the IBA, government and BSB were clear that its chances of success depended on a clear run free of new competition. So the other two DBS channels were to be held back until well after BSB started broadcasting, and in May 1988 BSB urged the government not to allow a fifth terrestrial channel until 1995. However, well before the IBA even advertised its DBS franchise, the government had, quite probably inadvertently, laid the regulatory basis for competitors to BSB.

In May 1985 a Home Office minister announced to the House of Commons that the government had decided to relax the licensing of Single Master Antenna Television Systems (SMATV). SMATV was a common dish servicing several households, and as events turned out it has not played a major part in satellite television development in the UK. But the May 1985 announcement contained what was to be a far more important relaxation. 'We have further decided', the government declared, 'that direct reception of low-powered satellite services on a single set of premises may also be permitted.' In other words, from 1985 on, anyone could have a satellite dish capable of receiving low- or medium-powered satellite services, subject only to planning permission. In the government's view this and other factors meant that such liberalisation would not be of great immediate impact. 'Because ... of the likely size and relatively high cost of a dish currently needed to receive these services,' the Home Secretary's Parliamentary Private Secretary, Tim Smith, told the Commons, 'it seems unlikely that this facility will be taken up in the short term by many members of the public, although some commercial organisations may wish to do so' (HoC Debates, 23 May 1985, col. 489).

This may well have been true at the time, and indeed until Sky's UK launch in 1989 individual household dishes were a quite marginal part of the British television environment. In 1988 one estimate put their number at only 18,000 (*Cable and Satellite Europe* October 1988 pp. 26–8, cited in Collins (1992, p. 35)). (Although this may well have had more to do with the low appeal to UK viewers of the 'pan-European' channels then on offer by satellite, rather than the size and cost of the dish required to see them.)

But, as the Home Office study on *Direct Broadcasting by Satellite* had pointed out four years before, technological advances meant that the dish size required to receive any given satellite was rapidly diminishing. The potential implications of such developments did not escape the notice of contemporary observers. A year after the lifting of restrictions on satellite dishes, the Peacock Committee observed:

> One aspect which the Government will keep under review is the extent to which the lifting of restrictions will lead to the growth of direct reception of ... services by individual households ... If it became clear that services were being established in this country intended exclusively for direct reception by individuals in the UK ... the government would wish to consider introducing further controls. (Peacock, 1986, p. 25)

The prospect of direct reception other than from the high-power 'official' DBS satellites was brought even closer by the scheduled launch of medium-powered satellites in Europe. The first of these, the Luxemburg licensed commercial satellite, Astra, was due for launch in June 1988. Even without improvements in receiver technology, these new medium-powered satellites required a smaller dish than the low-powered versions which the government had referred to in its May 1985 announcement.

By the beginning of 1988 it was commonly accepted among informed observers that there was now an alternative route to direct-to-home satellite reception. One academic article on satellite broadcasting in the UK published in that year confidently declared:

> Medium-powered satellites have stolen much of the thunder of the high-power satellites for national DBS. The size of TVRO [dish] required to receive the signal of a medium-powered satellite ... has shrunk to the point where it need only be a few centimetres larger than that required for a high-power satellite. The term DBS is, in fact now commonly used for both high-power and medium-power satellites. (Goodfriend, 1988, p. 167)

This technical potential of medium-powered satellites was also publicly recognised by the Home Office. In January 1988 a departmental memorandum to the House of Commons Home Affairs Committee stated:

A Luxemburg company, SES, has announced that it will launch later this year a medium-powered satellite called 'Astra' with a capacity for 16 channels which will be capable of direct reception by individuals with relatively cheap, small (60–85 cm) dishes. (Home Affairs Committee, 1988 II, p. 4)

Despite these numerous warnings, the possible threat to the official UK DBS plans posed by a UK-directed service from a medium-powered satellite was publicly dismissed by BSB. In March 1988, BSB Managing Director Graham Grist, made this response to an inquiry from the House of Commons Home Affairs Committee on the implications of medium-powered satellites, like Astra, for BSB's future:

> Really, the competition is with the BBC and ITV. If we cannot get an audience there we are not going to succeed. We are competing against the best English-speaking television in the world, and whatever comes on other marginal competitors is unlikely to be such that it would actually tip the balance between our success and our failure. Astra, as one example of a pan-european satellite, and there may well be others further ahead, is very much in that category: it is a pan-european charter, which means it is not really focused on the UK as we are. (Home Affairs Committee, 1988 II, p. 127)

From the early 80s until at least the launch of Sky in 1989, the government appeared to hold fast to its backing of official UK DBS, while absolving itself from possible failure on the grounds that 'there are strong arguments against the Government backing winners by artificially protecting one service or technology against competition from another'. In May, Home Office Minister responsible for broadcasting, Tim Renton, told the Home Affairs Committee:

> One of the key issues for our broadcasting system is timing ... we have made clear our desire to increase competition and consumer choice ... That does not in our minds imply that all the possibilities should be let loose simultaneously or as soon as possible. That would increase competition and advertising time and space in the short-term, but in the longer term it could mean that some services would collapse, which would be of no benefit to either the consumer or the industry. We have recognised the need to allow BSB to establish itself ... BSB will be crucially dependent on subscription income, particularly in the early years, and a new service financed by subscription and competing head-on with BSB subscription services – and I recognise this – would clearly be more of a threat to their viability than advertising financed services. That said, BSB is a commercial venture, they knew when they took on the contract of the risks – and I respect them for that – and that there could be no guarantees of success from the Government or elsewhere. (Home Affairs Committee, 1988 II, p. 275)

The widely forecast, but casually dismissed, challenge from medium-powered satellites to official UK DBS became a reality on 8 June 1988 when Rupert Murdoch announced that he was to launch a four-channel, *UK-directed*, direct-to-home service on the Astra satellite, which was then scheduled to be launched in November 1988.

By 1988 Murdoch had already held a commanding place in the British newspaper industry for several years. He had owned the pan-European Sky channel, broadcast on a low-powered satellite primarily for cable reception, since 1983, had been an unsuccessful contender for an ITV franchise many years before and more recently had been part of an unsuccessful consortium for the UK DBS franchise.

Here, then, was a serious challenge both to BSB's commercial prospects and to the DBS strategy that the government had formulated in the early 80s and still claimed to uphold. As *Broadcast* commented a week after the announcement:

> Murdoch's pre-emptive strike in announcing Sky Television has put a question mark over the viability of BSB's plans ... Murdoch also scored a marketing goal, creating an image of Sky television as the cheap and quick route into the world of satellite television. (*Broadcast*, 17 June 1988, p. 6)

To this challenge the government made no response.

BSB meanwhile continued on a course which seemed positively to invite disaster. Seeking to market its prospective service with an image based on its distinctive technology of reception, their slogan 'it's smart to be square' focused attention on the company's small square dish. But the technology for that dish and other aspects of BSB's delivery system (on MAC rather than the more established PAL system used by Sky) were still suffering teething problems. The thrust of the BSB campaign – technology rather than content – was probably misguided. It is programming that sells new television services, not technological wizardry. But the technological thrust of BSB's marketing had a particularly disastrous consequence. Unable to solve the technical problems with its delivery and reception system quickly enough, BSB was forced to delay the launch date until April 1990. Meanwhile, the Sky UK-directed direct-to-home service had launched on schedule in February 1989, a full fourteen months before BSB. By the time of the BSB launch Sky had already got over 600,000 dishes in place (Davis, 1991, p. 142).

In the six months that followed the BSB launch, it became clear that BSB's marketing pitch was quite unable to make up for Sky's early start. 'By the end of September it [BSB] had sold at most 120,000 squarials, against its target of 400,000 by Christmas' (Shawcross, 1992, p. 508). BSB was set to lose the UK direct-to-home duel in the first round.

But the precise outcome of the contest was also being shaped by the colossal finance needed to sustain it. Direct broadcasting by satellite was always bound to be a venture with high start-up costs and uncertain return. Competition between the two contenders increased those costs on both sides. For example, the two competitors bid up the price of movies from the Hollywood studios. By 1990 Murdoch's News Corporation was under serious pressure from its bankers, and Sky was the biggest drain on its finances. BSB was visibly losing the UK satellite contest, but Murdoch lacked the resources to drive his rival into extinction. The result was that secret merger talks took place between Murdoch and BSB shareholders in October, with the finally agreed merger – forming BSkyB – announced on 2 November 1990 (Shawcross, 1992, pp. 503–10).

The shotgun marriage between BSB and Sky caused one notable regulatory shockwave. As holder of the official DBS franchise, BSB should, under the terms of its franchise, have, at the very least, consulted the IBA before the merger. Among other changes produced by the deal, the official UK DBS franchise was effectively put under the control of a non-EC citizen, Rupert Murdoch. This was not something which the IBA would previously have countenanced. But no such consultation or prior warning took place:

It is clear . . . that the completion of the merger, for which the IBA's consent was neither obtained nor sought, gave rise to a serious breach of BSB's programme contract. The IBA is entitled, in consequence of the merger, to terminate that contract and intends to do so. (IBA News Release, 16 November 1990)

Murdoch may not have warned the IBA, but he did alert Margaret Thatcher to the merger deal a few days before it was publicly announced. The Prime Minister did not see fit to warn her Cabinet colleagues (most importantly the Home Secretary, David Waddington). Pressed in the House of Commons on that, Waddington replied: 'It certainly was no business of the Prime Minister to go phoning around the place to all and sundry, and me included, saying that she had already been told by Mr Murdoch what everybody already knew' (quoted in Shawcross 1992, p. 511; HoC Debates, 12 November 1990). Bowing, as it saw it, to the inevitable, the IBA did not terminate the BSB contract immediately, allowing a smooth, if forced, transformation of BSB subscribers into BSkyB customers.

Thatcher's prior warning of the Sky/BSB merger has since been interpreted as a crucial piece of evidence that the government had consciously helped a political ally in the media to circumvent regulation and gain broadcasting influence. In much the same way as Italian Socialist Prime Minister Craxi had oiled the wheels of Silvio Berlusconi's rise to broadcasting dominance in Italy in return for political support, so, it was alleged, the Thatcher government had smoothed her friend Murdoch's path to UK satellite dominance (see, for example, Hutton, 1995, p. 220).

There is much circumstantial evidence to support such a thesis. The UK government was not entirely powerless to act against foreign-based satellite services of which it disapproved. In subsequent years the Tory government, on four occasions, acted successfully to drive UK-directed pornographic channels out of business (DNH News Release, 5 March 1997). But none of the weapons that the government had at its disposal were ever used to curb Sky or BSkyB. Instead, from the beginning, the Tory government turned a blind eye to the possibility of regulatory infringements by Murdoch's UK-directed satellite operations.

Perhaps the most blatant example of this was over the question of European programme content. The British government was party to the 1988 European Broadcasting Directive, which required channels to broadcast at least 50 per cent of European programmes (with the exception of certain genres like news) 'where practicable'. The 1990 Broadcasting Act gave the government the power to require the ITC to enforce its international treaty obligations. But, far from using that power to force BSkyB to increase the European content of its programming (which on many BSkyB channels was way below 50 per cent), the Home Office, and later the Department of National Heritage, wrote to UK-licensed satellite channels (including BSkyB) informing them that the quota did not apply to, for example, movie channels. That said, there is very little direct evidence that the Tories at any stage positively and premeditatedly encouraged Murdoch's rise to UK satellite dominance. Rather, they simply did nothing to stop it.

But that still leaves a more fundamental, and perhaps more damning, accusation against Tory satellite policy. As we have seen, in 1981 the Conservative government had embarked upon a policy of early start for UK DBS for reasons of the benefits this would give to British industry. By the early 90s – admittedly later than anticipated – a substantial direct-to-home satellite broadcasting industry was indeed beginning to take hold in the UK. For two years after the 1990 merger, BSkyB's steady advance in viewers was accompanied by large financial losses, and the very future of the operation seemed threatened by News Corporation's massive debts. But by 1992 BSkyB claimed to have entered operating profit, and, as the 90s continued, its profits were to multiply. By the year ending 30 June 1996 they had reached £311 million (Syfret, 1996, p. 45). The shadow of the bankers had receded, BSkyB mustered a growing stream-subscription income, and a range of other channels clustered around Murdoch for UK direct-to-home transmission from Astra. From virtually nothing, when the UK-directed Sky service started in 1989, by the end of 1991 there were already 1.77 million households in the UK with satellite television. By mid-1996 that had grown to 3.56 million (p. 50). The overwhelming majority of these were BSkyB subscribers (as were the overwhelming majority of the 1.64 million UK households who subscribed to cable in mid-1996).

But this UK direct-to-home satellite industry that established itself in the early 90s was a very different one to that envisaged by government satellite policy of the early 80s. It did not use UK technology – the anticipated benefits to the UK aerospace industry had not materialised; it was dominated by a non-UK-controlled concern; and it broadcast heavily non-UK programming. In short, the UK industrial benefits which were the lynchpin of early 80s government satellite strategy simply had not been forthcoming. As we shall see in the next chapter, the picture was to be uncannily similar for cable.

# 5 New Technologies, New Approaches: 2. Cable

By 1979 the traditional British cable industry – narrowband and founded essentially on relaying the terrestrial broadcasts of the duopoly – had already entered terminal decline. But two different developments urged a new attempt at British cable broadcasting with additional services. They are summarised in a contemporary report for stockbrokers, Williams de Broe Chaplin & Co:

> Why then has cable reappeared with such force? The main reason is the coincidence of two individually powerful factors. These are:
>
> 1) The recent boom in cable TV in America.
> 2) The wish of this government to bring about a broadband communications network in the UK. (Littleboy et al., 1982, pp. 1–2)

In the USA, cable had started from the base of relaying terrestrially broadcast services to areas of poor reception (considerably greater than in the UK). In the second half of the 70s, with additional, paid for, channels like Home Box Office (HBO), American cable broadcasting had mushroomed. 'Starting from a negligible base in 1975, the number of [HBO] subscribers now approaches 10 million,' observed the Cabinet Office's Information Technology Panel in early 1982 (ITAP, 1982, p. 20). Such a boom in the world's leading television market was bound to bring calls for another round of experiment with pay-TV via cable in Britain. The Labour government's 1978 White Paper had already suggested further pilot schemes (Home Office, 1978, p. 63).

In November 1980 William Whitelaw announced a new series of experimental pay-TV licences to be run on existing (narrowband) cable systems. Eventually thirteen licences were issued to run on the services of seven companies. Each was for two years, and the first came into operation in September 1981 (Hollins, 1984, p. 47). Whether these experiments would have generated policy results any different from their predecessors was never put to the test. What soon determined the shape of Tory cable policy was the second factor we have mentioned – the desire to bring about a broadband communications network as part of the general development of information technology.

The incoming Conservative government had made a particular point of its general concern to foster development of information technology in the UK. As Margaret Thatcher put it in July 1981: 'The government fully recognise the importance of information technology for the future industrial and commercial success of the UK and the central role that government must play in promoting its development and application' (quoted in Negrine, 1988, p. 226). In keeping with this view, the government appointed a Minister of Information Technology, Kenneth Baker, in the DTI, and designated 1982 as 'Information Technology Year'. It also set up an Information Technology Unit in the Cabinet Office and, in June 1981, an Information Technology Advisory Panel (ITAP) to advise it on policy (Negrine, 1988, p. 226). ITAP's first extended study was on broadband cable. This was handed over to government in January 1982, and published under the title *Cable Systems* in March.

The policy recommendations contained in *Cable Systems* were not primarily based on broadcasting considerations. Rather, ITAP founded cable strategy squarely on what it saw as the central place of broadband cable within the general framework of information technology. *Cable Systems* began with the following vision:

> Modern cable systems, based on coaxial cables or optical fibres, can provide many new telecommunications-based services to homes and businesses. The initial attraction for home subscribers would be the extra television entertainment channels. However, *the main role* of cable systems eventually will be the delivery of many information, financial and other services to the home and the joining of businesses and homes by high-capacity data links. (ITAP, 1982, p. 7, my emphasis)

Here, broadcasting considerations (the expected demand for extra television entertainment channels) were being used simply as a lever to achieve the greater goal of a broadband network whose 'main role' was to be the delivery of 'information, financial and other services'.

In the light of current debate on the information superhighway, it is worth spelling out what ITAP envisaged these services would be. They would include: 'New ways of selling (a videotaped tour of a house for sale or a prospective holiday location perhaps) or of instruction (e.g. how to carry out a piece of car maintenance)' (p. 2). The videotaped house tours and holiday brochures are relatively sophisticated versions of what today would be termed 'home shopping'. The car maintenance example foreshadows current emphasis on the potentialities of the information superhighway for education.

ITAP's 1982 catalogue of services to be provided by cable also included the 'development of new relationships between work and home activities, and reduction in the need to travel' (p. 30). Today, all this would be referred to as 'tele-commuting'. ITAP also emphasised that cable would enable ' "film request" services to be developed' – what we would now call video-on-demand. Lastly, the panel listed a variety of interactive services, including home security (pp. 16, 44–5).

In other words, the list of benefits to be provided by a broadband network, as set out in *Cable Systems* in 1982, is almost exactly the same as that set out by information superhighway enthusiasts over a decade later. How was this vision of an information technology future to be translated into a strategy for the development of cable?

The first pillar of the strategy outlined by ITAP was that the cabling of Britain should rely entirely on private funding. As the report's summary crisply put it: 'Private sector finance is available for investment in cable systems – there need be no call on public funds' (p. 7).

The Panel were distinctly bullish about the prospects for commercial funding:

> Our investigations have revealed considerable interest by private firms (not only from established cable companies) in the possibility of participating in cable systems, and *we have no doubt that funds would be available from commercial sources to finance the installation of cable systems.*

Recognising that there was as yet little information available on the amount that consumers would spend on the range of anticipated additional services, the report cited the US experience that 'households will pay upwards of £10 a month for additional TV services'. Adding in other sources of income, including advertising, ITAP concluded:

> Even with less than 100 per cent take-up of the system, there would appear to be sufficient income from subscribers to give a reasonable return on capital ... *Cable systems offer large business opportunities with good chances of profit.* We see no need for any public funds to be used to establish them. (p. 33, my emphases)

ITAP saw the ultimate benefit of cable being in a general information technology future. Part of that benefit would be in the services that cable could provide for private and business consumers. But ITAP were equally definite that a major part of the benefits of cable would accrue in the stimulus that development of cable would give to British industries associated with information technology. Like the Home Office's DBS study, *Cable Systems* included a chapter (Chapter 5) on 'Economic and Industrial Considerations':

> 'The economic activity generated by a decision to encourage the growth of cable systems could ... be very large ... We suggest that (a) there would be a net employment generating effect, which could be substantial, (b) that insofar as manufactured products are involved these would at present ... be more likely British made than if the same consumer expenditure were devoted to cars, video cassette recorders, etc. and (c) that the resulting stimulus to programme and information producers would result in products that had significant international markets, given the high reputation of British broadcasting and information services. ... A decision to encourage cable systems would ... provide a large stimulus to developments in optical fibre technology, as well as in the industries associated with consumer electronics and the supply of programme material. (pp. 28–9)

This was the same argument that we have already seen articulated in the Home Office DBS study. An early domestic start with the new technology would put British hardware and, to a lesser extent, software manufacturers in poll position in a newly developing and major international market. From this vision, the ITAP report firmly urged a policy conclusion which we have also seen clearly formulated in the Home Office DBS study – the industrial imperative for an early start.

The only difference between the two reports was one of tone – whereas the Home Office study had couched its arguments for an early start to DBS in terms of a series of apparent alternatives, *Cable Systems* was altogether more direct:

> Unless firm policy decisions toward cable are taken in 1982 there is a high risk of overseas technological dominance ... The decision [to lift constraints on the programmes

that could be distributed by cable] must be made quickly to allow prospective operators and investors sufficient time to plan future systems before a change in Government policy can occur. This again points to a decision in 1982 ... If no decision is taken now to encourage the growth of cable systems, it will have to be taken later as public and business demand for wideband communications, fuelled by knowledge of the systems installed in other countries, increases. And the likelihood is that we will then become dependent on overseas cable technology and will offer foreign firms a rich market. (pp. 7, 8, 48)

There was a third parallel with DBS policy. If the potential advantages to British industry of cable development dictated an early start, they also dictated some measures to advantage British industry in that start. So ITAP proposed that 'the recommended design standards should offer maximum potential to United Kingdom manufacturers and operators' (p. 51).

If both DBS and cable were to be driven by their supposed potential for UK industry, that still left open what the relationship between the two distribution technologies should be. ITAP was in no doubt about the answer: 'The American experience demonstrates the close and supportive relationship that can be established between satellite and cable TV services, to the benefit of both.' On the one hand, 'the introduction of DBS services would provide cable systems ... with a very valuable asset'. This asset the report described as 'the extra choice of popular television programme services (e.g. feature films)'. On the other hand, 'cable systems could supply DBS signals to many subscribers at a lower cost than individual reception.' ITAP was therefore emphatic that 'the Government should announce as soon as possible its approval for an early start on DBS services'. This, as we have seen, Whitelaw had in fact done in early March 1982, in between the completion and publication of *Cable Systems* (pp. 22, 24, 50).

The final pillar of ITAP's cable strategy was the necessity of liberalising British broadcasting policy as it applied to cable. 'There is a direct connection between the degree of broadcasting "liberalisation" established for cable systems and the possibility of private sector investment in them', the Panel maintained. Private finance would only be forthcoming 'if the Government lifts the present constraints on the programmes that may be distributed by cable operation and allows a full range of programme services to be provided'. So 'the Government should urgently review the implications of cable systems for the financing and regulation of broadcasting and consider the need for a new statutory body to be the "broadcasting authority" for cable systems' (pp. 7–8, 34).

*Cable Systems* set the government a tight timetable, backed up by a stern warning:

Only through a set of speedy, positive and radical regulatory changes can the United Kingdom obtain the benefits offered by developments in cable technology. We must repeat, though, that for British industry a late decision is the same as a negative decision. (p. 52)

The government quickly followed ITAP's injunction. On 22 March 1982, less than three weeks after his announcement of the early start to DBS, William Whitelaw announced the establishment of an inquiry on cable and broadcasting, to be chaired by Lord Hunt of Tamworth. The inquiry was to submit its report by 30 September 1980, and would take

> as its frame of reference the Government's wish to secure the benefits for the United Kingdom which cable television can offer and its willingness to consider an expansion of cable systems which would permit cable to carry a wider range of entertainment and other services ... but in a way consistent with the wider public interest, in particular the safeguarding of public service broadcasting.

Within that framework, the Hunt Inquiry was to 'consider the questions which would arise from such an expansion, including in particular the supervisory framework' (Hunt, 1982, p. 1).

Hunt and his two colleagues met their deadline with just two days to spare. *The Report of the Inquiry into Cable Expansion and Broadcasting Policy* was presented to Parliament in October 1982.

The Hunt Report stood firmly on the foundations erected by ITAP. It accepted the Panel's general perspectives, and it picked up on and elaborated many of *Cable Systems* specific suggestions. Acknowledging ITAP's basic thesis, Hunt observed:

> There is one general point which needs emphasising. It seems to be generally agreed that investment in cable television for entertainment purposes will be the necessary base to which interactive services of economic benefit to business and the individual will be added. It is therefore very important that decisions about cable television should be taken with this in mind and that for example the award of franchises should positively encourage the development of interactive services. (p. 2)

Hunt had been specifically briefed to square ITAP's industrial- and information technology-driven perspective for cable with 'the safeguarding of public service broadcasting'. His report recognised that it would be 'a serious loss' if the quality and diversity provided by BBC and ITV were to be eroded by either a general lowering of standards or the siphoning off to paying cable subscribers of programmes previously universally available. But, Hunt went on, 'if the recommendations in our report are accepted we do not think this is likely to happen.' The report argued that

> multi-channel cable television should be seen as supplementary, and not as an alternative or rival, to public service broadcasting. ... Cable television is ... all about widening the viewer's choice. It should be innovative, experimental and sensitive to local feeling. It cannot be run as though it were another branch of public service broadcasting providing a balanced service for the country as a whole. (pp. 2–3)

From this position Hunt concluded that 'Cable television must ... operate within certain, albeit liberal, ground rules.' There would be the need for 'some continuing oversight'. The report rejected ITAP's proposal that self-regulation by the cable industry would be generally acceptable. But, it immediately added:

> We emphasise the word 'oversight' rather than regulation. The latter implies imposing detailed programming rules across the country whereas the whole idea of cable is that it should supplement public service broadcasting and be responsive to local demand. The concept should be one of cable operators accountable to observe a few general

guidelines and provide the service offered when given their franchises rather than one of a central body regulating in detail how they go about their business. (p. 8)

Among the few 'general guidelines' that Hunt proposed were a prohibition of pay-per-view (to prevent 'siphoning' off of popular programmes from universally available broadcasting) and requirements on cable for impartiality in news and 'taste and decency' (pp. 16, 24, 25). Hunt specifically rejected any restriction on cable advertising time or any requirements for programme diversity (pp. 15, 22).

Two other recommended stipulations have particular significance in view of subsequent developments. First, the report expressed the view that

> the supervisory body might have a role in encouraging the production and use of British material on cable and possibly even have power to impose restrictions in the longer term, if that was thought appropriate, on the amount of foreign material which could be included in programme channels.

Second: 'It would seem unacceptable for cable systems to be under foreign control' (pp. 26, 9). Both these recommendations were in keeping with the emphasis, in both the Home Office DBS study and the ITAP cable report, on maximising the benefits of the new distribution technologies for *British* industry. As we shall see, both recommended stipulations turned out to be deeply problematic.

ITAP had proposed a new body to franchise and oversee cable. Hunt concurred. The Hunt Report saw only two possibilities for a cable overseer: 'the IBA with different requirements on it in respect of cable television, or a new body'. It plumped for the latter, because 'there would be a suspicion that the IBA might have an over-protective attitude to public service broadcasting, and this could deter potential investors in cable'. Hunt therefore recommended 'a new cable authority' to award cable franchises and monitor performance. If legislation were not immediately possible, the Home Secretary should use his current powers to license cable operators, establishing the cable authority on a non-statutory basis (p. 32). Here again, this time on urgency, Hunt followed the lead given by ITAP.

Hunt distinguished between the *cable-provider* (who installed the physical infrastructure), the *cable-operator* (who managed the local cable system), the *programme-provider* (who assembled programmes into channels) and the *programme-maker*. 'Our conclusion', the report added, 'is that the key figure of these four will be the cable operator.'

So it was to be the cable operator who would be granted a franchise (effectively a local monopoly with certain obligations), but the report did

> not believe it necessary that the programme provider or programme maker ... be licensed. ... It will be the cable operator who determines what services are to be used ... it seems simplest to hold the cable operator responsible for the services he distributes. ... Programme providers will only succeed if they produce material which the operator is able to use. (pp. 6–7)

The Hunt Report therefore provided the loose regulatory framework for cable to develop along the lines set by ITAP, outside, but supposedly not in conflict with, the traditional British public service framework for broadcasting.

The government rapidly picked up most of Hunt's recommendations. First of all, in the House of Commons in December 1982 and then in its White Paper, *The Development of Cable Systems and Services*, published in April 1983, the Thatcher government indicated its acceptance of the cable television strategy developed by ITAP and refined by Hunt:

> Cable is in a sense the crossroads at which broadcasting and telecommunications meet. It has never been possible to look at the two sets of issues in isolation from each other ... The Information Technology Panel created by the Prime Minister in July 1981 ... focused attention on the industrial, economic and social opportunities of cable and underlined the importance of early progress if this country was not to be overtaken by others. The Government responded immediately by arranging, as the Panel had recommended, for the many important issues which it had not been able to study in depth to be examined further.

The government's broad strategy was that cable should be 'privately financed and market led'; 'regulation should be as light as possible so that investors are free to develop a wide range of services and facilities'; the regulatory framework should be flexible, but 'a small number of key safeguards are needed'.

In pursuit of this strategy, a new statutory body (the Cable Authority) was to be established 'to award franchises to cable operators and exercise a measure of supervision over the services provided'; 'cable should be able to finance itself by rental payments, subscription, advertising and sponsorship'; cable should be underground, via either coaxial or fibre optic and with a requirement for a two-way capacity; and local licences should be issued, in the first place, for a twelve-year period (Home Office and Department of Industry, 1983, pp. 7–8).

The 1983 White Paper parted company with Hunt on little. There were only two major disagreements. In contrast to Hunt, the White Paper argued for the need to set some limits on cable advertising time. Revealingly, its justification for this was not in terms of protection for the viewer, but in order to maintain a level playing field with existing commercial services: 'In equity either cable advertising should be subject to the same limits as the IBA applies, or independent television and local radio should themselves be deregulated.' The White Paper also proposed, in contrast to Hunt, that 'pay per view should be permitted except in those particular circumstances where it would pose a specific threat to public service broadcasting' (pp. 42, 49). These, however, were the exceptions. In overall thrust the 1983 White Paper was simply a government endorsement of the basic strategy for cable advanced by ITAP, and then refined with regard to broadcasting policy, by Hunt. That strategy finally reached the statute book in the 1984 Cable and Broadcasting Act.

Two further aspects of the White Paper's detailed proposals are particularly worth singling out at this stage. First was the desire to specifically advantage British industry, which we have already seen in *Direct Broadcasting by Satellite*, ITAP and Hunt. The White Paper was explicit that both cable programming and the operation of cable systems should be protected from North American dominance:

> The Government accepts that operators may need to use a significant amount of overseas material, particularly from the USA, in the early years; but the Cable Authority will

have a duty to work towards a progressive increase in the proportion of British programming.

The White Paper also unambiguously proclaimed that

> The Government accepts that control of a cable operating company should, as with ITV and ILR, not rest with a company or individual from outside the European Community. This will not preclude companies with experience of cable operation elsewhere, particularly the United States and Canada, from deploying their expertise and financial resources to the benefit of cable development in this country, provided they do not acquire what in the judgement of the Authority constitutes a controlling interest. (pp. 84 and 30)

We have already remarked that such requirements were to prove deeply problematic in practice. What needs emphasising here is that measures to advantage British (or, as was by now required by EC developments, EC) ownership of cable, and to foster British programming on it, were an explicit and central part of the cable strategy which the Thatcher government adopted in the early 80s. Both the duty to ensure a 'proper' level of European (effectively British) programming and the prohibition on non-European control of cable systems were to be included in the 1984 Cable and Broadcasting Act.

The second element in the 1983 White Paper worth singling out with the benefit of hindsight is what it said about cable in relation to the rest of the telecommunications market. At the same time as the Thatcher government was deliberating its cable strategy, it was also putting into place the foundations of an ambitious deregulatory telecommunications policy. When the White Paper was published a Telecommunications Bill (eventually to reach the statute book as the 1984 Telecommunications Act) was already before Parliament. This would end British Telecom's exclusive privileges and licensing function, convert it into a public company and provide for its privatisation. Alongside this formal change in BT's status and ownership, the other key plank of government telecommunications policy was to foster competition with the soon-to-be-privatised monopolist. The most notable step here was the licensing of Mercury to run a public telecommunications system in competition with BT.

How was cable to fit into this prospective Mercury/BT duopoly? The White Paper reported that it had received two directly contradictory sets of representations: that BT should *not* be allowed any role in the development of cable, and, alternatively, that *only* BT should be allowed to install wideband cable systems, which it should then be required to operate on a common-carrier basis.

The government rejected both of these positions. To give BT (or BT and Mercury) the exclusive right to run cable systems 'would be to reinforce the dominance of telecommunications currently enjoyed by the existing operators and would prevent competitive entry into the telecommunications market by cable system providers and operators'. However, 'the skills and expertise' of BT and Mercury could 'contribute to the development of cable'. So, 'it would be wrong to exclude BT and Mercury from competing freely with others for the provision and installation of cable networks'.

The White paper considered it likely that BT and Mercury would participate in many cable consortia, but 'the Government is however concerned at the prospect of BT and Mercury's financial position being eroded in the event of interactive services depriving them of local and national traffic'. Therefore, only BT or Mercury would be allowed to offer voice telephony services on cable systems, 'either alone or in partnership with a cable operator'.

Two other pieces of protection were proposed for the two national telecommunications providers. Cable operators offering data services to the business centres of London, Manchester and Birmingham would have to do so in collaboration with either BT or Mercury; and only BT or Mercury would be allowed to provide the links between the different local cable systems. 'Subject to these restrictions, cable systems will be free to provide subscribers any service whether of a switched or non-switched variety' (pp. 70–3).

So cable was fitted pragmatically into the government's plans to foster competition in the telecommunications market. It was partially sheltered from BT and Mercury, because these companies were not allowed to provide cable television over their own national network licences. But BT and Mercury could – and it was both hoped and expected would – apply for local cable franchises without restriction. Cable franchises could not provide voice telephony directly, but they could provide it in collaboration with BT or (more likely commercially) Mercury. That opened up a chink of opportunity for cable operators on voice telephony which was not available in other countries.

There was some delay in translating the proposals of the White Paper into legislation. The 1984 Cable and Broadcasting Act became law well over a year after the publication of the White Paper, and the Cable Authority which it established came into operation right at the end of 1984. However, in line with the stress on urgency which had characterised the ITAP report, the government did not wait for the new legislative framework to be in place before awarding the first of the new broadband licences. In the summer of 1983 the government invited applications for broadband licences in areas to be nominated by the applicants. It received thirty-seven applications. The government had said it would award up to twelve licences; in the event, at the end of November 1983 it awarded eleven. The UK's broadband cable revolution was under way – or was it?

## Cable in Practice

During the discussions on cable and satellite strategy in the early 80s considerable expectations had been raised about the likely pace of growth of the new technologies once a suitable framework for their growth had been established. In 1982 the then Minister of Information Technology, Kenneth Baker, predicted that 'by the end of the decade multi-channel cable television will be commonplace in-home countrywide – TV will be used for armchair shopping, banking, calling emergency services and many other services' (Henley Centre, 1993, p. 130). In the same year the report on *The Prospects for Cable TV in the UK* for stockbrokers Williams de Broe Chaplin forecast that

the period 1984 to 1987 should see the start of cable systems covering the more promising, higher density 50 per cent of the UK. These systems could take up to five years to construct but by 1992 we can foresee 5 million cable subscribers, out of a total of 20 million households. (Littleboy et al., 1982, conclusions pp. ii–iii)

And in 1984 a study for the Broadcasting Research Unit concluded that

> it is reasonable to assume that by the end of 1986 some four or five million households could have cable systems available to them on new and old systems. By 1990 many more systems will have been built but will to some extent have been offset by the closure of old ones. Perhaps eight million households will have cable available, mostly on new systems.

The same study suggested an admittedly 'optimistic' possible rate of take-up of cable of up to 55 per cent of homes passed. This, it suggested, would give, as the 'most optimistic of scenarios', 6.6–7.7 million cable subscribers in the UK by 1994 (Hollins, 1984, p. 303).

By 1986 such forecasts were already looking distinctly ragged. In May of that year, William Phillips, writing in *Broadcast* (16 May 1986, p. 6), dubbed the heralded 'explosion' in broadband communications and satellite television the 'revolution that can't get started'. This sort of scepticism was sufficiently widespread to goad the Chairman of the Cable Authority into response. 'It is remarkable how much has been achieved up to the end of our first reporting period [end of March 1986],' he wrote in his forward to the Authority's first report. 'It is perhaps just as astonishing that despite this progress, the feeling may still persist in some quarters that the cable revolution is not happening: it is' (Cable Authority *Annual Report*, 1984/6, Chairman's Foreword). However, the same report contained more than enough evidence to show that cable development was progressing far more slowly than had been expected, and it presented some of the reasons why.

Only one of the eleven pioneering broadband licences granted in November 1983 was in operation when the Cable Authority came into existence in December 1984. These eleven licences covered areas ranging in size from 22,000 to 136,000 homes, and in total this first tranche of broadband franchises covered over a million homes. In its first fifteen months the Cable Authority added to these pioneers nine more franchises covering another million homes. By the end of March 1986, of these twenty broadband franchises, the number actually in operation had risen to seven. So, after nearly two and a half years, not even all of the November 1983 awards had begun operation (pp. 4–8).

Nevertheless, the Authority's first report portrayed twenty franchises awarded and seven operational as a considerable achievement. But it also bemoaned the fact that the flow of finance into cable was 'less liberal than the speedy development of the industry would demand'. Lack of investment, it continued, was 'the major constraint on the development of the cable industry'. The Authority highlighted several reasons for this shortage of finance. Cable was new and unknown and there was now less public attention given to it than in the early 80s. More specifically, the 1984 Budget had announced the phasing out of capital allowances. Given the very considerable initial investment involved in cable construction, and the very long payback period, these allowances had been seen as important to companies contemplating investment in cable. The Authority reported that the removal of capital allowances was 'widely seen as a blow to the development of cable'.

This worsening of the tax position of cable investment was harmful enough in itself. But, in addition, an unsuccessful campaign against it by the cable industry may have had the perverse effect of scaring off potential investors even more. The Cable Authority acknowledged that, rightly or wrongly, the 1984 Budget decision 'became embedded in the minds of many people in the financial community as the factor which made investment in cable much less attractive than it might have been' (pp. 11–12).

Over the following two years, just three extra franchises were awarded by the Cable Authority. The reason for the tiny number of new awards, and the slow progress of the ones already awarded, was the same one that the Authority had already identified as inhibiting development in 1986 – lack of investment. 'Progress is slower than we had hoped,' commented the Authority's Chairman in 1987:

> Clearly investors are still not wholly convinced of the sense in investing in broadband cable systems. It is lack of finance which is restricting cable's development and causing problems both to existing operators and to those whose franchises are struggling to make a start. It causes problems too to the authority in inhibiting our ability to pursue continuing franchising programme.' (Chairman's Foreword)

So, by the end of March 1988 just twenty-three franchises had been awarded, covering fewer than 2.4 million homes (less than 12 per cent of total TV homes). Only ten of these franchises were operational, their total build passed just over 300,000 homes, of which just under 45,000 were connected. That represented a 14.5 per cent penetration rate. Not only was the franchising far less than had been predicted, and the rate of build within those franchised areas far slower, but the take-up among households where cable did eventually become available was also disappointingly low. The Cable Authority might congratulate itself on the number of new cable channels, but the attraction of these to potential customers was clearly less than overwhelming.

In retrospect, 1987 represented probably the nadir of cable's fortunes. After that things began slowly to improve. Surveying the year 1987/8 the Cable Authority continued to report that a shortage of finance was inhibiting the development of many of the franchises already awarded. But by mid-1988 there seemed to be some evidence of a pick-up in investor interest, so much so that the Authority felt confident enough to advertise another seven, on average rather larger, franchises, covering another 1.5 million households.

The new finance that began to come forward in 1988 was not the result of a rethink by British investors. They remained as reluctant as ever. Instead, as the Authority itself observed: 'Most of the current interest is based on North American investment. It comes from groups who know and understand cable better than do investors in the United Kingdom, who are still slow to recognise and seize the opportunities' (Cable Authority *Annual Report*, 1987/8, Chairman's Foreword).

However, this North American interest ran up against the provision of the

Cable and Broadcasting Act, which prohibited non-European control of a franchise. As early as 1987 the Chairman of the Cable Authority had called for this provision to be removed, and this was eventually done in the 1990 Broadcasting Act. In the meanwhile, and with the approval of the Cable Authority and the acquiescence of the government, North American investors found ways round the prohibition. This generally involved vesting control of the cable operating company in the UK with a discretionary trust in the Channel Islands. Such a legal expedient enabled North American investors to effectively control UK cable franchises, while leaving formal control in European hands (Cable Authority *Annual Report*, 1988/9, p. 6).

The North American investment in UK cable continued to grow in 1989 and 1990, prompting the Cable Authority to rapidly increase the pace of its franchising – twenty-six new franchises were advertised in 1988/9, followed by eighty-five in 1989/90.

Two other factors assisted the revival in cable's fortunes at the end of the 80s. First was the start of direct broadcasting by satellite by Sky in March 1989 and by BSB in May 1990. This provided a considerable increase in both the number and the attractiveness of channels available via cable. The satellite channels also had a level of national publicity which the cable-only channels had never achieved. And in the short period before November 1990, when there was competition between Sky and BSB, cable offered the considerable advantage over satellite of being able to deliver both programme packages without the complexity and expense of two satellite dishes. In March 1989, take-up in broadband franchises was only 14 per cent; by the end of 1990 it had risen to 18 per cent (Cable Authority *Annual Report*, 1988/9, p. 5 and Final Report). As the ITAP report had foreseen, satellite could be a positive factor in the development of cable.

The second factor that improved cable's position at the end of the 80s was voice telephony. As we have seen, the 1984 Act had opened a chink of opportunity here by allowing cable operators to offer voice telephony in partnership with BT or Mercury. Partnership between a cable company and Mercury offered benefits to both partners, enabling them to offer a more effective local challenge to BT's dominance in the voice telephony market than Mercury would have been able to do on its own.

The first cable franchises to take up this opportunity to offer voice telephony were Cable Camden and Windsor Television in 1987/8. The following year they were joined by a third franchisee. These were still only slight beginnings, but as the 1988/9 Cable Authority Report commented:

the experience of these developments – particularly in Windsor where the service was most extensive – did much to establish the credibility of cable as an alternative telecommunications medium. For the first time, the value of being able to derive a second stream of revenue from the infrastructure investment became quantifiable: it was possible to include in a cable operator's business plan some realistic projections for revenue from telecommunications services. (p. 5)

The possibility of combining cable television and voice telephony had a particular attraction for North American investors. These included cable companies, whose opportunities for further domestic expansion in their core business were narrowing as the North American cable market matured. They also included telecommunications companies. In North America the provision of cable television and voice telephony were then still rigidly separated. So, for both sets of transatlantic players, there was not only the intrinsic attraction of investing in a market where they were allowed to do both but also the added bonus of being able to gain experience in the less regulated environment, which sooner or later they would face back home. As the Cable Authority itself put it in 1990:

> The United Kingdom's unique regulatory environment, which encourages cable operators to be telecommunications operators within their area as well as television providers, is undoubtedly one reason why the North American telephone companies are taking such an interest. (*Final Report*, p. 6)

The Cable Authority oversaw the development of broadband cable in the UK for six years from the beginning of 1985, until (under the provisions of the 1990 Broadcasting Act) it handed over responsibility to the ITC at the end of 1990. Developments during the first half of those six years had, as we have seen, been desperately slow – owing to the reluctance of British investors to put their money into cable. In the second half of the period things had picked up, thanks to the boost in content and profile of programming from Sky and BSB, to the voice telephony opportunities offered to cable operators in the UK, and, above all, to the huge North American injection of finance, filling the gap which British investors were still unwilling to meet. But cash for cable was still in short supply even at the end of 1990. The Cable Authority's Final Report bemoaned the fact that

> a looming recession, coupled with a banking crisis in the United States from which most of the finance was expected to come, undermined the plans which many companies had drawn up for raising and investing the large sums of money which the construction of a cable system requires. Recession had arrived just at the point when the major expansion of cable was set to take place.

Nevertheless, the Authority still felt able to claim that 'the extent of activity in different parts of the country gave a definite feeling of cable having at last arrived' (*Final Report*, p. 5). How much justification was there for such a claim?

When the Cable Authority handed over responsibility at the end of 1990, a total of 135 franchises had been awarded – mainly owing to the frantic franchising activity of the Authority's last two years. These covered some 14.6 million homes, two-thirds of the UK's total. However, only twenty-nine of these broadband franchises were in operation by the end of 1990. They had built past only 828,000 homes (less than 4 per cent of the UK total), of which only 149,000 were subscribers (18 per cent of homes passed, and less than 1 per cent of total homes). These broadband subscribers were still outnumbered by the dwindling number (274,000) of subscribers to upgraded old-fashioned cable systems. All this was real enough, but it was quite definitely not on the scale of the forecasts of the early 80s. ITAP had claimed that the private finance was there to cable Britain. A decade later that initial assessment looked, at the very least, over-confident.

After 1990, cable build accelerated. From 828,000 at the end of 1990, the number of homes passed by broadband cable multiplied tenfold to 8.96 million by

April 1997, while the number of broadband television subscribers increased even faster, from 149,000 at the end of 1990 to 1.97 million by April 1997. Cable television penetration among homes passed crept up during the same period from 18 per cent in 1990 to 22 per cent in April 1997 (ITC News Release, 22 May 1997). This was, however, still far lower than most early forecasters had envisaged. The pattern of viewing in cable homes was very similar to that in satellite households. The most popular channels were all available direct-to-home via Astra, and were dominated by BSkyB (ITC, 1996, p. 9). To date, UK cable operators have been singularly unsuccessful in providing a 'cable only' programming offer and thus developing an independent pole of attraction to BSkyB's domination of the UK multi-channel market.

Two other planks of the ITAP strategy turned out to be even further removed from reality than its projections about the pace of cable build and take-up.

First, it should be remembered, ITAP had stressed the opportunities for *British* industry involved in the rapid development of broadband cable systems. So far as the cable franchises were concerned, this British involvement simply did not happen. The operators of the old narrowband cable systems showed no interest in the new broadband franchises and completed their withdrawal from the cable industry. Of the two British telecommunications operators, Mercury made no attempt to get involved in owning cable franchises; BT did in the early stages, but then, in the second half of the 80s, withdrew from most of what it had been awarded in the first half. Other UK takers of early franchises were often financially weak and gave up, or sold out, later on. The great bulk of franchises advertised in the Cable Authority's last two years went to North American-controlled consortia.

The net result of this was that when the Cable Authority handed over to the ITC, it had awarded 135 franchises. Eight of these were subsequently withdrawn for lack of activity. Of the 127 that remained, in 1993: '77 are controlled by US companies; 35 by Canadian companies; 5 by a French company; 4 are UK controlled; and 6 are UK/overseas joint ventures' (Cable Television Association, 1993).

During the 90s, British cable and satellite policy was increasingly justified by the government on the basis of its success in attracting 'inward investment'. 'The lightness of touch in our regulation provides the incentive and encouragement to invest,' Heritage Secretary, Virginia Bottomley proclaimed in 1997:

> By the end of the decade, £12 billion will have been invested in cabling the UK, invested by companies which have the assurance that the regulatory goalposts are not going to be moved on the basis of whim or short term populism. (DNH News Release, 27 February 1997)

Whatever the truth in this argument that stable light regulation would attract foreign investment into the UK broadcasting – it was not the argument advanced when the Thatcher government formulated its satellite and cable policy in the early 80s. Then the chief rationale of policy was articulated in terms of the benefits it would bring to British industry. As with satellite, so with cable, the idea that British private industry would, without the aid of government money, speedily finance the introduction of the new distribution technologies proved to be an illusion. After several years of uncomfortable hesitation, the new television industries did eventually get going – but on the basis of *foreign* finance and ownership. That development might have its own merits, but it was most certainly not the basis on which the Thatcher government formulated its cable and satellite policies a decade before. That was very clearly in terms of advantage for *British* industry.

The Thatcher government's cable strategy had a second leg which was largely lacking in terms of satellite strategy: namely, the potential of cable in terms of *interactive services*. Cable television was, remember, merely to be the sweetener for these services. Kenneth Baker's prediction, quoted earlier, that multi-channel cable television would be 'commonplace in-home countrywide' by 'the end of the decade', appears ridiculous enough in terms of the slow growth of cable in the 80s which we have already observed. But his rider – that 'TV will be used for armchair shopping, banking, calling emergency services and many other services' – turned out to be even sillier. In its 1987/8 report, the Cable Authority claimed that

> a great deal of effort and interest was devoted to the development of other new services. Westminster Cable exploited its British Telecom switched star system not only to provide new text-based interactive services (including the ordering of goods and payment for them by credit card through the system) and to introduce at the end of the year access to Prestel services but also to provide on a trial basis remote access to a library of interactive videodiscs. A range of other services was in the developmental phase elsewhere. (Cable Authority *Annual Report*, 1987/8, p. 4)

None of this, however, came to anything. By the time the Cable Authority handed over to the ITC at the end of 1990 there were precisely no special interactive services running on UK cable. Broadband cable provided television, and was beginning to compete with BT on voice telephony – but it did nothing else (and was to continue to do nothing else for the next seven years). A central plank of the Thatcher government's early 80s cable strategy was that broadband cable should be developed in order to provide, not just television, but a range of interactive services. In practice, by the time the Tories left office in May 1997, those services simply had not materialised.

# 6 The Peacock Committee

During Margaret Thatcher's first term, Tory television policy directed its innovating energies almost wholly to *new* developments in British television – a new terrestrial channel (Channel Four) and two new delivery systems (direct broadcasting by satellite and broadband cable). The public service core of the British television duopoly which the Tories had inherited – BBC and ITV – was left largely untouched.

After Thatcher's second election victory of 1983, right through to the 1990 Broadcasting Act, Tory television policy radically but unacknowledgedly shifted emphasis – away from new channels and new means of delivery, and towards an attempt to reform the established television system. We have already traced a negative side of this shift at work in satellite and cable. The ambitious if flawed strategy of the early 80s, concentrating on an early start for cable and satellite to gain a place in a new international market, stagnated from 1984 onwards, and policy on the new media had been allowed to drift in the wake of commercially driven events.

What replaced the focus on the new delivery systems was a desire to reform the existing core structure of the terrestrial television duopoly in a more commercially driven, consumer led and competitive direction. This new concern initially focused on one side of that core structure – the BBC – and resulted in the setting up of the Peacock Committee on *Financing the BBC* in 1985. However, the Committee's conclusions (Peacock, 1986) effectively turned the government's drive to reform the core terrestrial television system away from the BBC, and towards the advertising-funded side of the system – ITV and Channel Four. The government finally unveiled its plans for this new target of reform in the 1988 White Paper, *Broadcasting in the 90s: Competition, Choice and Quality* (Home Office, 1988) and – with some very significant modifications – embodied them in legislation in the 1990 Broadcasting Act.

The course of this attempt to reform the terrestrial core of British television is the subject of this chapter and the next. We must begin by asking why, after four years of leaving the BBC and ITV largely unchanged, the government embarked on such an exercise, and why its initial efforts at reform were directed almost exclusively at the BBC.

There were several strands in the growing impetus from 1983 onwards for the Tories to 'do something' about the mainstream television system (they are most fully detailed in O'Malley, 1994, pp. 13–92). One strand was the general blueprints for change, advanced most fully by the increasingly influential free-market think-tanks, the Institute of Economic Affairs (IEA) and the Adam Smith Institute. As we have seen, the free-market right had devoted little sustained intellectual energy to the subject of broadcasting since the 60s. This neglect continued for most of Thatcher's first term, and it was only towards the end of it, in February 1983, that the IEA published *Choice by Cable* by Cento Veljanovski and W. D. Bishop.

As its title suggests, *Choice by Cable* focused on the government's plans for broadband cable described in the last chapter. It appeared after the ITAP and Hunt Reports, but before the 1983 White Paper on cable, and was thus primarily designed to shift government policy on cable in an even more free-market and less regulated direction. But, in doing so, it also drew some general conclusions from the cable debate for the television system as a whole. *Choice by Cable* therefore forms an important intellectual link between the Tory government's new media policies of the early 80s and its efforts to reform terrestrial television during the rest of the decade. The intellectual link was probably also an influential one: Veljanovski was to be an adviser to the Peacock Committee and Peacock was a prominent member of the IEA. Several of the more important themes and proposals of the Peacock Report can be found in embryo in Veljanovski and Bishop's small book.

*Choice by Cable* began by observing that government acceptance of the general approach of the Hunt Report had 'effectively jettisoned the principles upon which the British broadcasting system has been based since its inception 60 years ago' (p. 17) – namely that broadcasting was a public service to be provided by public authorities. This conclusion, it should be noted, was in sharp contrast to the official claim of both Hunt and the government that cable (and satellite) were being developed as *supplements* to the core public service system. The traditional premise that broadcasting should be run as a public service was, argued Veljanovski and Bishop, in part, based on the *technology* of traditional broadcasting – the scarcity of channels available on the electro-magnetic spectrum. 'Cable, and the new technology of communications,' Veljanovski and Bishop continued, 'challenges this traditional philosophy and the argument for the government regulation of TV.' Cable was 'narrowcasting', they explained, 'it has unlimited channel capacity' (Veljanovski and Bishop, 1983, pp. 20–1).

Veljanovski and Bishop took this challenge to the 'old philosophy' beyond cable television. Not only was cable part of a wider market in communications, including terrestrial television, but also 'by extending the discussion to broadcast TV it can be shown that the scarcity of frequencies ... pose(s) no peculiar problems for a market, and thus one of the principal arguments for the regulation of broadcasting is seriously flawed' (p. 43).

Veljanovski and Bishop devoted a whole chapter (Chapter 3) of their book to arguing the proposition that the market could serve as a mechanism for the running of *all* television (not just cable). Two parts of their argument are worth singling out for further analysis. First, was an emphasis on *efficiency* in resource allocation as an important goal of policy in television. They drew attention to the fact that fostering efficiency by means of the discipline of the market was already a high priority in government telecommunications policy (pp. 44–6). By implication it should also be a high priority in broadcasting policy. Second, the *Choice by Cable* authors argued that the market could deal with spectrum scarcity – scarce frequencies could be allocated by auction. This idea they took from an article by Leo Herzel, published in an American law journal in 1951 (Herzel, 1951):

> Herzel's proposal differs radically from the way frequencies are allocated by the Home Office in Britain – namely free of charge to commercial and public operators. In effect the Home Office is giving away a valuable resource ... The present method of awarding ITV licences bestows large windfall profits on the programme companies, which government has taxed since 1964. (p. 53)

The authors later spelt out the practical conclusion of their discussion on frequency auctions: 'Consideration should ... be given to auctioning existing ITV franchises. ...' (p. 112)

These three general emphases in *Choice by Cable* – market mechanisms as the method for organising television; the end to spectrum scarcity as an incentive to use them; and efficiency in resource utilisation as a prime goal in broadcasting policy – were all to be key elements in the Peacock Report. So, too, was Veljanovski and Bishop's specific proposal to allocate ITV franchises by auction.

One other theme from *Choice by Cable* was to figure prominently in Peacock. Veljanovski and Bishop placed particular emphasis on the merits of pay-TV (either by channel or by programme) as a means of commercially financing television, and as an alternative to advertising. Pay was, they argued, the only method of funding television

> that provides TV programmers with a direct measure of the preferences of viewers ... Pay-TV can survive only if it provides the consumer with a package of programmes he chooses to continue to pay for. The more intense a consumer's preference for a type of programme, the more he will be willing to pay. Profit maximising cable programmers will thus offer a mixture of channels and programmes which caters for market demand and diversity.

Direct payment, they carefully added, would only be able to fulfil this potential when there was an unlimited number of channels (pp. 61–2).

In contrast to direct payment, advertising finance for television was, according to Veljanovski and Bishop, deficient. It did not distinguish between different intensities of preference for watching a programme. So, the *Choice by Cable* authors commented, 'the mass audience is crucial to the profitability of the ITV companies: thus they have a tendency to offer programmes which nearly everyone is *willing* to watch, even though no one wants very much to watch them' (p. 61). In relation to the standard British pro-public service argument about the narrow range of output of the US networks, Veljanovski and Bishop conceded that it was true that 'unregulated advertiser-supported TV has a tendency to screen mass appeal programmes which are aimed at the lowest common denominator'. But the problem, they maintained, was the *source* of the network's commercial funding, not their private ownership *per se*: 'The economic incentives for privately operated *pay*-cable TV are entirely different [from advertising-funded television]. Pay-TV with unlimited channels has a tendency to diversify rather than offer lowest common-denominator programmes' (p. 66).

Free-market-motivated belief in the virtues of direct payment for television, as opposed to advertising funding, and an emphasis on the importance of unlimited channels as a condition for the effective working of pay-TV were to figure as further central elements in the Peacock Report. But, as we shall see, they were not views that fitted neatly into Tory predilections.

*Choice by Cable* devoted very little attention specifically to the BBC. Its target was the general regulated public service framework of the *whole* of British broadcasting. The second free-market think-tank report on broadcasting was far more explicit about the Corporation.

From 1982 onwards the Adam Smith Institute started producing an ambitious set of blueprints for radical-right reform of a wide range of British institutions, ranging from Defence to Housing, and from Agriculture to Justice. These were finally all collected together as *The Omega File* in 1985 (Butler et al., 1985). Several of the different sections of the report were published separately before this, and the Omega Report on *Communications Policy* (Adam Smith Institute 1984) first appeared in May 1984.

In keeping with rest of the Omega project *Communications Policy* covered a wide range of areas – from the postal service to telecommunications. Its section on television and radio directly challenged what it saw as the traditional principle of British broadcasting – that broadcasting was a public service accountable to the people through Parliament:

> If television is to have a healthy future in Britain, then it must move towards the demands of its audience. Logically the only possible way this can occur is by moving away from the television licence fee to other forms of finance.

Although the *Communications Policy* authors conceded that pay-TV was a more direct method of charging than advertising, they did not place the same emphasis on pay as Veljanovski and Bishop. Nor did the Adam Smith Institute authors share the IEA pair's worries about advertising funding. 'Where the balance lies between advertising and charging is a decision only the market can make,' they pronounced. Either method of finance was superior to 'the decisions of the bureaucrat' (Adam Smith Institute, 1984, p. 38).

Answering the traditional defence of supporters of public service that commercialisation of television would lead to a decline in quality, *Communications Policy* had this to say:

> the 'quality argument' is clearly elitist ... The idea of a 'quality' programme is a highly subjective one. The only fair criterion for judging programme quality is by how many people like it ... High ratings ought to be accepted as the yardstick of what people want, and should not be regarded as the object of disdain. (p. 40)

This was a noticeably less sophisticated free-market position than *Choice by Cable*, and in terms of the Peacock Commission it was to have far less influence. But, as we shall see, the argument against 'elitist public service bureaucrats' (particularly in the BBC) was to have considerable currency in the press campaign leading up to the establishment of the Peacock Committee.

In keeping with its general approach, *Communications Policy* advocated a progressive loosening of restrictions on the types of advertisements permitted on television, and a variety of measures to reform both the BBC and the IBA. In the case of the BBC, it proposed breaking the Corporation up into 'an association of independent and separately financed stations, operating under the guidance of the BBC board of governors'. One unit would comprise BBC 1, BBC 2 and BBC Breakfast Time:

> [This] would be kept intact as one BBC TV unit, but their method of financing would be changed. BBC1 and BBC Breakfast Time would be financed by advertising, while BBC2 would be financed by a mixture of advertising, sponsorship, and subsidy from revenue gathered by BBC1 and Breakfast Time.

To preserve its integrity, 'BBC TV news would be formed into a separate entity financed by levies on all three channels, and from funds from other TV stations, possibly cable or satellite' (p. 41).

On the ITV side, the Adam Smith Institute urged that

> the IBA should be replaced by a body more akin to the FCC [Federal Communications Commission] in the United States – a body that allocates frequencies to prevent interference between stations but which maximizes the number of stations on air.

This reformed IBA 'should be a commercially-aware body that can effectively promote commercial broadcasting in Britain rather than acting as a body more concerned with control and restriction' (p. 42). Interestingly, although in other sections it advocated the allocation of radio frequencies by auction, in its 'Television and Radio' section *Communications Policy* did not specifically suggest an auction of the ITV licences.

The appearance of *Choice by Cable* in 1983 and *Communications Policy* in 1984 were important indicators of how the free-market right was, several years after 1979, turning its attention to challenging the general framework of British broadcasting. But the differences of emphasis between the two reports – on advertising as opposed to pay-TV, and on the amount of attention given to the BBC – also revealed that the 'ideological' free-market camp did not have one single recipe for the commercialisation of broadcasting. That fact was to prove of considerable significance for subsequent developments.

In 1984 and 1985 a combination of factors pushed the government in favour of concentrating its energies in the broadcasting area not just on the terrestrial public service core in general, but quite specifically on trying to put advertising on the BBC. ITV, in contrast, was the subject of comparatively little attention.

In the summer of 1984 the BBC began preparing its case for an increase in the licence fee. 'There had only been eight licence fee increases in our history,' recalled then Director-General, Alasdair Milne, 'but five of them had occurred, because of inflation, in the eight years between 1976 and 1984 and that had caused the licence fee to incur sharp political overtones' (Milne, 1989, pp. 124–5). So, without any other developments, a proposed increase in the licence fee would have drawn the finances of the BBC into the centre of political controversy in 1984/5.

But there were other factors which sharpened the focus on the BBC. One was the new interest in broadcasting by the intellectual free-market right which we have described above. A second was the traditional Conservative Party hostility to the output of the BBC as a hotbed of leftism. This had recently been fuelled by controversies over elements of the BBC's Falklands War coverage and its reporting of Northern Ireland. So, for reasons of its supposedly biased political content, by the mid-80s the BBC was, at the very least, not the Conservative Party's favourite broadcaster.

A third new factor was the scale of the increase in the licence fee that the BBC felt compelled to propose in 1984. For a number of reasons television programming costs have tended to rise faster than the general rate of inflation (Collins, et al., 1988, pp. 15–18). In the 70s and early 80s the BBC licence fee did not need to fully reflect this, because television viewers were moving in huge numbers from black and white to colour, and thus from paying the black and white licence to the much more expensive colour licence. By the mid-80s, however, this move was coming to an end (Peacock, 1986, p. 14). So any new hike in the licence had to reflect more truly the increases in broadcasting costs, as well as any expansion in the scope of BBC operations, which, in keeping with its tradition of taking up new developments in the medium, the Corporation wanted to pursue. The result was that when Milne and his colleagues publicly launched the BBC's bid for a rise in the licence fee at a press conference in December 1984, their declared target was to increase the fee from £46 to £65 – a rise of 41 per cent (Milne, 1989, p. 125).

The bid prompted an extensive and hostile press response. Predominantly pro-Conservative, the press had already begun to articulate some of the general free-market hostility to the BBC before the Corporation unveiled its licence fee bid. In a carefully documented survey of the press coverage of the BBC in this period, Tom O'Malley persuasively suggests that the campaign against the BBC was particularly strong in the papers owned by Rupert Murdoch. Press hostility to the BBC was therefore not simply motivated by general ideological considerations, but also, O'Malley argues, by Murdoch's desire to expand into television and thus his desire to destabilise a major state-funded potential competitor (O'Malley, 1994, pp. 36–46). Whatever the motivations, it is clear that after the BBC's December 1984 press conference press coverage hostile to the traditional basis of the BBC increased. Most notably, on the 14, 15 and 16 January 1985, the Murdoch-owned *Times* took the quite exceptional step of running a series of three consecutive leaders on the same subject – 'something it had not done since the abdication of King Edward VIII in 1936,' observed Alasdair Milne (1989, p. 127). The *Times* leaders went under the collective title, 'Whither the BBC?'

'The BBC', pronounced the first of these leaders, 'should not survive this Parliament in its present size, in its present form and with its present terms of reference intact'. Four reasons were advanced for this. 'First, since the arrival of independent television, the BBC has found it harder to win the audience necessary to justify to itself its licence fee monopoly.' Second, the BBC's traditional goal of expanding along with the general expansion of broadcasting now faced 'the enormous cost of technical enhancement from satellites in space and cables beneath the city streets'. Third, technical developments 'are extending consumer choice, making it all the harder for the BBC to achieve its chosen level of domination in the market'. Fourth, and we might surmise, most important, 'the political climate has changed. Today a duopoly has to be justified. So does a poll tax such as the BBC licence fee, particularly one that is fast rising and looks set on present policies to rise still faster' (*Times*, 14 January 1985, p. 9).

By 1985 all these arguments had gained a considerably wider currency than the *Times* leader writers. And, as we shall see, they were to resurface nearly a decade later in less strident form, and in a rather different political climate, in the debate around the 1996 BBC charter renewal (see Chapter 8).

The second *Times* leader explored a fifth issue. 'We need', it argued, 'more open discussions about the use of public funds.' Ideally the licence fee should not be used to fund programmes which could be provided by advertising finance. Advertising funding could, the *Times* maintained, support considerably more good television than the British public service tradition had allowed:

> The Government might consider critically the question of whether British television really is better than that of the Americans . . . The BBC and its independent competitors have set a standard within the British tradition. What reason is there to be certain that finance by advertising will overthrow this?

Faced with financial pressure, the *Times* continued, the BBC should cut back on entertainment areas which 'could be remade by others if the money is not there for the corporation' (*Times*, 15 January 1985, p. 13). (The 'others' it may be observed would include the commercial television operations which Murdoch and other newspaper proprietors hoped to develop.) As we shall see, this notion that public service should be narrowed down away from what might be provided commercially was to feature prominently in subsequent discussion of the BBC, from Peacock through to the charter-renewal debate of the early 90s.

In the third of its series, the *Times* leader writers came to the question of positive proposals for reform. They were clear that 'the Government should concede no increase in the BBC licence fee', but immediately qualified this with: 'nor should it jump to an ill-considered conclusion that advertising be taken immediately on Radios 1 and 2 and BBC1'. But they concluded: 'advertising must eventually pay for some of the "quality television" now financed by the BBC licence'. The nearest the *Times* got to a concrete method of how this change should come about was the slightly confusing proposal (bearing some of the hallmarks of the Adam Smith Institute Report) for a new broadcasting commission to auction franchises that were currently operated by the BBC:

> These franchises could form one or more than one of the services that the Corporation currently controls. Public service criteria would be constructed and strictly enjoined on the franchise holders, all of whom would be allowed to take advertising under as little regulation as the commission thought appropriate to the smooth establishment of the new arrangements. (*Times*, 16 January, 1985)

These last specific proposals were not to prove influential. The general thrust of the *Times* leaders was.

We have already mentioned the suspicion that these leaders, along with similar coverage of the BBC in the rest of the Murdoch press, were the product of particular commercial interest as well as ideology. That accusation of vested interest was vigorously contested at the time (see Milne, 1989, pp. 129–30) and, however powerful the circumstantial evidence, it remains difficult to prove conclusively. But there can be no room for doubt about one other special interest which in 1984 began to call publicly for a change in the BBC's source of revenues. This was the advertising industry itself – with, in the early and mid-80s, considerable credibility and influential links to the Conservative Party. (For a full account, see O'Malley, 1994, pp. 22–9.)

The interest of the advertising industry was clear, and had already been articulated – but rejected by the government – in debates surrounding the fourth channel. ITV was effectively a monopoly seller of television airtime, with a limited amount of space to sell. It could therefore bid up prices. Advertising on the BBC would mean more airtime for sale and thus introduce serious competition. Prices to the advertising industry would therefore fall. In September 1984 the agency D'Arcy MacManus Massius published *Funding the BBC from Advertising*, and the next month Saatchi and Saatchi followed up with *Funding the BBC – The Case for Allowing Advertising*. In November the Institute of Practitioners in Advertising (IPA), one of the advertising industry's main trade associations, received a report advocating advertising on the BBC, and in December the IPA called for a committee of inquiry into the funding of the BBC (O'Malley, 1994, pp. 24–9).

This advertising-industry campaign not only added to the pressure for the Conservative government to 'do something' about the core of British television, it also reinforced the feeling that 'something' would be done about introducing advertising on the BBC.

One other factor contributed to the BBC-directed thrust of Tory television policy. Margaret Thatcher had become personally convinced of the desirability of putting advertising on the BBC. Milne recalls a meeting with Thatcher in the autumn of 1984 at which she suggested this and dismissed his objections (1989, p. 124). In December, on the same day that the BBC press conference launched its campaign for a licence fee increase, Thatcher's Press Secretary, Bernard Ingham, let it be known to the press that the Prime Minister personally favoured the Corporation taking advertising. In her memoirs Thatcher maintains: 'I would have liked an alternative to the licence fee. One possibility was advertising ...' Interestingly, she adds: 'Willie Whitelaw ... was fiercely opposed to it and indeed threatened to resign from the Government if it were introduced' (Thatcher, 1993, p. 636).

As Whitelaw's own memoirs reveal he was, and remained, a firm defender of the traditional core public service duopoly (Whitelaw, 1989, pp. 217–18). That it was Whitelaw who headed the Home Office (the centre of the formulation of broadcasting policy) between 1979 and 1983 was no doubt a contributory factor to the Tories' largely leaving the public service duopoly alone during Thatcher's first term. Whitelaw left the Home Office after the Tories' 1983 election victory. His replacement as Home Secretary, Leon Brittan, while by no means an enthusiast for advertising on the BBC, did not share Whitelaw's particularly positive support for the existing system. This change in departmental responsibilities, coupled with the Prime Minister's personal predisposition to put advertising on the BBC, seems likely to be one extra reason why Tory television policy shifted direction in Margaret Thatcher's second term.

At the end of March 1985 Leon Brittan announced the government's response to the BBC's licence fee bid. The response consisted of two parts. The licence would be increased from £46 to £58 (a 26 per cent increase rather than the 41 per cent the BBC had asked for) and a committee of inquiry into the financing of the BBC was to be set up under the chairmanship of Professor Alan Peacock. It was to report by July 1986 (HoC Debates, 27 March 1985).

Establishing such a committee of inquiry offered a number of advantages to the government. Independent inquiries – like the Pilkington Commission before the allocation of the third channel to the BBC, and the Annan Commission before the fourth channel – had traditionally preceded major innovations in broadcasting. Thatcher may have been convinced personally of the need for advertising on the BBC, but there was continued opposition to it from Whitelaw (still in the Cabinet) and the Home Office. An external examination of the subject which came out in favour of advertising would therefore be useful for government unity. A committee of inquiry provided just that sort of considered 'independent' examination without the great delay that would have resulted from the setting up of a full-blown Royal Commission.

The Committee's composition was widely seen as being stacked to favour advertising on the BBC. In fact its members turned out altogether more independent-minded than either friends or critics expected. But suspicions that they had been selected to come up with such a result appeared well grounded.

Peacock himself was an economist of a distinctly free-market persuasion, a member of the advisory council of the Institute of Economic Affairs and a former Vice-Chancellor of Britain's only private university, Buckingham. He was joined on the Committee by Samuel Brittan. Brittan was a *Financial Times* economic journalist and leader writer, and brother of the Home Secretary, Leon. Samuel Brittan later described the membership of the Committee as, from the start, being divided into three groups:

> There were Peacock and myself, who were inclined towards market provision of goods and services. ... At the other end were Alastair Hetherington and Judith Chalmers ... who were keen to preserve the achievements of British broadcasting and suspicious of what they perceived as market ideology ... The third and middle group consisted of Lord Quinton ... Sir Peter Reynolds ... and Jeremy Hardie ... These three were not committed either to the existing institutions or to any particular alternatives; they were thus the swing voices on the Committee. (Brittan, 1991, p. 340)

This range of predispositions did not, however, mean that the seven members were fully representative of the political spectrum. The Committee contained no one publicly associated with the Labour Party. Of the two members who Brittan saw as 'suspicious of market ideology', one (Chalmers) was a supporter of the Conservative Party, as were two of the 'middle group' (Quinton and Reynolds; the third, Hardie, was a member of the SDP).

In the event it was Peacock and Samuel Brittan, and their 'inclination to the market provision of goods and services', which quite clearly set the tone for the Committee's conclusions in July 1986. Those conclusions, however, were very different from what many in government had intended, and most observers had expected. As Samuel Brittan later recalled, the mistake observers made was to confuse his and Peacock's strong free-market views with '(a) enthusiasm for advertising finance, (b) support for commercial pressure groups and (c) a desire to please the Thatcher Government' (Brittan, 1991, p. 340). As Peacock and Brittan were to show, none of the latter three positions necessarily flowed from general advocacy of the free market. The Committee was to prove far more willing to pursue its own course than either its composition or the circumstances of its creation might have initially suggested.

The Peacock Committee was set up with the following terms of reference:

(i) To assess the effects of the introduction of advertising or sponsorship on the BBC's Home Services, either as an alternative or a supplement to the income now received from the licence fee, including
(a) the financial and other consequences for the BBC, for independent television and independent local radio, for the prospective services of cable, independent national radio and direct broadcasting by satellite, for the press and the advertising industry and for the Exchequer; and
(b) the impact on the range and quality of existing broadcasting services; and
(ii) to identify a range of options for the introduction, in varying amounts and on different conditions, of advertising or sponsorship on some or all of the BBC's Home Services, and with an assessment of the advantages and disadvantages of each option; and
(iii) to consider any proposals for securing income from the consumer other than through the licence fee. (Peacock, 1986, p. 1)

This brief was, on the face of it, highly focused on the immediate issue of advertising on the BBC. But (iii) clearly extended discussion to subscription funding, while (i) (a) and (b) opened up the possibility of the Committee extending its deliberations far beyond the immediate question of financing the BBC to the whole of the broadcasting system. This wider remit was apparently what the Home Secretary himself intended (Brittan, 1991, p. 338), and the Committee seized the opportunity to the maximum. Indeed, positive recommendations for ITV and Channel Four in the final report were to prove considerably more influential than many of its long-term proposals for the BBC.

The Peacock Report that emerged, on schedule, in July 1986 can most usefully be analysed under four headings: first, its general approach to broadcasting; second, its treatment of the immediate question of financing the BBC; third, its more general approach to the longer-term future of the BBC; and, lastly, its recommendations on the rest of the broadcasting system. Each of these affected the subsequent course of government television policy in very different ways.

The core of the Peacock Report's general approach was that

British broadcasting should move towards a sophisticated market system based on consumer sovereignty. That is a system which recognises that viewers and listeners are the best ultimate judges of their own interests, which they can best satisfy if they have the option of purchasing the broadcasting services they require from as many alternative sources of supply as possible. (Peacock, 1986, p. 133)

This statement is a clear indication that Peacock and Brittan's free-market economist approach had won out with the rest of the Committee. Framing the future of broadcasting as a whole in terms of the market was a fundamental theoretical break with all previous official reports on broadcasting in Britain – including Annan – all of which had stressed public service as their central organising principle.[1]

However, although the market replaced public service as the Peacock Committee's goal for the organisation of broadcasting, this did not mean that the Committee foresaw public service disappearing altogether. Indeed the quote above was immediately followed by this qualification:

> There will *always* be a need to supplement the direct consumer market by public finance for programmes of a public service kind ... supported by people in their capacity as citizens and voters but unlikely to be commercially self-supporting in the view of broadcasting entrepreneurs. (p. 133, my emphasis)

The Peacock Committee was quite explicit that public intervention in broadcasting should not just be confined to enforcing laws on decency and defamation, or preventing monopoly. It should also include some element of collective and collectively funded provision:

> Viewers and listeners themselves may be willing to provide finance for broadcasting activities in their capacity as voting taxpayers ... A simple illustration makes our point. Many citizens who never go near our National Galleries value their existence and are prepared to contribute as tax-payers to their upkeep. Public patronage has long been a source of support for the arts, alongside direct consumer support, since the time of classical Greece or earlier.

The Committee listed a range of the types of programmes which were 'suitable for public patronage'. These included: 'news, current affairs, documentaries, programmes about science, nature and other parts of the world, as well as avowedly educational programmes, all of which require active and not passive attention and which may also contribute to responsible citizenship'; 'high quality programmes on the Arts'; and 'critical and controversial programmes, covering everything from the appraisal of commercial products to politics, ideology, philosophy and religion'. There might also be a case for public patronage for experimental entertainment. The report put just two – rather important – stipulations on such state support: it should be 'visible and not achieved by cross-subsidisation or "leaning" on programme makers', and it should 'account for a modest proportion of total broadcasting' (pp. 127–8).

So, although the Peacock Committee decisively shifted the parameters of broadcasting debate from public service to the market, within this envisaged market-dominated future, it still saw a continued and permanent, if subordinate, place for public service and state support.

A second, important point to note about the Peacock Report's pro-market approach was its conclusion that 'what we do expect to disappear is the need for negative or censorious controls' (p. 133). If broadcasting were to become increasingly like the press, governed by the market, then it would also become, like the press, subject only to the general 'law of the land'. 'The end of all censorship arrangements', declared the Committee, 'would be a sign that broadcasting had come of age, like publishing three centuries ago' (p. 150).

Samuel Brittan later explained that this link between the market approach and the liberal tradition of free speech was an important element in winning over members of the Committee who were sceptical about the role of the market in broadcasting (Brittan, 1991, p. 341). He also recalled that 'it was the linkage of the Report with the long tradition of Western writing (from Milton to Mill and beyond) in favour of free expression that gave me more pleasure than anything else' (p. 342). But it was also an aspect of the report that stuck in the throats of the Conservative government, who were, at the time, as concerned with controlling the content of broadcasting, on political or 'moral' grounds, as they were with developing market forces within it. 'Just how far removed the Thatcher Government really was from the main Peacock conclusion became apparent when the Whips applied pressure on the "payroll vote" to ensure the Second Reading of the Obscene Publications Bill on April 3, 1987,' Brittan commented. 'This was a highly illiberal measure inspired by the "moral majority" campaign of Mrs Whitehouse' (p. 352).

The third major element in the Peacock Committee's overall philosophy was its emphasis on *efficiency* of resource allocation as a prime goal of broadcasting policy. Chapter 11 of the report was entitled 'Improvements in Efficiency':

> We received a fair number of letters and memoranda from both the general public and figures prominent in the broadcasting world recommending that the Committee should look into the question of the efficiency of the BBC and the extent to which this depended on the duopoly situation ...' (Peacock, 1986, p. 120)

The Committee certainly did not take such representations uncritically, nor did it attempt to gloss over the problems involved with the different strategies involved in trying to improve efficiency. But the very concern with efficiency in resource allocation, which occurs throughout the report, and is not confined to the BBC, represented a fundamental departure from previous official discussions of broadcasting.

Like the 'industrial' considerations on satellite and cable we have highlighted in the last two chapters, efficiency of resource allocation had not figured prominently in either the Pilkington or Annan Reports. The prominence of 'efficiency' in Peacock was to prove one of the report's most important and lasting legacies.

The final feature of the general Peacock approach particularly worth noting is its advocacy of a *move* towards a *sophisticated* market system. Both of these qualifications, made by the Committee in its advocacy of the market, were important. The first implied that not every immediate apparently 'pro-market' reform would necessarily operate in favour of the final goal of sovereignty of consumer choice, especially if the conditions of multiplicity of channels were absent. As academic economists, Peacock and Brittan may have been starry-eyed about the theoretical workings of the market, but they were also readily familiar with the standard conditions which free-market theory considers necessary for the market to properly work. Advocacy of a 'sophisticated' broadcasting market not only meant a recognition that a multiplicity of channels was necessary if the television market was to work according to free-market ideals but also entailed a strong preference for pay-TV. Pay was a direct way for the consumer to exert financial preference in contrast to the considerable imperfections of advertising. These two qualifications took on great practical importance when it came to the Committee's recommendations on its immediate remit of putting advertising on the BBC.

The Peacock Committee spent a considerable amount of effort trying to accumulate evidence on the likely prospects for the growth of television advertising expenditure. Its witnesses were sharply divided in their prognoses, and on the whole the Committee tended to side with the more cautious estimates. However, as the Peacock Committee itself stressed, its final conclusion was not dependent on these estimates:

> Our primary consideration has been the satisfaction and range of choice available to viewers and listeners. The main defect of a system based on advertising finance is that channel owners do not sell programmes to audiences, but audiences to advertisers. The differences between the two concepts would narrow if there were sufficiently large numbers of channels, without concentration of ownership. In that case there could well be pressure on suppliers to transmit a wide range of programmes, covering minority and medium appeal programmes. But these conditions do not prevail and are unlikely to for some time. *So long as the present duopoly remains in being and competition is limited to a fringe of satellite and cable services, the introduction of advertising on [BBC] television is likely to reduce consumer choice and welfare.* It could do this both by driving the BBC into a ratings war and by putting financial pressure on ITV companies, which would make it more difficult for them to meet IBA requirements. The result could be an inadequate supply of programmes which many of us watch most of the time, but which do not achieve top audience ratings. One consequence of not introducing advertising on the BBC television services is that the growth in advertising revenue in real terms projected by our economic studies will provide additional finances for the new technologies of cable and DBS. (p. 137, my emphasis)

Such a verdict, delivered by a committee dominated by pro-market economists and generally regarded as having been set up with the specific purpose of introducing advertising on the BBC, was a devastating blow to any such project. Regardless of Margaret Thatcher's personal preferences, the Peacock Report effectively removed advertising on BBC television, not only from the practical political debate of the mid-80s, but also for the following decade.

The Peacock Report's specific proposals for the BBC followed from its long-term desire to move towards a sophisticated market system for broadcasting, coupled with its recognition that the complete end to spectrum scarcity was necessary to achieve this. In the meantime, 'the BBC, and the regulated ITV system, have done far better, in mimicking the effects of a true consumer market, than any purely *laissez-faire* system, financed by advertising could have done under conditions of spectrum shortage' (p. 131).

So, reform of the broadcasting system would have to be based on a series of stages through which broadcasting would move. The Peacock Report distinguished three stages of likely broadcasting developments. During stage one, 'satellite and cable develop, but most viewers and listeners continue to rely on BBC, ITV and independent local radio'. During stage two there would be a 'proliferation of broadcasting systems, channels and payment methods'. This would lead finally to stage three, where there would be an 'indefinite number of channels', 'pay-per-programme or pay-per-channel' would be available and technology would reduce the 'cost of outlets and of charging system' (p. 136). It was central to the Committee's recommendations that policy measures had to be appropriate to each stage. Only with stage three would multiplicity of choice lead to a full broadcasting market.

To facilitate the transition to that final stage, quite different measures were required in earlier stages, particularly stage one, than would be necessary once a full broadcast market was established. We have seen that, during stage one, when the ITV/BBC duopoly would continue, the Peacock Report rejected advertising funding for the BBC. Instead it proposed retaining the licence fee 'for the time being as the principle source of BBC finance'. It was 'important to have a systematic and agreed formula for determining it', and, therefore, 'the licence fee should be indexed on an annual basis to the general rate of inflation'. This, the Committee believed, 'would bring a measure of insulation of the BBC from political influence'. General inflation was chosen in preference to either average earnings or the BBC's own level of pay costs, because either of the latter courses 'would build in incentives to inefficiency, waste and lax pay settlements' (pp. 137–8). In other words, the Peacock Committee expected indexation to the retail price index to bring some downward pressure on BBC costs.

Finance of the BBC from the licence fee was not, however, to continue indefinitely:

> In Stage 2, which is likely to begin well before the end of the century, we recommend that subscription should replace the licence fee. We regard it as the way in which all broadcasting organisations, including the BBC, can sell their services directly to the public. We do not see it simply as an alternative way of collecting the licence fee.

This medium-term shift to subscription for the BBC did not, in the Peacock Committee's view, obviate the continued need for some public service provision:

> We must face the possibility that if broadcasting finance is confined to subscription and advertising there would be some erosion of public service broadcasting in the narrow sense. As broadcasting becomes more competitive the ability and the desirability of detailed IBA regulation of the independent sector will also weaken. Rather than engage in a fruitless battle to maintain regulation ... it would be better for parliament to take more positive action to make finance available for public service broadcasting. (pp. 147–8)

This finance – either from general taxation or a continuing licence fee – would be distributed by a Public Service Broadcasting Council (PSBC), allocating grants for particular programmes which it deemed merited public service support on any channel. 'Whenever a PSBC grant was given, the PSBC would have the right to stipulate where programmes should be broadcast, and these should be broadcast in non-encrypted form.' Public service programmes so funded 'would be likely to be a narrower group than "everything the BBC at present does" but a larger group than what has been called rather gracelessly "an arts and current affairs ghetto" ' (pp. 148–9).

In short, the Peacock Report recommended an indexation of the licence fee and no advertising in the short term, and subscription supplemented by grants from a PSBC in the medium to long term. This was a free-market strategy with considerable sophistication and intellectual coherence behind it. But it was not one that the government found completely palatable.

Alongside its proposals for the BBC, the Peacock Report made a number of other important recommendations for the rest of the broadcasting system, all of them to take place during stage one, and all of them presumably designed to pave the way to stages two and, ultimately, three – 'multiplicity of choice leading to a full broadcasting market'. One of these recommendations applied to both sides of the 'comfortable duopoly': 'the BBC and ITV should be required over a ten year period to increase to not less than 40% the proportion of programmes supplied by independent producers'. At the time, it should be remembered, virtually all BBC and ITV programmes were produced in-house. The independent television production sector was new, essentially brought into being by, and still largely confined, to Channel Four.

It is important to note the Peacock Committee's reasoning behind this recommendation:

> We are concerned about the level of costs and efficiency in broadcasting generally ... There is suggestive evidence that BBC costs are higher at least in some cases than those of small independent producers ... and that ITV costs are higher than those of the BBC.

This situation resulted from the very nature of the 'comfortable duopoly': 'One way of introducing competition, even while the duopoly remains, is by enlarging the scope of independent programme makers to sell to existing authorities, as already occurs in the case of Channel Four.'

The Committee continued:

> there are many reasons for wanting to enhance the role of independent producers apart from the greater range of cost comparisons which greater competition would ensure.... Requirements for in-house production are at the root of union restrictive practices at least in the major ITV network companies. If ITV programme makers were separate entities from ITV contractors, they could less readily be blackmailed by the threat to black channels out ... Apart from its value as a check on costs, minimum prescribed proportions for independents would have the great advantage of encouraging new small-scale units in preparation for the more competitive regime of Stages 2 and 3. (pp. 141–2)

In short, the Peacock Report recommended an independent production quota, not primarily in order to diversify the types of programmes being produced, but so as to exert a downward pressure on programme costs, most specifically by weakening union bargaining power in the television industry.

The Peacock Report's two other major recommendations were clear examples of how the Committee stretched its brief way beyond the BBC. One was concerned solely with ITV, the other with Channel Four.

Recommendation 10 of the report asserted that 'franchise contracts for ITV contractors should be put to competitive tender'. The Committee saw this as a necessary extra measure 'to produce more efficient use of resources':

> The [ITV] levy was designed to cream off some of the monopoly gains resulting from the restriction of entry into the sector: but even after its 1986 reform the levy system offers too little incentive to economise in costs, which may be inflated in order to reduce the net profit which is the tax base of the levy. A more suitable device, which would both act as a revenue raiser and an incentive to economise in resource inputs, would be for those seeking a franchise to bid against each other in competitive tender. The success-ful bidder would then have monopoly profits creamed off in advance of operating the

franchise, and the subsequent earning of profits would depend on close attention to economy in the use of resources.

This was the stated rationale for what was to turn out to be the notorious 'ITV franchise auction' of 1991. It displayed both the Peacock Committee's general concern to introduce efficiency into broadcasting through market mechanisms and a liberal economist's technical solution to the problem of ITV's monopoly profits. Given the subsequent history of the franchise auction, it is important to note a number of extra details about its original formulation.

First, the Peacock Committee were concerned that at this stage in the duopoly the quality of service might be reduced. So, it stated, 'we would still expect the IBA to lay down the minimum quality, schedules and range of criteria which companies bidding for franchises for programme packaging must meet.' In addition, 'the IBA could decide that a company offering a lower price was giving more "value for money" in terms of public service and, accordingly, award the franchise to them'. Lastly, 'where there was only one bidder for a franchise, the IBA might lay down a "reserve price" on the allocation of a channel' (p. 143). These qualifications were all to prove of major importance in subsequent debates on, and operation of, the auction system.

But despite the qualifications, Recommendation 10 gained the support of only a bare majority (four out of seven) members of the Committee. The other three (Judith Chalmers, Jeremy Hardie and Alastair Hetherington) appended the following note of dissent:

> Three of us ... do not recommend this system, certainly as long as the duopoly lasts. First, it would be very hard for the IBA to choose between a high cash bid and a bid which offered less money but a better chance of high quality public service broadcasting. The present system of allocating franchises has been much criticised as arbitrary and unpredictable. The proposed system would reinforce these criticisms. Second, we do not think the public service undertakings given by bidders can be made sufficiently precise to be legally enforceable; and if it is the IBA, not the courts, who decide when there has been a breach, that will give rise to concern about unnecessary and arbitrary decisions. Third, a system of competitive tenders is designed to reduce profits. It therefore makes it more likely that companies, through bad luck or bad management, will make losses or poor profits. The examples of TV-am and many ILR stations show how hard it is in practice for the IBA to enforce standards in those circumstances. (p. 143)

We shall see in Chapter 8 just how prescient or otherwise those objections were to be.

The Committee's specific recommendation on Channel Four was unanimous, but less clearly explained: 'Recommendation 14: Channel 4 should be given the option of selling its own advertising time and would no longer be funded by subscription from ITV companies.' The only justification offered for this was that 'Channel 4 is now at a point where its costs are of a similar order to the revenue from advertising'(p. 144). In other words Channel Four was now in a position to fend for itself. Any implication this might have for the channel's fulfilment of its special remit was not considered. We can only speculate on any other reasons which may have lain behind this recommendation. One consequence would, of course, be to introduce some measure of competition into the sale of television airtime. The advertising industry's preferred option for this – advertising on the BBC – had, as we have seen, been rejected by the Committee. For Channel Four to sell its own advertising could therefore be taken as a consolation prize for the advertising lobby.

For all their range and radicalness, every one of the above recommendations related to one aspect or another of *broadcasting* as traditionally understood. In the last part of the report that merits special mention the Committee extended their recommendations to *telecommunications*:

> At the time of writing, a likely route to the full broadcasting market we envisage appears to be the development of an optic fibre network by the telecommunications industry, which could be used for broadcasting and other services. In our first stage proposals we suggest the removal of the obstacles to such a development. (p. 135)

So the Peacock Report's Recommendation 15 was that 'national telecommunications systems (e.g. British Telecom, Mercury and any subsequent entrants) should be permitted to act as common carriers with a view to the provision of a full range of services, including the delivery of television programmes.' BT had put the case to the Committee that pay-TV could become available at a modest price to the consumer as homes were connected to a fibre-optic grid, but

> if the government were to stick to its current line of hoping that existing cable systems will develop on an entertainment basis and that a competitive telecommunications network will be established, then the whole communications enterprise could get bogged down.

The Peacock Committee saw its proposal to allow BT and Mercury to act as common carriers for television and other services as a way out of this impasse.

This approach was in keeping with the tendency to view television as part of the general telecommunications policy which had characterised the Tory policy of the early 80s, particularly on cable. By the middle of the decade, with the Tories tending to compartmentalise broadcasting and telecommunications issues more rigidly, it fell on stony ground. The recommendation was largely neglected in discussion when the report was published, and in 1990/1, when the government conducted its telecommunications duopoly review, the Peacock recommendation was ignored (DTI, 1991). The ban on BT and Mercury carrying broadcast entertainment was retained. It was only in the mid-90s, as we shall explain in Chapter 10, that the subject returned to the centre of the television policy debate.

The Peacock Report threw Tory television policy into disarray. A committee appointed by the government had devastatingly rejected the Prime Minister's favoured policy of putting advertising on BBC television. The alternative policy it put forward, for a long-term move to subscription by the BBC, represented both a quite new proposal for most of the Cabinet and was viewed with hostility by the Home Office, Tory paternalists, the Opposition and a large section of the television industry. On top of this, the Peacock Committee's anti-censorious liberalism brought a major aspect of its general approach into sharp conflict with the Prime Minister's determination to be more censorious with television over 'taste and decency' and politics.

The Peacock Committee's findings were well leaked in the weeks before its official publication on 3 July 1986. Samuel Brittan subsequently claimed that this had been deliberately done by the Home Office with the object of denigrating the report and 'putting it into the long grass' (*Daily Telegraph*, 30 July 1986, p. 4). Whether or not this was true, many observers at the time thought that conflicts within the Cabinet would result in the report being put on the shelf. The possibility for such conflicts had been exacerbated by another shift in departmental responsibility. In the interval between the establishment of the Committee and its report, Leon Brittan had been replaced as Home Secretary by Douglas Hurd. Hurd may not have been as committed to the public service duopoly as Whitelaw, but he was distinctly more in tune with the traditional pro-status quo Home Office position than Brittan.

So, in the not untypical view of one trade paper at the time, the report

> has been virtually written off even before its publication today ... After the frustration of seeing the committee refuse to do the one thing she wanted from it – to press for the introduction of advertising on the BBC – the Prime Minister is said to have dismissed the alternative proposals as neither strong nor immediate enough ... Hurd apparently opposed the proposals because he believed they were too radical and could spell the end of public service broadcasting in Britain. The result now seems to be that the Prime Minister and Hurd have decided, for opposite reasons, that the report should be shelved ... (*Television Today*, 3 July 1986, p. 17)

Against this background, the government's initial public reaction to Peacock bore all the signs of a holding operation. Hurd's first official response was cautious in the extreme. The government, he maintained, saw much merit in the Committee's emphasis on consumer choice, 'which is very much in tune with the Government's general philosophy'. Its proposals 'deserve and will receive careful study'. Peacock's rejection of advertising on BBC television 'could not be lightly put aside'. The government also saw merit 'in a number of the committee's shorter-term proposals designed to pave the way for the free broadcasting market'. But, Hurd rapidly added, 'the best way of achieving this will need careful consideration' (HoC Debates, 3 July 1986, cols. 1176–8). This 'careful consideration' was to last well over two years. The government only finally felt able to put forward an agreed menu of proposals for reform of the television system at the end of 1988, with the publication of the White Paper, *Broadcasting in the 90s: Competition Quality and Choice*.

By November 1986, when the House of Commons had its first full debate on Peacock, it was clear that the government had begun to set some of the parameters for its post-Peacock strategy. Hurd informed the Commons that it was likely to accept the Committee's verdict against advertising on the BBC:

> The committee made out a powerful and detailed case based both on economic principle, on the committee's assessment of price elasticity of demand for advertising, and on research of experience abroad. *The arguments were pretty forceful and I believe that the onus now rests on those who disagree with the committee's conclusions to disprove the arguments underpinning those conclusions.* (my emphasis)

The government, Hurd made clear, favoured the Committee's recommendation to index the licence fee to the RPI. And it leant towards doing something about Peacock's 'important recommendations for the independent television system'. The government needed time to decide on the changes that should be made, explained Hurd. So, in order not to foreclose on the options, the Home Secretary announced that 'there should be early legislation which would have the effect of enabling the IBA to extend existing contracts ...' (HoC Debates, 20 November 1986, cols. 716–18).

This legislation was soon forthcoming. In 1987 the ITV licences were extended – from the end of 1989 to the end of 1992. Taking full advantage of this breathing space, internal government debate on the framework for the new franchise round was conducted in a Cabinet Committee chaired by the Prime Minister. One member of that committee, Nigel Lawson, the Chancellor of the Exchequer from 1983 to 1989, has since given a distinctly jaundiced account of its workings:

> The future of broadcasting, and in particular television, ... occupied a surprising amount of my time in 1987 ... Faced with the need to devise a coherent Government response to both the Peacock Report and the enormous technical possibilities that were opening up, which clearly required a whole new statutory framework, Margaret [Thatcher] set up a Cabinet Committee on broadcasting on which I served. It was not the most cost-effective way of spending time. Broadcasting was a subject on which Margaret held a great many firm views and prejudices, which she would air at some length, irrespective of whether this had any bearing on the Committee's pressing need to reach decisions on a number of complex and critical issues. Indeed, her Chairmanship became so discursive, and hence indecisive, that, with her knowledge and consent, I took to chairing smaller meetings between the meetings of the main committee, without which it is hard to see how decisions would ever have been taken. At these smaller meetings ... the key participants were the two Ministers with the main departmental interest in broadcasting: Douglas Hurd, then Home Secretary, and David Young, then Trade and Industry Secretary ... (Lawson, 1992, pp. 720–1)

Alongside the personal ideological divisions between the members of the Cabinet Committee, there were equally important divisions based on different departmental loyalties – the Treasury's desire to maximise revenue from ITV, the Home Office's protectiveness over the traditional British broadcasting framework and the Department of Industry's predisposition to see broadcasting as simply another industry to be made more efficient and competitive.

That Young and the DTI were now centrally involved in formulating general television policy was seen by many contemporary observers as being a key indicator of the drift of government thinking. We shall see in the next chapter that this involvement left a rather less lasting imprint on government policy than critics might have feared. But, it should also be noted, this involvement of the DTI constituted an important element of continuity with the 'industrial' orientation of early 80s cable and satellite policy described in Chapters 3 and 4.

Any members of the Cabinet Committee who were tempted to take early action on Peacock's long-term goal of turning the BBC over to subscription must have had their enthusiasm dampened by the one major piece of research that the government commissioned on the subject. Soon after the Peacock Committee had reported, the Home Office decided to commission independent consultants to examine the technical and economic implications of Peacock's subscription proposals The contract for the study was awarded to Communications Studies and Planning Limited (CSP) in October 1986. CSP was taken over by Booz Allen and Hamilton before the study was completed in April 1987, and it was eventually published under the title *Subscription Television* (Booz Allen, 1987) in May.

At over 200 pages, *Subscription Television* was a weighty assessment of the then available evidence about the prospects in Britain for the new form of television finance. The report was to prove perceptive in identifying the potential UK consumer demand for 'premium channels'. But what mattered in 1987 – with subscription for the BBC already viewed with much suspicion in the Home Office and elsewhere – was the study's conclusions about switching the BBC's existing channels to subscription. And these were, in the immediate term, distinctly unfavourable to Peacock's hopes of a subscription-based future.

Subscription television in the UK, Booz Allen concluded, presented no great technical problems – although even on technical grounds the study pointed to 'the need to introduce any future subscription service on a gradual basis rather than by a sudden switch-over of an existing channel from clear to scrambled transmission'. The key problem was financial. In the opinion of the study, neither BBC 1 nor BBC 2 could finance themselves from subscription. BBC 1 could raise only half its running costs, BBC 2 could do better, but still not break even. Although UK viewers were willing to pay for more television, this was primarily for, what Booz Allen called, 'premium' programming – first-run movies, major sporting events, etc. – and not for the current programming mix on the terrestrial channels (p. 160). To this gloomy assessment of the financial viability of a subscription-financed BBC, Booz Allen added a second, damning conclusion:

> All options involving subscription funding of the existing channels are undesirable when evaluated from the standpoint of economic benefit-cost analysis. Applying the methodology of welfare economics to assess the value of television services to UK consumers under various financing options, we find that the substitution of the licence fee by subscription results in a large loss rather than a gain in economic welfare ... Indeed the economic analysis suggests an optimal licence fee would be set at a level higher, not lower, than the present figure ... (p. 161)

This was clearly not a line of argument that fitted in well with Conservative thinking. And indeed, Booz Allen recognised it as a political impossibility.

Nevertheless the study was not totally negative about the prospects for subscription television in the UK in general. 'Our study has identified', it continued, 'considerable consumer demand for extra television programming, backed up by willingness to pay for such material. ... A category of programming which is particularly under-supplied in the UK is premium material ...' (p. 162). The correctness of this prognosis was soon to be borne out by the success of Sky and then BSkyB's subscription movie and sports channels. But in 1987 Booz Allen saw considerable advantages in fostering this latent demand for subscription payment for premium programming, not on satellite, but on terrestrial channels. To this end it made three proposals:

1. Use of night-time services on BBC 2 and Channel Four for downloading premium material;

2. Replacement of some parts of the BBC 2 schedule by encrypted and subscription-financed premium material;
3. New terrestrial subscription channels. Another study carried out by Booz Allen for the Home Office in 1987 had already shown that such extra terrestrial channels, covering a substantial part of the country, were technically possible.

There was implicit in these suggestions a course of development along the lines already pioneered by Canal-plus in France – subscription funding in one or a few terrestrial channels as an add-on to the 'free' public service system. This option was not taken up by the British government. The overall effect of the Booz Allen study was to put one more nail in the coffin of Peacock's long-term goal of subscription funding for the BBC as a matter of practical policy.

It surfaced just once more. On 10 June 1988 a joint statement by the DTI and the Home Office revealed that Young and Hurd were in discussions with the BBC and IBA about the possibility of moving BBC 2 and Channel Four to satellite so as to free the terrestrial frequencies occupied by them for new advertising-funded commercial channels (*Independent*, 11 June 1988, p. 2). The proposal was greeted with considerable astonishment and hostility within the industry, and was widely seen as an example of the DTI's attempts to encroach on broadcasting policy. It sank without trace in a few weeks.

The burial of a long-term subscription future for the BBC as a practical guide to policy still left much to disagree about in the Cabinet Committee on broadcasting. In the two years that these disagreements were hammered out inside the administration, the government nevertheless managed to begin to implement two of Peacock's immediate key proposals: independent production quotas and licence fee indexation.

In the November 1986 Commons debate on the Peacock Report, Douglas Hurd's most positive comments were reserved for independent production:

> The Peacock Committee argued forcefully that an increase in independent production [on BBC and ITV] would help the general move towards a more competitive broadcasting market ... and have a good effect on the level of costs and efficiency in broadcasting generally.... We agree with that view and believe that independents, too, deserve a place in the sun.

Hurd added that, having been in touch with independent producers, he believed the goal of 25 per cent, advanced by the independent producers' lobby, was 'more realistic', although the government looked for 'somewhat faster progress' on this than Peacock's ten-year target. 'I have, therefore, arranged', Hurd concluded, 'to meet the chairmen and directors general of the BBC and IBA soon to discuss the means of achieving the broad targets that we have in mind' (HoC Debates, 20 November 1986, cols. 718–19).

On 14 January 1987 Hurd announced to the House of Commons that the government had definitely accepted that the BBC should not be financed through advertising and 'for the time being the licence fee should remain the main source of income'. That fee, which Hurd had already announced was to remain at £58 until March 1988, would thereafter be indexed to move annually in line with the RPI. This arrangement would last for three years from April 1988. 'Given the past tendency of BBC costs to rise faster than inflation,' said Hurd, 'this form of indexation will form a strong incentive to practise efficiency and care in undertaking fresh commitments.' The base from which this indexation would be made – a notional £60 for the year 1987/88 – put further pressure on the BBC's finances, as Hurd explained:

> By April 1988 the BBC will be spending at substantially above the level of the £60 licence fee. We shall be applying a *double squeeze* – a once-and-for-all squeeze, inasmuch as we have chosen a notional figure of £60 and not a higher figure, although the BBC will be spending at a higher figure, and a continuous squeeze inasmuch as we have chosen for the index the retail prices index and not the higher index that the BBC tended to favour ...' (HoC Debates, 14 January 1987, cols. 263–5, my emphasis)

The considerable hostility with which the Peacock Report was initially greeted by both the Opposition and much of the television industry continued during the two years between the report and the White Paper. However, despite that continued and widespread hostility, there were indications that at least some of Peacock's general philosophy was becoming increasingly regarded as the common sense of debate on television policy and that some of the Committee's still controversial recommendations were increasingly being seen as inevitable.

On publication in July 1986 Shadow Home Secretary, Gerald Kaufman rubbished the Peacock Committee's findings:

> In most of its recommendations [it] goes wildly beyond its terms of reference and seeks, arrogantly and impertinently, to restructure the whole of broadcasting ... We reject the plan for BBC TV as a subscription service. That would either turn the BBC into the television equivalent of junk food, or drive it into a cultural ghetto ... We reject the proposal to privatise TV during night time hours. This could introduce a completely unregulated system of television which would become a playground for pornography and violence ... We reject the indexing of the licence fee. Such a system would be unrelated to the BBC's financial needs ... The proper place for the report is not a pigeon hole but a wastepaper basket. (HoC Debates, 3 July 1986, cols. 1178–9)

In the full November debate on the Peacock Report, Kaufman's tone was rather more considered, but he still reached a damning conclusion:

> If the Government follows the Peacock proposals, they will destroy the standards which have brought distinction to British broadcasting and television ... We condemn the Government's present anti-BBC vendetta and oppose the Peacock prospect of a free-for-all future ... (HoC Debates, 20 November 1986, col. 731)

This absolute Labour hostility to virtually the whole of Peacock's approach and proposals continued throughout 1987. It is unusual for issues of broadcasting policy to figure in election manifestos. But in the 1987 general election, broadcasting figured in both Labour and Tory manifestos. The Conservatives pledged to bring in a 'major new' Broadcasting Bill. Apart from the 25 per cent quota and the extra regulation of taste and decency, the commitment was short on specifics as to what the Bill would contain – probably reflecting the uncertain state of Conservative response to Peacock in the summer of 1987 (Craig, 1990, p. 451). Labour was short, negative and more specific: 'We reject subscription for the BBC and the auctioning of the ITV franchises,' its manifesto declared (p. 472).

In 1988, however, despite continued hostility from the Labour front bench, there were indications of some cross-party consensus about the reform of British broadcasting. That consensus apparently extended to at least the principle of introducing money into the allocation of ITV franchises. In December 1987 the House of Commons Home Affairs Committee announced an inquiry on the future of broadcasting and produced a unanimous report – *The Future of Broadcasting* (Home Affairs Committee, 1988) – in June 1988. The Home Affairs Committee Report is an interesting indicator of how the post-Peacock concerns had become accepted and of the consensus that was being established among back-bench politicians of all parties on the eve of the government's November 1988 Broadcasting White Paper. Among the Committee's many recommendations was an endorsement of the principle of a franchise 'auction':

> There would be obvious advantages in introducing a more commercial element into the allocation of ITV franchises. The Exchequer would gain maximum revenue from the sale of frequency space, while the ITV companies, faced with reduced profits in a more competitive market, would not need to pay back a bureaucratically-determined percentage of their revenue. Tendering would also be a simple way of ensuring cost efficiency within ITV companies. The levy system has historically been difficult to administer satisfactorily and effectively, and is unlikely to prove suitable to the radically changing broadcasting environment of the future. A suitably regulated tendering process would continue to provide a good return to the Exchequer, while satisfying the demand for quality television and good housekeeping by the television companies. We therefore recommend that such a system be introduced when the ITV franchises are next due for renewal. (pp. xxxiv–xxxv)

This was both a succinct restatement of the classic liberal economist's argument for a franchise auction and an endorsement of the Peacock's general concern for efficiency in resource allocation in broadcasting. The fact that it was endorsed by all the Labour members of the Committee is strong evidence about how far these ideas had permeated in the two years since the report. The Labour front bench might appear to continue its opposition to an auction in principle, but thereafter the real – although still fierce – arguments were in practice about the precise mechanism of the auction. The ITV auction itself had become regarded as inevitable.

The Peacock Committee left a hugely important but complex legacy. The Committee had been set up by a government whose Prime Minister, at least, was set on radically reforming the core UK television system by putting advertising on the BBC. By explicitly rejecting Thatcher's preferred option, the Peacock Committee effectively spiked advertising on the BBC as a practical political option for the next decade. The Committee's own long-term strategy for the BBC presented numerous technical problems and was for a variety of (often opposing) reasons unacceptable to the government. Tory television policy was therefore forced to redirect its target towards the already advertising-funded side of British television. Here it took up a number of the Peacock Report's specific proposals.

So far as the general philosophy of the report was concerned the government, keen to placate the 'taste and decency' lobby, rejected Peacock's anti-censorious twist to the free market. But the Committee's emphasis on 'efficiency' in broadcasting was eagerly accepted by the government and soon became part of the political and industry conventional wisdom. As for the Committee's goal of pushing towards a broadcasting market, that too became a slogan of Conservative policy, but one whose practical meaning was susceptible to numerous interpretations.

Both the Peacock Report and its reception in Conservative circles are proof, if proof were needed, of the deep divisions among free-marketeers about how their message should be applied to broadcasting.

## Note

1. In this respect Jean Seaton's formulation in the standard work *Power without Responsibility* is seriously misleading. She states, correctly, that up until the 70s official thinking on broadcasting in the UK had been dominated by the notion of 'public service, unified in structure and aim' and based on the 'assumption of commitment to a unified public good'. The Annan Report, she claims, abandoned this assumption in favour of 'liberal pluralism'. 'For Annan and those who supported and inspired him,' the ideal became 'a free market-place in which balance could be achieved through the competition of a multiplicity of independent voices' (Curran and Seaton, 1988, p. 17).

   This is to confuse two things. The first is a move from the notion of a unified public to be served by public service broadcasting to a more pluralist conception of public service. Here, Seaton is right – Annan did mark an important break in official thinking. The second is the move from public service itself as the underlying principle of broadcasting to a notion that broadcasting should be organised as a marketplace for independent voices. Annan did not make this move, Peacock did. For Annan, pluralism in broadcasting was to be provided not only within, but actually *by*, the continuation of public service as the overriding principle of broadcasting organisation.

# 7 The Great Reform – From White Paper to 1990 Broadcasting Act

It took nearly two and a half years from the publication of the Peacock Report for the government to decide precisely how to respond to Peacock's recommendations and to present its own detailed plans for reform of the broadcasting system. These plans were finally unveiled on 7 November 1988, when Douglas Hurd at long last published the White Paper, *Broadcasting in the 90s: Competition, Choice and Quality* (Home Office, 1988).

*Broadcasting in the 90s* announced changes across the whole range of television services – including the BBC, cable and satellite, and a proposed fifth terrestrial television channel. But the main thrust of the White Paper's plans was directed at the existing advertising-funded terrestrial channels – ITV and Channel Four. Here, *Broadcasting in the 90s* made three central proposals:

- First, the IBA was to be replaced by a new 'lighter touch' regulator, the Independent Television Commission (ITC).
- Second, the new licences for ITV were to be allocated (subject to significant qualifications) to the highest bidder.
- Third, Channel Four was to sell its own advertising.

*Broadcasting in the 90s* maintained that the new framework it proposed would enable a more open and competitive broadcasting market to be attained 'without detriment to programme standards and quality' (Home Office, 1988, p. 1). Few outside observers shared that confidence. Each of the three measures outlined above had the potential to fundamentally transform the terrestrial core of UK television to the detriment of both standards and quality. Each was to be criticised on those grounds. And, in response to that widespread criticism, each measure would be substantially modified as the 1988 White Paper was translated into legislation in the 1990 Broadcasting Act.

In the light of these critical responses and subsequent modifications, it is tempting to see *Broadcasting in the 90s* as an essentially dogmatic blueprint motivated primarily either by free-market ideology or the industrial concerns of the DTI. Up to a point this is true. The 1988 White Paper was clearly premised on a free-market vision of the future of broadcasting, and many of its specific proposals were derived from the equally clearly free-market Peacock Report. But *Broadcasting in the 90s* was also very much a product of uneasy compromises within government – compromises between DTI and Home Office concerns, between the desire for heightened authoritarian controls over the content of television and the desire to open it up to the market, and between different free-market strategies. As one contemporary critical account put it:

A careful reading of the document reveals signs of the tug between ... two aims ... In the case of the White Paper it is possible to detect ... the work of two hands, one belonging presumably to the Home Office (worried about taste and decency and standards) and the other to the Department of Trade and Industry (determined to let slip the dogs of the market). (Hood and O'Leary, 1990, p. 121)

This tug, and the compromises it involved, resulted in what turned out to be some highly ambiguous major formulations in the White Paper.

*Broadcasting in the 90s* specifically acknowledged two intellectual debts – to the Peacock Report and to the 1988 Home Office Select Committee Report on *The Future of Broadcasting*. It presented the background to its proposals in firmly free-market and technologically determinist terms:

In a rapidly changing environment, the existing framework for broadcasting in the UK must change too. But change is desirable as well as inevitable. Through it the individual can exercise choice from a greater range and variety of services. The growth of choice means that a rigid regulatory structure neither can nor should be perpetuated. It would not be sensible for the Government to try and lay down a detailed blueprint for the future. The Government should not try to pick winners. It should enable, not dictate, choice. A new enabling framework must be flexible to allow for technological change. As new services emerge and subscription develops, viewer choice rather than regulatory imposition, can and should increasingly be relied upon to secure the programmes which viewers want. (Home Office, 1988, p. 5)

But, if its general premises were superficially as free-market as Peacock's, the White Paper departed from the Peacock Report in two quite fundamental ways. First, it effectively rejected Peacock's equation of the move towards a broadcasting market with a move towards the complete abolition of censorious controls. Margaret Thatcher's concern to tighten up on standards of 'taste and decency' in broadcasting remained, quite unpersuaded by Peacock's libertarianism. So the free-market premises of the White Paper cited above were immediately followed by the qualification that 'rules will still be needed to safeguard programme standards on such matters as good taste and decency and to ensure that the unique power of broadcasting is not abused' (p. 5). Indeed, a whole chapter (Chapter VII) of the White Paper was devoted to 'programme standards'. This argued that 'further steps are need to meet public concern' about the portrayal of violence and sex in television programmes. *Inter alia* this chapter proposed to remove the previous exemption of broadcasting from the 1959 Obscene Publications Act; to establish on a statutory basis the Broadcasting Standards Council, which was already established on a non-statutory basis to monitor and enforce standards of taste and decency in broadcasting; and to extend legally enforceable taste and decency standards to all satellite services.

The second way in which the White Paper departed from Peacock was in its downplaying and effectively indefinite postponement of Peacock's long-term plans for the future of the BBC. *Broadcasting in the 90s* stated that 'the Government agrees with the Home Affairs Committee that the BBC "is still and

will remain for the foreseeable future, the cornerstone of British broadcasting"'
(p. 7). This meant that for the moment the licence fee would remain and advertising would not appear on the BBC. But, the White Paper maintained:

> the BBC has a role in the Government's desire to enable subscription to develop ... The
> Government looks forward to the eventual replacement of the licence fee ... The
> Government intends to encourage the progressive introduction of subscription on the
> BBC's television services. (p. 8)

However, this purported ultimate aim was not reflected in any specific proposals in *Broadcasting in the 90s*. Instead, the White Paper cited approvingly the
views of the 1987 report on *Subscription Television*:

> the Government's consultants advised against the wholesale immediate switch of exist-
> ing services to subscription, mainly because this would result in a loss of consumer wel-
> fare since some viewers would not subscribe to services now available to them ... the
> Government accepts the advice of its consultants that a sudden, wholesale switch to
> subscription would be undesirable and damaging. (p. 8)

The White Paper also rejected Peacock's proposal to make the fitting of peri-
television sockets mandatory on new televisions (pp. 9–10).

There was therefore only one practical step towards subscription for the BBC in
*Broadcasting in the 90s*: namely, that the Corporation's traditionally unused night
hours be utilised for subscription. Focus on the night-time hours as a possible
vehicle for subscription derived from Peacock and from *Subscription Television*.
Debate on it was much concerned with the dilemma of whether the night-time
hours of BBC and ITV should be allocated to their former owners to exploit commercially, or whether they should be allocated separately to new commercial operators. By the time of the White Paper the BBC had already started downloaded
night services in conjunction with a commercial partner (pp. 8–9). These services
were not to prove particularly successful. But even if they had been, provision of
downloaded material for paying customers in the night-time hours was at best
quite marginal to the BBC's finances, and scarcely amounted to a major stepping
stone on the road to more general subscription funding for the Corporation.
Services on the BBC night-time hours were generally business-oriented, not the
premium entertainment that *Subscription Television* had envisaged.

So, despite its formal protestations to the contrary, *Broadcasting in the 90s* effectively shunted a subscription future for the BBC to the sidelines of government
policy. This sidelining of Peacock's long-term strategy for the BBC meant that
*Broadcasting in the 90s* signalled a more general shift in focus for Tory television
policy, away from the BBC and towards, what pre-Peacock had been little considered, the advertising-funded segment of the public service system.

Once these two quite fundamental qualifications are taken into account it can
be readily acknowledged that many of the major positive proposals of the White
Paper derive from the Stage One recommendations made by the Peacock Report.
In other words, there was the extensive 'cherry-picking' that the Committee's
Chairman described.

But without the Peacock Report's broader context, the White Paper's proposals were viewed with considerable scepticism by the report's main authors. Samuel Brittan wrote of the White Paper that

> Unfortunately, the selective way in which the Government picked up some specific proposals from the [Peacock] report, while failing to accept its basic import, was unpromising. *To the extent that the Government endorsed some Peacock recommendations it is the letter that was accepted, and the spirit that was rejected.* (Brittan, 1989, pp. 39–40)

The central proposals of *Broadcasting in the 90s* were directed towards a reform of the ITV system. The proposed reform had several elements. The IBA, which had owned the the transmission system for ITV and Channel Four, and had legally been their publisher, was to be replaced by the ITC: 'The Government proposes that the ITC should be a licensing body rather than a broadcasting authority. This means that it will supervise, but not itself provide, programme services, applying the same light touch regulation across the board.' The ITC, which would now also be responsible for all cable and satellite television services, would no longer own transmitters or have the right to preview programmes. The ITC would enforce on all services – terrestrial, cable and satellite – what the White Paper called 'consumer protection requirements'. These stated that news and political and religious stances should be 'impartial' and that 'nothing should be included in programmes which offends against taste and decency or encourages crime or disorder or is offensive to public feeling' (p. 20). In addition to these requirements, *Broadcasting in the 90s* proposed that ITV (called 'Channel 3' in the White Paper) be given extra positive programme requirements. These were, most importantly, that ITV should show 'regional programming' and 'high quality news and current affairs', and should 'provide a diverse programme service calculated to appeal to a variety of tastes and interests'.

In explanation of this stance the White Paper, on the one hand, asserted that these programme requirements '*are not, and need not be, as extensive as those now governing ITV*' (my emphasis). But, on the other hand it acknowledged that

> the Peacock Committee [had] warned against a policy of commercial *laissez faire*, under which there would be no constraints on the ability of broadcasters to sell audiences to advertisers, leading to curtailment of the range and diversity of programmes provided. (p. 21)

The key ambiguity about *Broadcasting in the 90s* lay in this 'lighter touch' regulation that it proposed for ITV. In formal terms the White Paper was clear what that lighter touch involved: the regulator of commercial television would no longer be its legal publisher and no longer have the right to preview. But in the substantial terms of programme content, things were altogether less clear. The White Paper in no way even began to spell out *how much* lighter a touch the ITC was supposed to exert, or *how much* programme 'quality' and 'diversity' on ITV it was willing to sacrifice for increased commercial competition. In public, the government often appeared to be trying to have its cake and eat it. This lack of even a vaguely detailed vision of how far deregulation of ITV was to go in programming terms reflected the divisions within government we have already described. Over the next two years, as the details were filled in under the pressure of public debate and private lobbying, this ambiguity would be effectively exploited by opponents of ITV deregulation. As we shall shortly see, the opponents of deregulation enjoyed considerable success in securing positive programme requirements on the new ITV system established by the 1990 Broadcasting Act, which were considerably nearer to those of the old ITV than many readers of *Broadcasting in the 90s* either hoped for, or, more likely, feared.

Alongside its proposals for the existing Channel 3 (ITV and commercial Breakfast Television), the White Paper proposed a new, virtually national, terrestrial channel – Channel 5. The technical possibility of such a channel had, as we have seen, emerged clearly during the post-Peacock debate. 'The Government proposes', said the White Paper, 'that Channel 5 should come on stream from the beginning of 1993, when the new Channel 3 licences will start.' It added that the 'same regulatory requirements (although without the regional programming obligations) and the same licence allocation and review arrangements' that applied to ITV should also apply to the new channel (pp. 23–4). In effect, this meant that the fifth channel was seen as another advertising-funded commercial channel, allocated by competitive tender, with some public service requirements as ITV. This was of course quite different from the use of the fifth channel proposed by *Subscription Television*. The Booz Allen Report had envisaged the new channel as a British version of the French Canal-plus – a subscription-funded terrestrial provider of premium entertainment. There is no direct evidence as to why the government rejected this strategy in favour of what would in practice turn out to be an advertising-funded channel. But we may speculate that the desire to appease the advertising industry lobby, who had lost the battle for the BBC, was a not unimportant motive.

The second central plank of the White Paper's proposed reform of ITV concerned the method by which the ITC allocated ITV licences. Previous arrangements had, it explained, been 'widely criticised as arbitrary and opaque'. The government agreed with the House of Commons Home Affairs Committee Report that there was 'advantage in introducing a more commercial element into the allocation of ITV franchises, and ... [so] a suitably regulated tendering process should be introduced'. The mechanisms of this tendering process were as follows:

> The ITC should operate a two-stage procedure. In the first place applicants would have to pass a quality threshold ... All applicants passing this threshold would go on to a second stage in which they would offer financial tenders for the licence. The ITC would be required to select the applicant who submitted the highest tender ... This two-stage procedure will provide a more objective method of licence allocation which will be fairer to all applicants, and will at the same time secure a proper return for the taxpayer for the use of a public resource. (pp. 22–3)

Here was the second key ambiguity in the White Paper. The rationale for the franchise auction was clear, but the practical details of its operation were not. First, just how high was the quality threshold to be? This was to become a central point of argument over the next two years. Second, would the ITC be able to prefer a lower bid in return for higher quality? The Peacock Committee's majority recommendation for a franchise auction had, as we have seen, explicitly allowed for precisely that option. The White Paper's formulation appeared to rule it out. Again, the issue was to figure highly in subsequent debate, as opponents of the franchise auction tried to reintroduce an element of discretion into its operation.

Alongside Peacock's recommendations for an auction of ITV franchises, the White Paper also took up the Peacock Report's recommendation that Channel Four should be allowed to sell its own advertising. 'The programming remits of Channel 4 and S4C have been a striking success,' proclaimed *Broadcasting in the 90s*. So, it continued, that remit should remain:

> The Government accordingly proposes that Channel 4 should be required to cater for tastes and interests not served, or underrepresented by, other parts of the independent television sector: to encourage innovation and experiment in the form and content of programmes ...

But acceptance of the Channel Four remit did not, the White Paper maintained, mean that the structural arrangements of Channel Four should remain unchanged:

> It is now clear that under the present arrangements the revenue from Channel 4's air time could sustain its service. There is a strong case that it should be funded from this source. Greater competition between those selling television air time – a pressing demand from those whose expenditure on advertising has paid for the independent television system – is essential.

A change in the structure of Channel Four was also unavoidable, according to the White Paper, because 'the Government's wider proposals for a more competitive independent television sector mean that a place for Channel 4 within ... an integrated ITV system will no longer be available'.

The White Paper was definite about the general principles of the new structure:

> The Government believes that Channel 4's special role is best fulfilled by an independent organisation subject to ITC oversight, but without direct structural links to the Channel 3 licensees. Advertising will be sold separately from the advertising on Channel 3 or other channels ...

But within these general principles *Broadcasting in the 90s* outlined three possible options for a new Channel Four structure. These were:

1. 'A private sector company licensed by the ITC in much the same way as services on Channel 3', with the special Channel Four remit written into the licence conditions.
2. 'Channel 4 could remain as a non-profit-making body, in the form of a subsidiary to the ITC and given freedom to raise funds through advertising, subscription and sponsorship ... However, to avoid Channel 4 being wholly dependent on these sources, a minimum level of income could be guaranteed.' This would provide a safeguard against erosion of the remit.
3. 'A further possibility would be to establish some kind of link between Channels 4 and 5, with the former pursuing a special remit and the latter being subject to the more commercial regime already described.'

The White paper appeared genuinely open-minded when it came to considering these options:

> A fully privatised Channel 4 would have greater incentives to efficiency ... But there are fears that if Channel 4 were to be operated by a private company anxious to maximise profits, it might be tempted to weaken the remit ... On the other hand if Channel 4 remains in the public sector, and particularly if it does so under an arrangement which, like the present system, guarantees its income and accordingly insulates it against any market disciplines, then the incentive to efficiency will be diminished, and in programming matters, it may be vulnerable to sterile elitism or precious self-indulgence. (pp. 24–5)

Here, for a third time, but in this case quite explicitly, the underlying ambiguities of the White Paper are apparent. On Channel Four, as on ITV, the government was clear that it wanted to change the structures of the non-BBC side of British broadcasting to make it more commercial. But it was uncertain about how far it was willing to go along this route. Just as with ITV, the uncertainty was barely concealed under the public pretence of having one's cake and eating it – commercial independence for Channel Four without in any way affecting the channel's special remit.

One other major Peacock recommendation found a place in *Broadcasting in the 90s*. Peacock had recommended an independent production quota for BBC and ITV. The government had, well before the White Paper, declared itself in favour of a 25 per cent quota and set a target for the broadcasters to reach this goal. The White Paper toughened this up by proposing to make the 25 per cent independent production a *statutory* requirement for both BBC and ITV. As the White Paper made clear, 'the Government has already set the BBC and the ITV companies the target of original material from independent producers as quickly as possible', with a target date of 1992 for achieving the full quota.

The White Paper's general rationale for the quota was twofold: 'independent producers constitute an important source of originality and talent which must be exploited, and have brought new pressures for efficiency and flexibility in production procedures' (p. 41). More specifically, *Broadcasting in the 90s* argued that 'the Corporation's acceptance of the Government's independent production targets' had been 'a further stimulus for change at the BBC' (p. 10). The White Paper not only proposed that the 25 per cent independent quota should be mandatory on ITV (p. 21) but also added that 'no licensee should be required by the ITC to maintain any in-house production capacity as a condition of obtaining a licence' (p. 41). This last proposal opened up the possibility of ITV licensees being what were to become known as 'publisher-contractors', contracting out *all* their programme production to independent producers.

A further important strand of *Broadcasting in the 90s* was its proposal to reorganise the regulation of cable and satellite television. Previously the UK's 'official' DBS services had been allocated and regulated by the IBA, its cable services by the Cable Authority. Services from low- and medium-powered satellites receivable directly by homes in Britain had been unregulated. The White Paper proposed to abolish the Cable Authority and put all cable and satellite services under the authority of the new ITC. Recognising that 'since 1985 direct reception of low and medium power satellite services has been permitted in the UK', the White Paper proposed to bring them within the regulatory framework. The 'consumer protection regulation of programme content' proposed for the ITC would extend 'to cover all satellite services uplinked from this country but received direct …' And satellite services uplinked from abroad would be monitored by the ITC and the BSC to ensure that they were not 'obscene or grossly offensive'. If they were, the government would take action (p. 36).

The White Paper therefore rationalised regulation of the services provided by new delivery mechanisms under the authority of the new regulator for terrestrial commercial television, the ITC. Development of these services would be on a purely commercial basis, with regulation essentially confined to the government's particular concern with 'taste and decency'. By the time the White Paper was published, Rupert Murdoch's plans to provide a UK-directed service from the medium-powered Astra satellite were already clear, and the service went on air several months before the new Broadcasting Bill went before Parliament. Whether Murdoch's potentially powerful new service should be regulated more strongly than just for 'consumer protection' would therefore be another important issue of contention in the debate that followed *Broadcasting in the 90s*.

The last major strand in the White Paper was its insistence on the need for extra measures to foster competition in the television industry. The government's approach was to 'counter the excessive degree of vertical integration which has characterised broadcasting in the UK as an industry. A greater separation of the different economic activities making up broadcasting will help to promote competition and efficiency.' Such an approach underlay the independent production quota. In addition, the White Paper proposed to privatise the transmission networks previously run by the IBA (p. 39) and to require that some shares in ITN be held by bodies external to ITV (p. 22). The White Paper also emphasised that the government had, in March 1988, already referred possible restrictive labour practices in television and film production to the Monopolies and Mergers Commission (MMC): 'The Government will take account of its conclusions in preparing legislation and hopes that the report will help the industry to face up to an increasingly competitive environment and succeed in international markets' (p. 41).

In summary, in the 1988 White Paper the government expressed the aim of attaining 'a more open and competitive broadcasting market'. Change in this direction, it maintained, was both inevitable, because of technological and international developments, and desirable so that 'individuals can choose for themselves from a wider range of programmes and types of broadcasting' (p. 1).

Responses to *Broadcasting in the 90s* adopted two (often overlapping) tones. One was general and apocalyptic about the supposedly dire consequences of the whole projected reform. The other was critical – and often severely critical – of particular details of the proposals. Together, these two types of critical response were to produce considerable modifications as the White Paper blueprint was translated into statute in the 1990 Broadcasting Act. These modifications rarely altered the letter of the White Paper strategy, but they did effectively exploit its ambiguities, shifting their interpretation towards the maintenance of many aspects of traditional public service practice.

The apocalyptic responses to the government's reform of commercial broad-casting began well before the publication of *Broadcasting in the 90s*. In September 1988, South of England ITV licensee, TVS, ran a series of advertisements in the broadsheet press warning of the dangers of television deregulation. The most notorious of the advertisements featured a woman doing a striptease, with the caption: 'Italian Housewives Do it on TV'. Videos of stripping housewives were, the advertisement alleged, the sort of cheap programming that had appeared on Italian television following on deregulation – 'with around 600 national and local TV stations now competing for a finite number of viewers, standards have dived and so have airtime costs'. 'Do you really want it here?' the copy continued. 'We don't. The best way to ensure it doesn't happen is to preserve the environment in which British television operates' (*Guardian*, 19 September 1988, p. 5).

The details of the TVS ad were almost immediately discredited – the picture was posed by a British model and striptease channels were no longer a feature of Italian television (*Independent*, 28 September 1988, p. 15). But the spectre of deregulation prompting a downward spiral of programme standards and quality – with Italian television as a terrible warning – remained central for the White Paper's critics. It was echoed in the comments of Labour broadcasting spokesman Robin Corbet during the first major House of Commons debate on *Broadcasting in the 90s*, in February 1989:

> In the White Paper, any specific obligation of public service goes out the window. That is because the Government simply want to hand over ITV to the men with the deepest pockets who will meet a so-called quality threshold no higher than a pile of £50 notes ... It is not the so-called market value of a franchise which should guide the Government if they have the genuine interest of viewers and listeners at heart. It should be the quality and diversity of content, and the need to ensure that what happened in the United States of America, and lately in France and Italy, will not be allowed to happen here. (HoC Debates, 8 February 1989, cols. 1069–72)

This warning could have been dismissed as simply overblown parliamentary rhetoric, if it had not echoed the more detailed criticism of the White Paper pro-posals which came from the established commercial television industry, its regu-lators and a range of more independent commentators.

The trade association of the ITV licensees, the ITV Association, purported to welcome the White Paper's general philosophy, but went on to present a list of White Paper proposals which it regarded as 'questionable or outdated'. These included both 'the system of competitive tendering as at present planned' and 'the likely separation of Channel 4 from ITV' (ITVA, 1989, pp. 1, 11). The IBA adopted a similar position. As Chairman, George Russell, put it in his forward to the Authority's official response: 'The IBA shares Government's objectives, put for-ward in the White Paper, but we question whether all the particular proposals are workable in the form in which they are put forward.' Among the main ones with which the IBA 'had difficulty', continued Russell, 'are the proposals for the ten-dering process which allocates Channel 3 and 5 licences simply to the highest bid-der'. He added that in his opinion, 'the ability of Channel 3 licensees to provide the range and quality of programmes so far produced by ITV is likely to be reduced if all the White Paper proposals are put into effect' (IBA, 1989, pp. 1–2).

Whether framed in general or detailed terms, these widespread criticisms of *Broadcasting in the 90s* added up to one overall accusation – the government was planning a deregulation of British television which – whether the government desired it or not – could put established standards and quality in peril. The mechanisms of this supposed peril were various. There were at least four logically distinguishable ways in which the White Paper proposals could, and was said to, threaten the established standards and quality of UK television:

1. By making the regulator employ a 'lighter touch', the White Paper proposals necessarily made it less able to enforce public service requirements. The ITC would inevitably have less clout than the IBA.
2. The White Paper had itself narrowed down those public service requirements.
3. Auctioning the licences necessarily meant that money – and quite possibly irresponsible amounts of money – would prevail over quality.
4. Lastly, forcing Channel Four to sell its own advertising would inevitably compromise the channel's remit as it was forced to compete head to head with ITV.

The history of Tory broadcasting policy from the 1988 White Paper to the final passage of the 1990 Broadcasting Act is a history of modifications to the original White Paper proposals in an effort to meet these objections.

The first major modification came over Channel Four. As one review of the responses to the White Paper noted:

> With the possible exception of the proposals regarding franchise auctions, this part of the White Paper provoked more alarm and hostility than any other. Broadly speaking, advertisers argued that C4 should become financially self-sufficient, while just about everyone else concluded that the remit was not sustainable unless C4 had a guaranteed level of support. The overwhelming weight of opinion argued against C4 competing for advertising revenue with Channel 3 and supporting arrangements, accepting option 2 if the changes were insisted upon. (No submission expressed fears about elitism or self-indulgence.) (Stevenson and Smedley, 1989, p. 54)

In February 1989 the House of Commons held hearings on the White Paper proposals for Channel Four. The previous year, in its report on the future of broadcasting, the Home Affairs Committee had declared that Channel Four had been 'well received by viewers', and added that 'we feel certain that a major contributory factor to its programming success has been its indirect link with its source of income'. It therefore recommended that 'Channel 4 should remain substantially as it is at present. For the time being the current system of financing would seem to be the best way of achieving this end' (Home Affairs Committee, 1988, pp. xxxv–xxxvi).

That was before the White Paper. In February 1989 this Conservative-dominated committee now had to consider government proposals which ran counter to its previous recommendation. The Committee took evidence from the IBA, the ITVA and Channel Four itself. All were, to varying degrees critical of the White Paper proposals, but they exhibited certain differences when it came to the precise remedies.

All were agreed on maintaining Channel Four's remit and on White Paper

Option 2 – a non-profit-making trust – as their preferred future organisation of the channel. Neither of the White Paper's other two options – Option 1 (privatisation) or Option 3 (links with Channel 5) – found any significant supporters. All agreed on the need for continued cross-promotion between Channel Four and ITV. The ITVA went on from this to conclude that

> the remit of C4 would be best protected in the Nineties by a fully complementary relationship with the mass audience channel. C4 would do better to see itself, not as a pensioner of ITV, but as a partner with ITV.

It therefore made a final plea for the government to consider 'an extension of present arrangements, suitably modified' (*Home Affairs Committee*, 1988, pp. 36–7).

However, in its submission, Channel Four appeared less than eager to accept this ITV embrace:

> Channel 4 is confident that it can continue economically to provide its wide range of programming in an expanding broadcasting market. We are fully prepared to exploit the revenue opportunities offered by the move to separate selling of the Channel's airtime.

The Channel 4 submission then pointed out the 'central dilemma' of the White Paper: how to reconcile its three different objectives – increasing competition in the advertising market by separate selling of Channel Four airtime; guaranteeing the independence of the channel and its remit against the dangers of financial erosion; and, at the same time, maintaining incentives to efficiency in the channel.

The reconciliation Channel Four proposed was to take up the White Paper's suggestion of a baseline underwritten by the ITC:

> We have calculated the Channel's needs in the new environment, and have determined that the safety net for the ten year period of the Channel 3 licences should be set at 14 per cent of all terrestrial Net Advertising Revenue (NAR) [the joint revenue from advertising of Channel Four, ITV and – when it started broadcasting – Channel 5. (p. 1)

Channel Four's proposal for a safety net set at 14 per cent of total television advertising revenue was based on its calculation that the channel's costs for the previous financial year (1987/8), adjusted to take account of the extra costs that would incur under the new arrangements, would be 14.9 per cent of the year's total terrestrial advertising revenue. The channel's confidence that it would not have to use the safety net were supported by its calculations that in 1987/8 the actual percentage of net advertising revenue 'attributed to Channel 4 by ITV' was 15.6 per cent, and that its percentage share of joint Channel Four/ITV audience was 17.4 per cent (p. 9). In other words, Channel Four potential revenue was already performing well above the 14 per cent baseline.

The Channel Four argument was supported by the IBA, and endorsed in virtually its entirety by the Commons Home Affairs Committee when it reported in March 1989. Like almost every other response to the White Paper, the Committee supported Option 2 on the future structure of Channel Four. It hoped that Channel Four and ITV would continue cross-channel promotion, and accepted that Channel Four selling its own advertising would be an 'integral part of the new arrangements' (noting that 'Channel Four welcomes the opportunity to set up a national network advertising sales operation'). Most importantly, the Committee endorsed Channel Four's 14 per cent backstop. 'In proposing a safety net base line of 14 per cent of Terrestrial NAR,' it commented, 'Channel 4 is wisely offering to limit its guarantee to below the present level of support. This represents an incentive to maximise efficiency and its own income ...' (p. x).

Three months later, the government, in turn, effectively accepted the Committee's – and the channel's – main recommendations on Channel Four. On 13 June 1989 Douglas Hurd announced to the House of Commons that 'the Government has decided that it would not be feasible at the present time for Channel 4 to become an independent commercial company competing with other broadcasters if, as we consider necessary, it is to retain its remit'. The uncertain financial outlook and pressure to maximise profits could 'put too much pressure upon Channel 4 finances and place its remit in jeopardy'.

So, the government had now decided, Channel Four would become a public trust which would continue to provide the service set out in its special remit. Although it would be licensed by the ITC, it would not be owned by the Commission, because 'we see some difficulty in Channel 4 continuing to be owned by the authority responsible for regulating its output ...' The channel would, Hurd continued, sell its own advertising, 'and would be subject to a baseline of 14 per cent per annum of terrestrial net advertising revenue'. If the channel's revenue fell below the baseline, the difference would be funded by the ITC up to a maximum of 2 per cent NAR met by a levy on Channel 3 companies.

There was one sting in the tail – not included in any of the previous public submissions: 'Any surplus revenues *above* the baseline would be shared equally between Channel 3 and 4' (HO Press Release, 13 June 1989; HoC Debates, 13 June 1989 [my emphasis]). In other words, if Channel Four performed better than its safety net, it would pay out to ITV. At the time, this provision was little remarked on. As events turned out (see next chapter), Channel Four did perform well above the baseline, the payouts to ITV proved substantial, and Channel Four was to cry foul.

But in June 1989 such a possibility was not at the forefront of discussion. Hurd's announcement effectively seemed to remove one central threat to existing programme quality. The White Paper had toyed with the idea of full-blooded competition for revenue between Channel Four and ITV. Faced with the almost universal objection that such competition would imperil the channel's remit, and unwilling to abandon that widely admired remit, the government had rapidly backtracked. The letter of separate selling of advertising for Channel Four was preserved, but the substance of real competition for revenue was reduced to the margins.

With Hurd's June 1989 announcement, later embodied in the 1990 Broadcasting Act, the Channel Four issue receded from the centre of the broadcasting debate.

The franchise auction issue took much longer to settle. The government's proposal to allocate ITV (and the new Channel 5) franchises by means of an auction prompted widespread public criticism of the very idea, and elicited scarcely any positive enthusiasm for the principle. As the BFI analysis of formal responses to the White Paper noted:

The overwhelming weight of opinion was strongly opposed to the auctioning of franchises to the highest bidder. Submission after submission argued that sealed bid auctions, as proposed in the White Paper, would encourage over-bidding to secure the franchise, with the successful bidder having to reduce expenditure on programmes to ensure any profit. This tendency would be reinforced by the levy on revenue, rather than on profit, and the minimal standards of programme requirements which can be demanded by the ITC. So, the argument ran, money otherwise available to spend on programmes will be diverted to the Exchequer, and a group of under-resourced television companies will struggle with each other to gain maximum audience ratings from large volumes of the same, largely imported, mediocre populist material. (Stevenson and Smedley, 1989, p. 35)

Interspersed with this generally expressed outright rejection of the auction system as intrinsically harmful to the quality and diversity of UK broadcasting were two other types of response to the White Paper's auction proposals.

One was a series of technical examinations of the auction process, chiefly commissioned by the ITV companies as part of their response to the White Paper. Perhaps the fullest of these was the work of consultants, NERA (ITVA, 1989, pp. 97–9), later developed into an academic paper (Cheong and Foster, 1989). Also notable was the contribution made by Cento Veljanovski, the free-marketeer who, as we have seen, had been one of the early advocates of an auction system (ITVA, 1989, pp. 85–7). What such technical discussions stressed was that there were a variety of different auction mechanisms, each of which would prompt different strategies by bidders, and therefore different outcomes. We shall return to the question of bidding strategies in the next chapter, when we look at how the franchise auction turned out in practice. In the period from the 1988 White Paper to the eventual passage of the 1990 Broadcasting Act, the technical discussion of auction mechanisms opened up to question, from an impeccably free-market framework, the distinctly primitive and unthought-through auction mechanisms advanced in the White Paper.

The last strand of response was less theoretically rigorous, but instead placed its emphasis on the need to retain the supposedly high existing standards of UK television. The two most notable members of this camp were the Campaign for Quality Television, a lobbying group formed by programme-makers with the backing of some of the ITV companies, and the IBA itself. Both these groups were probably opposed to the very principle of the auction. But both chose tactically to accept the letter of auction, while arguing for a wide range of detailed modifications in its application, so as to preserve – what was to become the buzz-word of the debate surrounding the 1990 Bill – 'quality'. Both would be extravagantly praised by the minister chiefly responsible for the passage of the bill through Parliament, David Mellor (see, for example, CQT, 1990, pp. 1–2).

The first substantial results of this barrage of criticism came well before the Broadcasting Bill was published. On the 13 June 1989, during the same announcement to the House of Commons in which he accepted the safety net for Channel Four, Douglas Hurd announced two major changes to the original White Paper auction proposals.

First, the quality threshold was to be significantly strengthened. Channel 3 and 5 bidders would now be required to provide 'a reasonable proportion of programmes (in addition to news and current affairs) of high quality and to provide a diverse programme service calculated to appeal to a wide variety of tastes and interests'. It would be up to the applicants, Hurd continued, to decide what exactly this meant when drawing up their programme proposals. But 'those who fail to satisfy the ITC that they can meet this requirement will not have their financial bids considered'.

Second, Hurd proposed to introduce what he called an 'element of flexibility' into the auction procedure. This was not to be a full-blown weighing of fine distinctions about the relative quality of different bids. That, Hurd maintained, was impractical and unnecessary in light of the strengthened quality threshold, and risked returning to the 'opaque and sometimes arbitrary selection procedures of the past'. But Hurd was now prepared to grant the ITC the power, 'in exceptional circumstances ... to select a lower bid'. If it chose to exercise this power, the ITC would be required to give its full reasons, and its decision would be subject to judicial review (HO News Release, 13 June 1989, pp. 1–3).

Taken together, these two measures had the potential to substantially shift the operation of the licence auction in the direction of preserving the existing programming mix and standards of ITV. But they by no means satisfied the critics of the White Paper, who continued to bombard the government with further proposals to strengthen 'quality' during the whole of the passage of the Broadcasting Bill through Parliament, from its publication in December 1989 right through to the granting of royal assent in November 1990.

The government was by no means unresponsive to this continuing pressure. After the committee stage of the Broadcasting Bill in the House of Commons, left-wing Labour back-bencher Tony Banks observed: 'I have done 14 or 15 bills at committee stage. This was the one in which most movement was achieved' (*Broadcast*, 23 March, 1990, p. 7). And in a speech to a forum organised by the Campaign for Quality Television in March 1990, David Mellor listed eight changes passed in the committee stage which would 'beef up the quality threshold'. These included a new statutory requirement for children's and religious programmes, and a significant bolstering of regional requirements (CQT, 1990, pp. 4–5).

Later on in the year the government also bowed to pressure to spell out quite explicitly in the legislation that the 'exceptional circumstances' clause announced by Hurd before the bill could be used by the ITC to make an award on the basis of quality. A new sub-clause (17.4) was added specifying that the Commission could consider it appropriate to make an 'exceptional circumstances' award to a lower bidder if the quality of the service that bidder proposed was both 'exceptionally high' and 'substantially higher' than that proposed by the highest bidder.

There were, however, limits to which the government was prepared to go in these concessions. Some element of cash bid remained sacrosanct. An ingenious formula floated by the Campaign for Quality Television for a 'quality auction' – keeping the name but removing the cash-bid element – was not taken up. Indeed, the wording of the new 'exceptional circumstances' sub-clause was clearly designed to ensure that the ITC did not overstep the mark and try to make the 'fine distinctions' on quality of which Hurd had complained when he originally granted it the power to exceptionally overrule the highest cash bid.

Another indicator that the government was willing to go only so far in its concessions to critics came towards the end of the bill's passage through Parliament.

During the Lords Committee stage, amendments were passed adding educational, social action and documentary programmes to the already expanded list of programme types in the statutory quality threshold required for ITV. A provision was also added requiring programmes of each kind to be scheduled at appropriate times of the day and week. The government used its majority in the House of Commons to reverse these amendments. 'It is unsatisfactory for Channel 3 licences to be required by statute to show a long and detailed list of individual programme types,' David Mellor pronounced (HO News Release, 4 September 1990).

Nevertheless, the sum total of amendments to the quality threshold and auction procedure represented a qualitative change from what had been proposed in the White Paper. 'I am persuaded', Mellor declared at the same time as he proposed to reverse the House of Lords amendments on extra statutory programme requirements:

> that in order to pass [the quality threshold] ... applicants will need to offer the full range of programmes which are currently available on ITV – it would be a brave applicant who was so confident of his ability to pass the quality threshold regardless that he chose to offer appreciably less. (HO News Release, 4 September 1990)

As we shall see in the next chapter, Mellor's confidence had considerable substance. Alongside the amendments to the original White Paper proposals on quality threshold and auction procedures, there was one other important reason for this. The amendments, and the nature of the debate surrounding the bill, effectively made the ITC distinctly less of a 'light touch' regulator than *Broadcasting in the 90s* had orginally appeared to envisage. Hurd had portrayed his general strengthening of the quality threshold as leaving the applicants themselves to make a judgment on quality and diversity. But a seemingly rather technical amendment to the bill during the House of Commons Committee stage, proposed from the opposition benches and accepted by the government, radically changed this. When inviting applications for the Channel 3 and 5 licences, the Commission would have to publish 'general guidance to the applicants' containing 'examples of the kinds of programme whose inclusion in the service proposed by the applicant would be likely to comply' with the quality and diversity requirements (Broadcasting Act, 1990, clause 15.2). So the ITC could effectively set out before the auction more detailed – and therefore more stringent – requirements for the future services than those listed in the Act itself. That gave the Commission considerable initiative, further reinforced by the 'exceptional circumstances' clause.

The tone of the debate on the bill ensured that the ITC would make the most of these opportunities. ITC Chairman designate, George Russell, had early on in the debate declared that the quality threshold would be a 'Beecher's Brook' (the most difficult fence in the Grand National). Government spokesmen constantly referred favourably to this declaration, particularly when they resisted critics' demands for yet more statutory requirements to be included in the threshold. Russell and the ITC therefore ended up with both sufficient statutory power to set a high and detailed quality threshold and the political endorsement from the government to do so.

This potential power and discretion of the ITC extended not merely to programming promises but also to the bids themselves. Much of the concern among critics of the White Paper's auction proposals was directed at the likelihood of 'overbidding' – bidding that was too high to sustain the programmes promised, thus leading either to bankruptcy or, more likely, to the eventual reduction of expenditure on programming and therefore failure to meet the programme promises.

The government responded to such criticism with a number of changes to the original White Paper proposals designed to lessen the dangers of successful applicants making what might turn out to be financial over-commitments. Payments to government by licensees would comprise two parts – a percentage of advertising revenue, set on a licence-by-licence basis before the bid by the ITC, and the value of the bid itself. The bid would be payable on a yearly basis (to avoid advantaging those with deep pockets) and would be index-linked (to prevent dangers arising from any inaccurate estimation of inflation).

And here, too, extra discretion was given to the ITC. Russell had declared that he would interpret the quality threshold as including 'the quality of money', and this phrase was continually favourably cited by government representatives. The ITC was given the power to take this concern with 'overbidding' into account by two, again seemingly technical, sub-clauses in the Act. First, the Commission could only consider a bid if it was satisfied that the applicant could 'maintain ... [the proposed] service throughout the period for which the licence would be in force' (Broadcasting Act, 1990, clause 16.1.b). Second, applicants were required to supply to the ITC 'such information as the Commission may reasonably require as to the applicant's present financial position and his projected financial position during the period for which the licence would be in force' (clause 15.3.g). In other words, the ITC had to require applicants to supply a detailed business plan and could rule them out if they did not believe it was up to scratch. Russell's pronouncement on 'the quality of money', and the government's endorsement of this, gave every indication that the ITC would use these provisions to the full.

All this made it clear, by the time the Broadcasting Act received royal assent, that, at least so far as the licence allocations were concerned, the ITC would be far removed from the 'lighter touch' regulator outlined in the White Paper. Far from simply checking whether applicants had met a limited programme quality threshold and then awarding to the highest bidder who had satisfied this requirement – which was what the 1988 White Paper had envisaged – the new ITC would have a wide-ranging discretion as to whom it allocated licences and what it demanded of them. Highest bid was now only one element among many. Not merely Russell's pronouncements, and the government endorsement of them, but also the professional staffing of the ITC – essentially a continuation of the IBA apparatus stripped of its transmission function – made it likely that this discretion would be exercised to try to perpetuate a programme service very similar to that provided by the existing ITV companies.

A host of substantial changes had been made in the two years between the 1988 White Paper and the 1990 Act. How effective those changes would be in preserving the existing ITV system would only finally be determined in practice – by the conduct of the 1991 franchise auction and by the operation of the new ITV system it established.

# 8  The Reform in Action

## The ITV Auction

The Broadcasting Act received royal assent in November 1990. The existing ITV licences ran for two further years – until the end of 1992. It was generally agreed that any new licensee should be given a year to get up and running before it went on air. Before that, the ITC would need several months to process applications and make its decisions. And, prior to that, prospective applicants would also need a similar amount of time to prepare their applications.

That added up to nearly two years between the start of the race and the winners coming on air. So, in late 1990, the Commission had to move quickly. It was up to the ITC to decide how many licences would be issued – in other words how the regional map would be drawn – but several months before the Broadcasting Act became law the (then shadow) ITC had indicated that it would advertise exactly the same division of the Channel 3 map as had existed before the Act – fifteen regional licences with the same boundaries as before (London continuing to be divided between weekday and weekend), plus one national (breakfast) licence. This decision had been endorsed by government during debate on the bill as further support of its contention that the new arrangements would involve no dilution of the regional basis of ITV.

In the same month that the Broadcasting Act became law the ITC published for consultation draft invitations to apply for Channel 3 regional and national licences (ITC, 1990a and b). These drafts were not the subject of much significant criticism. And the invitations to apply were issued, substantially unchanged, in final form on 15 February 1991 (ITC, 1991a and b), formally marking the start of the 1991 ITV franchise race. They called for applications to be submitted by 15 May 1991.

The ITC's invitations to apply were formidable documents. The regional invitation was 100 pages long and the (very similar) breakfast invitation only slightly shorter. They set down the parameters for the race in great detail, and would have enormous effect on the sort of ITV system that eventually emerged. The invitations were, therefore, quite crucial indications of just how far the ITC was prepared to exercise the discretion given to it by the much-amended Act, and just how far it would attempt to preserve the range and quality of existing ITV programme services. They are, therefore, worth very close examination.

The invitations to apply set down in great detail the statutory obligations under the Broadcasting Act which the applicants would have to fulfil for their bids to be considered. But they also interpreted and amplified these statutory requirements in a number of crucial ways.

First, and most important, of these extensions of the bare letter of the Act's provisions came under the heading of 'Diversity in the Service'. The ITC was, the invitations explained, required by the new Act to ensure that, taken as a whole, programmes in an applicant's proposed service were 'calculated to appeal to a wide variety of tastes and services'. That was as far as the Act went. But the invitation to apply then expanded on this: '*in considering the diversity of the proposed service, the ITC will have regard to the programme range in the present ITV schedule*' (my emphasis). Taking full advantage of the amendment accepted at the House of Commons Committee stage in the passage of the Act, the invitation to apply for Channel 3 licences devoted more than a page to listing nine strands, some with as many as three sub-strands, and all further detailed, which were currently carried by ITV. We may take one of these (no. 6) as an example. The invitation to apply specified it as follows:

> *Education*, including
> – *adult education*, usually backed by specially prepared literature advertised on screen and in other appropriate ways.
> – *social action*, covering programmes which reflect social needs or promote individual or community action. (ITC, 1991a, pp. 29–31)

It will be remembered that, towards the end of the passage of the Act through Parliament, the government had reversed House of Lords amendments requiring educational and social action programming on Channel 3, because, in David Mellor's words, 'It is unsatisfactory for Channel 3 licences to be required by statute to show a long and detailed list of individual programme types.' But, only a couple of months later, precisely such a 'long and detailed list of programme types' – indeed longer and more detailed than any critics had attempted to introduce in the statute – was precisely what was being required by the ITC. There was no word of objection from government.

A similar, though shorter, shopping list was included in the invitation to apply for the Channel 3 breakfast-time licence (ITC, 1991b, p. 23). This too reflected the range of output currently being broadcast – in this case on TV-am. Both regional and breakfast-time invitations stated explicitly that 'the ITC considers that there should be some programming in each of the ... strands'. It made it formally possible to miss out some of the sub-strands, but insisted that applicants would have to *demonstrate* why they had left any of them out. It warned in the regional invitation that 'applicants should note that a service with more limited range than is indicated here is unlikely to pass the quality threshold' (ITC, 1991a, p. 31). Mellor had said that it would be a brave applicant who offered less than ITV. The invitations to apply went further – they made it clear that it would be a positively foolhardy one. To offer less than the ITC's codification of existing ITV best practice was to invite the Commission to reject the application.

On regional programming, the (regional) invitation to apply was even more specific. It laid down the weekly hours of regional programming for each region which applicants '*must* at minimum include', and for four regions also the minimum number of average weekly hours of sub-regional output (pp. 27–9, my emphasis). In both cases, the figures were based on existing practice, but in some instances they may have actually gone beyond it.

Lastly, on 'quality' – a statutory requirement – the invitation to apply offered the following elucidation:

> The ITC considers that categorisation of programmes as of high quality is a matter which cannot be reduced to a single formula ... it is important that programmes of wide audience appeal should also be of high quality. High quality cannot be guaranteed by any particular combination of talent and resources, although both are normally crucial elements. (p. 31)

This was a formula that gave every incentive to applicants to maximise their offered talent and resource package over every strand, but still left the ITC with a tantalising amount of discretion when it came to their final decision.

One of the few significant changes from the draft invitation to apply to the final document demonstrates the ITC's determination – and ingenuity – to set a pro-gramme-quality threshold at least at the level of the existing ITV service. ITV had long been characterised by its huge proportion of domestically produced product, and its comparatively low level of US imports. In the draft invitation a require-ment was set that 75 per cent of programming should be of European (which in terms of UK popular television effectively meant UK) origin (ITC, 1990a, p. 26). This was roughly the figure then being offered by ITV. Lobbying from the US embassy forced the ITC to reduce this figure in its final draft to 50 per cent. But the Commission then added a new condition – 65 per cent of programmes had to be 'originally produced or commissioned for Channel 3 services' rather than acquired (ITC, 1991a, p. 23). Given that virtually all originally produced or com-missioned programmes would be UK-produced, and that a few percentage points of acquired programmes would be of UK origin, this new formula in practice pro-duced the same result as the original draft. The ITC thus effectively blocked an extra flood of US (or Australian) imports on the new ITV.

Commenting at the end of 1990, the then Director of Programmes for Thames Television, David Elstein, observed that for him the best thing that had happened in the year was the ITC draft invitations to apply:

> Some people in ITV will see them as dauntingly over-regulated. But to people like me who want to see the best of ITV retained into the Nineties it was very reassuring that the ITC had the courage to put into the application what I would call 'ITV plus'. (*Broadcast*, 20 December 1990, p. 17)

*ITV plus* – this was a neat and accurate phrase to sum up what the ITC had done in its invitations to apply. The Commission had used every element of discretion given it by the 1990 Act to codify the best in public service terms that ITV had achieved, and to ensure that applicants for licences under the new regime would have to commit themselves to at least that in order to stand any chance of having their bids accepted.

However, commitments were one thing, performance was another. But here too, in its invitations to apply, the ITC displayed both initiative and ingenuity in squeezing the maximum amount that it could out of the Act so as to preserve the existing standards and range of ITV programming into the new regime.

First, the invitations to apply gave the ITC ample means to deal with the much-debated problem of 'overbidding'. The Act required that the ITC ensure that a successful applicant could maintain its promised programme service throughout the licence. Under the heading 'Maintaining of the Service', the invitations to apply developed on this theme. The ITC would require detailed financial information as a basis on which to judge whether the applicant could, in their judgment, successfully maintain the promised service. 'Key to questions in this area concern the financial resources of the applicant'. So the Commission demanded:

- profit and loss projections;
- cash flow projections; and
- projected balance sheets. (ITC, 1991a, p. 38)

The details of how these were to be presented and justified were specified, again in considerable detail, in section c of the invitation, which ran to just over seven pages (pp. 68–75). Among many other things, applicants were required to project television advertising growth and the share of it that would go to their licence.

So, the ITC armed itself in advance with the information it believed necessary to eliminate 'overbidders'. This was not only a clear warning against overbidding, it also added considerably to the problems and cost of bidding for all applicants, because it required any applicant who hoped to succeed to provide a detailed business plan which the ITC would find credible. The applicant had to second-guess at what level of projections for, for example growth in advertising revenue, the ITC might decide that an ambitious bid had turned into an overbid. For the Commission was not just laying down a complicated step of hoops through which any successful applicant would have to jump. It was, in addition, clearly leaving open its option to decide whether or not it found a particular bid credible, regardless of how meticulously that bid provided the required formal details.

In addition to providing itself with a potentially powerful defence against over-bidding, the ITC also put into its invitation to apply a potentially powerful weapon to ensure compliance. The invitations said:

The licence granted by the ITC will include ... conditions with regard to programme content and other matters relating to the service. *These will reflect the proposals made by the winning applicant as to the service to be provided as set out in the information supplied by him to the ITC.* (p. 21, my emphasis)

In other words, successful bidders would be contractually bound by the promises they had made in their application. This was a departure from previous practice. And – given the incentive provided, by both the detailed quality threshold and the possibility of an exceptional circumstances award, to maximise programme promises in the applications – it was a potentially very important departure. The ITC had laid down a standard of 'ITV plus'. No serious applicant would offer less than that. So any successful applicant would be contractually locked in to 'ITV plus'.

The franchise race may have officially started in February 1991, but for potential contenders preparations had begun months, and in some cases years, before-hand. For the incumbents this had involved cutting costs, most notably staff; rationalising structure by divisionalisation and out-sourcing; and in some cases, improving output, by, for example, subdividing regional news provision. For prospective challengers, it involved forming credible consortia. And in both cases it involved developing business plans.

The process gave ample room for backstabbing, gaining intelligence about opponents and second-guessing both opponents and regulators, and all the associated skullduggery that such practices might involve. (A well-informed account of the manoeuvres indulged in by the contenders for most of the major franchises can be found in Davidson, 1992.) What were the results of this hectic preparation?

First, the final line-up for the 1991 ITV contest was on much the same scale as the line-up for the previous contest in 1980. In 1980 there had been forty-four contenders for sixteen franchises – thirty-six for the fifteen regional franchises and eight for the new breakfast franchise. In 1991 there were forty contenders for the same sixteen licences – thirty-seven for the fifteen regions and three for breakfast (IBA News Release, 9 May 1980; Davidson, 1992, pp. 297–8). So the new 'com-mercial' auction system in 1991 did not produce significantly more challengers than the old 'beauty contest'.

Nor did it greatly change the make-up of the contenders. The 1991 contest, like the 1980 contest, was overwhelmingly British, despite the fact that under the new rules a licence could be wholly European-owned and non-European players could have a substantial (generally considered to be up to 30 per cent), although non-controlling, share. As events turned out, few of the European and even fewer of the US television giants entered the race (although there were exceptions – for example, CLT was a major stakeholder in an unsuccessful bid for the East Anglia licence and Rizzoli Corriere della Sera was a minor stakeholder in Carlton Television). The Americans may have been put off by the prohibition on control from outside the EU. Both they and the Europeans were probably also put off by the complexity of putting together a credible bid. Nor were the British contenders of 1991 much different from those under the old regime. Of the two major mul-tiple bidders in 1991, one, Carlton, had been a previous contender for an ITV franchise, and both Carlton and Virgin (the other 1991 multiple bidder) had par-ticipated in the 'beauty contest' run under the old rules for the UK DBS licence.

There were just two significant new factors in the eventual make-up of the chal-lenging consortia. Most challengers included independent producers either in their consortium or as promised suppliers to it. This independent production sec-tor had, by and large, not played a part during the last contest, and what inde-pendent production had existed had very little credibility with regulators. In 1991 the situation was quite different. Perhaps independent production was cheaper, but, more importantly, by 1991 tying in credible independent producers was the easiest, and in practice probably the only, way for challengers to offer a credible production base to pass the quality threshold. Also, all bidders, whether incum-bents or challengers, had to be able to demonstrate that they could meet the 25 per cent independent production quota.

The other difference was that having local worthies on the board was no longer the *sine qua non* of a successful challenge that it had been in 1980. In 1991 most challengers played safe and included such figures, but one challenger, Carlton, did not. Its gamble proved successful. Under the new system their absence from the board was not to prove an obstacle to a successful regional ITV bid.

The second main feature of the 1991 contenders was a complete split in approach between incumbents and challengers. Despite divisionalisation, all the incumbents bid as producer-broadcasters (i.e. making their own programmes), while all the challengers bid as publisher-contractors (i.e. contracting out their programme production to – generally named – independent producers). In the run-up to the contest there was much debate in the industry about which model was cheaper. But the sharp divergence in strategies points to another factor – the quality threshold. For incumbents, that meant above all resting on their record – as programme producers. For challengers, the safest method of guaranteeing programme quality was to sign up proven independent producers.

The third notable fact about the 1991 bids was their lack of innovation. The ITC had, as we have seen, set tight parameters for the contest and provided detailed incentives that encouraged challengers to promise to replicate the old ITV schedules, and incumbents to guarantee more of the same. Only one challenger, North West Television, proposed significant changes to the schedule (and this only in the little-watched night-time hours), and it failed the quality threshold.

The one obvious new element in the 1991 contest was the cash bid. Here the contestants adopted radically different strategies. Some, notably incumbents Central and Scottish, took the view (as it turned out correctly) that they would not be faced by a serious challenge for their franchise and therefore put in what was effectively a zero bid. One other, LWT, took the view that it would win on quality (either through its challenger failing to pass the quality threshold, or by an 'exceptional circumstances' award). But it also believed (probably mistakenly in the light of the Central and Scottish awards) that its application would only be taken seriously by the ITC if it put in a significant cash bid (albeit one that it did not expect to be the highest). Some other incumbents may have adopted the same reasoning. The other contenders, both incumbents and challengers, simply bid as high as they could. But even here contenders were restrained by two strategic considerations in addition to the basic question of whether they could make a profit after their bid.

All contenders were sensitive to the fact that they had to pass the quality threshold – and more. They also either had to (if they were incumbents) maximise their chances of an 'exceptional circumstances' award in their favour, or (if they were challengers) minimise the possibility of an 'exceptional circumstances' award being made against them. In both cases that meant pitching programming commitments somewhat above the basics of the threshold. The other strategic consideration for straightforward high bidders was the danger of being seen to 'overbid' – and therefore having their application ruled out by the ITC. This danger put an extra premium on applicants refining credible business plans based upon a sober projection of likely advertising revenues.

Despite the very clear awareness among applicants about both the level of the quality threshold (reinforced by the perceived possibility of an 'exceptional circumstances' award) and the perils of overbidding, a good number of them got it wrong. Twelve of the twenty-four challenges to incumbents were judged by the ITC as failing to meet the quality threshold, and three bids which did pass the quality threshold were ruled out by the Commission as too high. These rejected bids included ones made by applicants with considerable experience and credibility in the industry. Challengers backed by companies as prominent as Virgin and leading independent producer Mentorn were ruled out on quality grounds. Two of the three ruled out for overbidding were incumbents, TVS and TSW. This suggests that the ITC was exercising its discretion to the maximum, not merely in setting the rules for the game, but also in adjudicating on the outcome.

A comparison of the outcome of the 1991 franchise race with that of 1980 reinforces that belief. In 1980, of the fifteen regional franchises, three were unchallenged and three incumbents were unseated (one as a result of a forced amalgamation). In 1991 the figures were exactly the same: fifteen regional races, three unchallenged and three incumbents unseated. The only reason why the 1991 race may appear to involve slightly more upsets than 1980 is because the incumbent of the breakfast licence (a quite new franchise in 1980) was also unseated. Of the 1991 losing incumbents, two (TVS and TV-am) had been widely criticised beforehand, and one other (TSW) was at best a lacklustre and quite marginal contributor to network programming. In other words, all three would have been prime candidates for a fall under the old rules.

So, the only way in which the auction system produced an obviously different outcome to the race than might have been anticipated from a rerun of the previous 'beauty contest system' was in Carlton Television's successful outbidding of Thames for the London weekday licence. Thames was widely perceived to be a pillar of quality in the old ITV system. It has often been claimed since that Thames was a political victim as a result of showing *Death on the Rock*, a critical documentary on the killing by the SAS of three unarmed IRA members in Gibraltar. There is no evidence for this. And indeed, both the old IBA's behaviour over that programme and the new ITC's general conduct of the franchise auction suggest that the regulators were perhaps surprisingly immune to any such nakedly political considerations. George Russell has subsequently claimed that the ITC sought legal advice as to whether it could successfully make an exceptional circumstances award to Thames, but was told that this would not stand up to challenge in court (Thames's quality might be acknowledged as higher than Carlton's – but not 'exceptionally' higher). Those who want to see a political element in the ITC's awards might perhaps suggest that such legal advice was itself based on a recognition that Carlton was the outsider who had previously made most effort to break into the ITV system and who had been closest to Thatcher in the attempts to change it. That limited speculation apart, the outcome of the 1991 franchise race pointed to the ITC, perhaps unexpectedly successfully, managing to preserve the substance of the existing ITV system while observing the letter of the substantially qualified auction. In other words, the outcome of the 1991 franchise race was in many respects a testament to the triumph of regulatory persistence over legislative change.

A consequence of this was that one supposed virtue of the auction system of franchise allocation fell flat on its face. Whatever advantages might be claimed for it, an auction system, the government had maintained, would at least produce a transparently fair result. Ten million pounds was clearly objectively higher than £9 million, and would be seen to be so. But the ITC's decisions on quality thresholds and overbidding ensured that of thirteen contested franchises only five went to the highest bidder. The result was a press outcry (see the editorials in daily morning press for 17 November 1991). It was not the specific decisions of the ITC that were challenged – few outside observers strongly suggested that x rather than y should have won a particular contest. It was rather that the overall decision procedure appeared just as opaque as it had done under the old 'beauty contest'.

None of the challengers who had been ruled out on 'quality' grounds challenged that ruling in the courts. However sore they may have felt, they were no doubt advised that the courts would be unlikely to overturn the ITC's judgment in this, its expert field. There was, however, a serious legal challenge from one of the incumbents (TSW) ruled out for overbidding. In the end this challenge was not successful, but the case did give some insight into the ITC's procedures on this question.

## The Channel 5 Auction

The concessions made by the government since the publication of the 1988 White Paper, and the determination of the ITC to exploit them, together ensured that the 1991 franchise auction had rather less to do with cash bids and much more to do with the discretion of the Commission. This was even more the case in the 'auction' of the Channel 5 licence. The licence for the new channel was, according to both the 1988 White Paper and the 1990 Act, to be allocated by exactly the same procedure as the ITV licences. But the fact that the channel was new gave the ITC even more discretion than it had had with ITV. Applicants could not make the same assumption that applicants for ITV licences had made – that the quality threshold meant effectively a repeat of past performance. Quite new schedules would have to be produced – with the risk that these might prove unsatisfactory to the ITC. And the credibility of business plans for a new service was an even more subjective matter than for a service that had been running for more than three decades. Channel 5 applicants would also be required to provide a credible plan for retuning the millions of video recorders that would be affected by the frequencies used by the new channel.

The Commission advertised Channel 5 twice. In April 1992 it issued its first *Invitation to Apply for a Channel 5 Licence*. When the deadline passed in July there was just one bidder, Channel Five Holdings Limited, whose most notable member was Thames Television, the prestigious loser of the London weekday ITV licence. In December 1992, having twice deferred its decision at the applicant's request, the Commission issued its verdict. The licence would not be awarded to Channel Five Holdings, explained the ITC, because the Commission were not satisfied with some aspects of its business plan or with the level of investor commitment. This decision effectively removed additional and unpredictable competition from ITV during the early and uncertain years of the new commercial regime. This may not have been entirely unwelcome to the ITC, although Commission spokesmen strenuously denied that this had been a factor in the decision.

After another extensive round of consultation, the ITC issued a second (amended) invitation to apply for Channel 5 in November 1994, with the deadline for applications set for May 1995. This time there was considerably more interest – perhaps because of the upturn in the economy, and consequent growth in advertising revenues that had occurred in the two years since the first attempt. Participants in the four consortia bidding for Channel 5 in 1995 presented an impressive range of British and foreign media companies (indeed, foreign interest for this one new channel was as great as for all sixteen ITV licences in 1991).

Easily top bidder of the four was UKTV Developments, a consortium dominated by Canadian broadcaster Canwest, which had made a very late marriage with a British independent producer. Tying for second place were two consortia with rather more substantial input from British media companies – Channel 5 Broadcasting, backed by Pearson and MAI, and Virgin Television, backed by Richard Branson's Virgin group. Finally, with a far lower bid came New Century Television, whose most noted component was Rupert Murdoch's News Corporation.

This line-up presented the ITC with some intriguing dilemmas. The top bidder was clearly dominated by a non-European company. Although a legal formula had been found to get round this, it can safely be assumed that the ITC would remain worried about what this meant for the new service. That there was a tie for second place raised the (subsequently judged unfounded) suspicion of collusion. It also raised the possibility of the two contestants having to rebid, which given the already high level of their bids (£22 million) cannot have been an attractive option for the Commission. Lastly, if all the top three bids were ruled out, that would leave as winner the consortium backed by Rupert Murdoch, a prospect widely criticised in the run-up to the bids, and one unlikely to be eagerly welcomed by the ITC.

In the event, the Commission neatly sidestepped these dilemmas. It ruled out top bidder UKTV and one of the tied bidders, Virgin Television, on programme quality grounds. This left Channel 5 Broadcasting to successfully outbid the Murdoch-backed consortium. Deft use of its discretion on quality threshold had once again enabled the ITC to achieve the result which it would surely have come to in a 'beauty contest' without cash bids.

As in 1991 the press was unconvinced about any transparency in procedures, but, unlike 1991, unperturbed by their end result. There was another, again ultimately unsuccessful, challenge in court by one of the losers. This perception of unfairness was not changed by the fact that in 1995, unlike 1991, the ITC offered some explanation of its decisions on passing the quality threshold. That explanation was, however, couched in formal and cursory terms. Virgin, said the ITC, had not devoted enough time to news and current affairs of high quality, and neither Virgin nor UKTV had given sufficient time to other programmes of high quality or offered a service which, taken as a whole, appealed to a wide variety of tastes and interests. There was no amplification.

## The New System in practice

The 1988 Broadcasting White Paper had contained crucial ambiguities between the government's desire to maintain the overall programming standards of the existing ITV system and its desire to fundamentally change that system to a more commercial model. The 1990 Broadcasting Act incorporated numerous concessions to critics who sought to emphasise the virtues of the old system against the perils of deregulation. And the ITC ran the 1991 franchise race so as to preserve as much as it could of the existing ITV system. But all this still left open the question of just how the new system would work in practice. Once the licensees started broadcasting, how much would the new regime established by the 1990 Act and the ITC actually differ from the old?

The new regime came into full operation on 1 January 1993 when the new licensees came on air. Before that, two things were required, each of which would greatly affect how the new ITV regime operated. The ITC had to agree the details of licences with the winners of the 1991 race, and the new licensees had to agree arrangements for running a national network which were satisfactory to both the ITC and to competition regulators.

The first of these requirements proved easy. The ITC did as it had promised in the invitations to apply, and incorporated as an annexe to each licence the whole of the detailed programme proposals the successful bidder had made in its application. For good measure, each licence also spelt out the precise number of hours for each programme strand that the licensee had promised. The licences were signed with very little demur in late 1991 and early 1992. (Copies of the licences can be found in the ITC library.) As we shall see, these very detailed contractual obligations were soon to be used by the ITC, and used effectively, in a key dispute with the commercial desires of the new ITV broadcasters.

Agreeing arrangements for a national network proved rather more difficult. The government had set the goal that there should be 'fair competition' in the supply of programmes to the network. In other words, rather than programme supply being largely carved up between the 'big five' ITV companies, as had traditionally been the case, the programme proposals of the smaller ITV companies and independent producers should be considered for the network on their merits. So the network arrangements had to involve some degree of formal separation between the ITV companies as network programme commissioners and the same companies as potential network programme suppliers. The 1990 Act required that both the ITC and the Director-General of the Office of Fair Trading (OFT) had to approve network arrangements.

Not unnaturally, the 'big five' companies were reluctant to abandon entirely their previous privileged position on network programme supply. Provisional network arrangements proposed by the ITV companies were approved by the ITC in May 1992, but the OFT decided that they did not adequately meet the competition test. The arrangements were then referred to the MMC, and eventually modified network arrangements were accepted by the regulators (ITC *Annual Report*, 1992, pp. 4–5). However, there continued to be complaints from independent producers that the ITV companies were abusing their position as broadcasters in order either to secure more production for themselves or to retain rights in independent productions. Significantly, this latter complaint was directed not only at the old producer-broadcasters but also at some of the new publisher-contractors.

Under the new commercial television regime, the ITC on the face of it no longer had the formal power to determine the scheduling of programmes. It had set the amounts of particular programme genres, but could not, unlike the IBA, prescribe when these were to be shown. That raised the possibility of 'public service' programming on ITV being moved out of peak viewing hours in favour of more audience-maximising (and therefore revenue-maximising) entertainment. A small but revealing indication that the ITV companies would take advantage of this came right at the start of the the new licensees' transmissions, when ITV abandoned its traditional early Sunday evening 'God slot' and instead broadcast its quota of religious programming at times when smaller audiences were available. The ITC took no action on this.

But later in 1993 a further move along the same lines resulted in far greater controversy. A number of ITV companies felt that broadcasting their main weekday evening news bulletin at 10 o'clock prevented the scheduling of unbroken feature films – which would have provided larger audiences – in late peak time. The issue was discussed at an ITV strategy conference in June, and the desire of the ITV companies to reschedule their late evening news was leaked to the press. The news provoked vocal criticism, particularly among politicians of all parties – for whom *News at Ten* had the particular attraction of maximising coverage of their activities to a peak audience. The ITC promptly sided with these critics, and wrote to the ITV companies reminding them that a majority of companies had pledged to continue the 10 o'clock news slot in their applications, that these pledges were included in their licences and that therefore they would be in breach of their contractual obligations if they moved the time of their late weekday news bulletin. ITV promptly abandoned the attempt to shift *News at Ten* (ITC Annual Report, 1993, p. 23). The affair was an early, and important, indicator that the ITC had sharp regulatory teeth, and was prepared to use them in order to maintain some of the central pillars of ITV's traditional public service traditions.

The following year those regulatory teeth were bared again, this time over the issue of the 'undue prominence' given to commercial goods and services in programming. In December 1994 the ITC fined Granada Television for repeated breaches of the 'undue prominence' code in one of its regional programmes. It was the first time the ITC had imposed a financial penalty, and the fine – of half a million pounds – was generally seen as a substantial one (ITC *Annual Report*, 1994, p. 27).

While the ITC displayed a readiness to enforce the rules it had set after the 1990 Act regarding the ITV companies' on-screen performance, pressure was mounting from the companies for the government to change the rules it had set about their behind-the-screens organisation. Using the powers given him by the Act, the Home Secretary had in December 1990 set down the details of ownership limits on the ITV companies. Regional licences were divided, according to advertising revenue, into nine large and six small. No one company was allowed to control more than two licences, and no one company was allowed to control two large licences. Only one takeover took place under these rules. Before the new licensees started transmitting (small) Tyne Tees agreed (with the ITC's approval) a takeover by neighbouring (large) Yorkshire. However, mergers between a large and a small company, or between two small ones, still blocked the large economies of scale that could be gained by mergers between large companies. Some in the ITV industry (most notably Central Television's Chief Executive, Leslie Hill) had long argued that ITV should be concentrated into a handful of companies. In the arguments over the White Paper and the Broadcasting Act, ITV as a whole had argued for maintaining separately owned regional companies. However, once the new licensees started broadcasting, the balance in ITV shifted, with a number of key ITV companies (notably Granada and Carlton) now arguing that companies should be allowed to own more than one big licence.

The argument was not simply in terms of the merits of concentration. It also seized upon an anomaly in the 1990 Act's ownership provisions. European companies could control ITV licences. So, whereas one large ITV broadcaster was not allowed to take over another large ITV broadcaster, that broadcaster could be taken over by a European television giant. Granada, for example, was not allowed to take over LWT, but Silvio Berlusconi or CLT were. The spectre was therefore raised of British commercial television falling into foreign hands unless the ownership rules were relaxed.

In November 1993, Heritage Secretary, Peter Brooke, bowed to this pressure by announcing that from now on a company could own two 'large' licences (apart from one company owning both the London licences). In his announcement, Brooke presented the apparently simple case that had influenced his decision: 'Changes are taking place in broadcasting throughout the world. The Government has been urged to relax the present restrictions on the ownership of ITV companies to enable them to compete more effectively in world markets' (DNH News Release, 24 November 1993).

In the following months Carlton took over Central, Granada took over LWT, and MAI, which already owned Meridian, took over Anglia. In those few months a bigger concentration took place in ITV than had occurred since its very earliest days. All three new pairings shed further numbers of staff as they rationalised their merged ventures.

So, relaxation of the ownership rules certainly allowed the merged ITV companies to achieve significant economies of scale in the home market. Whether that would mean a more active role for ITV companies in the world market was altogether less clear.

There was also pressure for change in the rules set by the 1990 Broadcasting Act for Channel Four. The Act had forced Channel Four to sell its own advertising, but buffered it from competition (and so protected its remit) by providing it with a safety net of 14 per cent of commercial terrestrial advertising revenue. If Channel Four fell below this, then ITV would have to make up the difference. The channel had viewed the prospect of selling its own advertising with some confidence, because by the time of the 1990 Act its share of commercial terrestrial television audiences (and hence of likely advertising revenue) was well above 14 per cent. However, Channel Four's continued audience success in the first years of the new regime raised a new problem with the funding formula.

When it announced the 14 per cent safety net, the government had added a rider, incorporated into the Act, that if Channel Four earned *over* the 14 per cent then it would pay 50 per cent of the surplus to ITV (plus 25 per cent to a Channel Four reserve fund). So, with 18.2 per cent of terrestrial advertising revenue in 1993, the first year of the new regime, Channel Four ended up paying £38.2 million to ITV, with the prospect of even bigger figures in subsequent years.

In 1994 Channel Four launched a vigorous campaign to get the formula abolished – well before the 1997 review that the Act allowed for. 'We believe', argued the channel's 1994 position document, 'that the present terms of the Act will result in Channel 4 diverting an average of £50 million a year from its programme expenditure – thus greatly weakening the channel's competitive position' (Channel Four, 1994, p. 6).

The channel's argument gained considerable political support, including from former Broadcasting Minister and Heritage Secretary, David Mellor. It was, naturally, vigorously opposed by the ITV companies, whose financial interests were directly and substantially at stake, and who could argue that the existing funding formula was the one under which they had made their bids. The government resisted Channel Four's argument for over two years, finally making a very limited concession to the channel in the 1996 Broadcasting Act (see Chapter 9).

Ultimately the most important test for the new regime was the standard of programming broadcast under it by the new licensees. Any judgments here are bound to be both impressionistic and subjective. From the start of the new licences the ITC adopted the practice of publishing detailed annual 'Performance Reviews' about both the ITV network in general and individual licensees. In the years 1993 to 1996 these reviews dealt with a host of issues, and handed out praise and blame in good measure. Perhaps the most important pronouncements were made at the end of the first year of the new regime:

> Although many individual programmes and series displayed high quality production standards and creative ability, the overall feel of the [ITV] network schedule was cautious and predictable. There was little evidence of adventure or the surprise of one-off events.

The ITC particularly singled out the fact that 'the predominance of crime-based stories narrowed the range of drama overall'. On current affairs, the Commission considered that ITV's overall performance 'was better than some of its eager critics asserted and there was no significant narrowing of the agenda compared to the recent past'. But it then added: 'nevertheless, the pressure to deliver ratings was never far away and occasionally showed in loss of nerve in the choice of subject and treatment'. In this first performance review the ITC made a specific point of criticising the major newcomer, Carlton, for failing to deliver on its promises for network programming. What Carlton did provide was, the Commission commented, 'with some exceptions not distinctive or of noticeable high quality'. There would need to be 'significant improvement' (ITC *Annual Report*, 1993, pp. 53, 55, 61).

The Performance Reviews for the following two years were in general less harsh. Some of the Commission's warnings about the first year had presumably been heeded. But the general thrust of those early criticisms continued to be a feature of comment on ITV programme output under the new regime. The Performance Review for 1996 reiterated them with a new sense of concern:

> The preoccupation with crime, police and emergency services in drama and factual programmes was no worse, but has not diminished since 1995 and was again, with some justice, criticised by the Viewer Consultative Councils. *Network First* and *The South Bank Show*, two flagship series regularly praised by the ITC for their high quality, were scheduled less frequently and with a narrower range of subject matter than in previous years. ... The strength of ITV's continuing commitment to regular serious documentary and arts coverage, clearly set out in the licence applications, appears to be in question. (ITC *Annual Report*, 1996, p. 61)

The wilder prophecies of doom for 'quality' programming on ITV made during the debate on the 1988 White Paper and the 1990 Act had not been fulfilled. But there were scarcely any outside observers to be found who claimed that ITV programming under the new regime was in any way an *improvement* on the old.

In its early years of operation, thanks to the concessions made in the passage from the 1988 White Paper to the 1990 Act, and thanks even more to the continued willingness of the ITC to exploit these to the full, the advertising-funding side of British terrestrial television did not show the catastrophic decline in public service standards which many critics of the 1988 White Paper had anticipated. In formal, and many substantive terms, the elements of public service programming established in the old ITV persisted. Meanwhile, Channel Four continued to fulfil its remit, at least in the terms which it had done so in the years immediately before the new regime. But there has been a clear and substantial commercialisation of the culture of ITV – and Channel Four – over those years. And that has had a real, if difficult to pin down, effect on-screen.

Alongside regulation, there was another reason why, up to the mid-90s, the worst of the feared prospects of the government's post-Peacock reforms to advertising-funded terrestrial television had been avoided. Competition for television advertising, within commercial terrestrial broadcasting, had been dampened by the Channel Four funding formula. And competition for television advertising from outside – i.e. from cable and satellite – was still relatively small. Cable and satellite's main source of revenue was subscription, not advertising. So, when the Tories left office in 1997, ITV and Channel Four still maintained the relatively secure revenue stream that had underpinned their public service provisions. That stream was, however, becoming less secure. ITV viewing figures seemed to be hit harder by the rise of cable and satellite than the viewing of either BBC or Channel Four. By 1996 cable and satellite had 8 per cent of television advertising revenue. And in March 1997, the start of Channel 5 – a third terrestrial advertising-funded channel – added to the increasing squeeze on ITV's and Channel Four's dominance of the television advertising market. Real competition in that market may have developed more slowly than many observers expected, but if it continues at its present pace, it will upset the relative financial security which ITV and Channel Four still enjoy, and with that, put qualitatively greater pressure on their public service remits.

In that important respect, the full consequences of the new regime for commercial terrestrial television by the 1990 Broadcasting Act are only now beginning finally to work themselves out.

# 9 Back to the BBC

Once the Tories had shaken up commercial television with the 1990 Broadcasting Act, it seemed to most observers to be only a matter of time before the government turned its attention to the BBC. In 1991 the organisers of the annual University of Manchester Broadcasting Symposium neatly captured the mood of expectation and foreboding by calling their gathering 'And Now for the BBC ...' (Miller and Allen, 1991).

This might have been more accurately phrased as 'and now *once again* for the BBC'. For, as we saw in Chapter 6, the whole Conservative excursion into reforming ITV, which culminated in the 1990 Broadcasting Act, had originally started in 1985 with an attempt to decisively change the BBC. After the passage of the 1990 Act and the 1991 ITV franchise auction, it seemed reasonable to expect that the Tories would return to implementing their unfulfilled mid-80s agenda for the BBC.

The government did indeed turn its attention back to the BBC in the early 90s. But it did so for rather routine administrative reasons. The BBC's charter was up for renewal in 1996. So, whether they contemplated any change or not, the Tories were bound to address the question of the future of the BBC in the years preceding that renewal.

The government approached the task at a leisurely pace. Before the 1992 election the Home Office drew up a draft Green Paper, which apparently reflected the then Home Secretary Kenneth Baker's desire to reopen the argument about putting advertising on the BBC (Barnett and Curry, 1994, p. 169). But such an approach did not command the support of Baker's colleagues, and after the election work started on a new draft, this time under the auspices of David Mellor. Mellor had been the key government protagonist in the passage of the 1990 Broadcasting Act, and had been widely seen as the willing broker of the many concessions which opponents of the original bill secured during that process. After the election of 1992 he became the first Secretary of State for the new department which would, from then on, have responsibility for broadcasting: the Department of National Heritage. The Green Paper on *The Future of the BBC* (DNH, 1992) was finally published by Mellor's successor as Heritage Secretary, Peter Brooke, in November 1992. Less than a week later, the BBC followed suit with its own strategy statement (written well before), *Extending Choice* (BBC, 1992).

The most obvious feature of the 1992 BBC Green Paper was the enormous contrast in tone between the way the Conservative government in 1992 approached the BBC and the way the Conservative government in 1988 had approached ITV. In 1988 there had been no Green – or consultative – Paper. The Tories had moved directly to publishing a White Paper, which set out, as policy, a series of radical, if often ill-thought-through, proposals for reform to a generally hostile industry and public. Having failed to convince almost anyone else of the merits of these proposals, the government proceeded to push their core into legislation, while grudgingly backtracking on many of their more controversial elements.

The tone of the 1992 Green Paper could scarcely have been more different from the 1988 White Paper. One newspaper leader (*Independent*, 25 November 1992, p. 22) aptly described the 1992 document as 'long on options, refreshingly short on recommendations'. This change in tone undoubtedly reflected a real political shift. It was two years since Margaret Thatcher had been ousted from the Conservative leadership. The débâcle of the ITV franchise auction had scarcely whetted the appetites of Tory politicians for more of the same. And David Mellor, who as Broadcasting Minister had piloted the ITV reforms through Parliament and, as Secretary of State for National Heritage, presided over the first drafts of the Green Paper, now took great glee from the back benches in warning his colleagues about the dangers of listening to 'glinty eyed pamphleteers'. By that he meant the free-market think-tanks. These had seemed very close to government broadcasting policy in the mid-80s but were now distinctly out of fashion in government circles.

What did this change in tone mean in practical terms? Behind a set of apparently open questions which formed the bulk of the Green Paper, the government undoubtedly had its own agenda for the BBC; but it was a markedly undraconian one – at least in formal terms – and, it should be added, one much more modest than it would have been had it been formulated at virtually any time since 1984. By 1992 the government seemed to have no intention of replacing the licence fee as the major source of BBC funding, no intention of getting the BBC to take advertising, no intention of cutting the BBC's two television channels to one (a seriously canvassed[1] outside possibility in the years before) or of breaking up the Corporation. The one 'radical' scheme, rather lamely canvassed in the Green Paper, was that of establishing a Public Service Broadcasting Council which would distribute licence money for public service broadcasting to both the BBC and other channels – an option first advocated by the Peacock Committee.

Why had the Conservatives so shifted their ground on the BBC between the establishment of the Peacock Committee in 1985 and the publication of the Green Paper in 1992? One reason is, of course, the intervening years of debate and the generally poor reception that greeted the government's ITV reforms, both in theory and practice. But more important is what had happened to the BBC itself in the intervening period. Perhaps the key reason why the Tories, from 1992, opted for a 'steady as she goes' course on the BBC was that the Corporation itself was already steering a course which conformed with Tory political objectives. It is to this development that we must now turn. In what ways did the BBC change from 1985 to 1992? And how much was this change a consequence of Tory policy?

# The BBC from Peacock to Green Paper

With the important exception of the 25 per cent independent production quota, the Peacock Committee generated scarcely any legislation to change the BBC. But, aside from legislation, the government had three other weapons available with which to influence the Corporation. It could exert financial pressure, because the government set the level of the licence fee. It could change the policy of the BBC through its ability to appoint the Chairman, Vice-Chairman and the rest of the Board of Governors. And it could generate political flak, either directly or through its press and back-bench supporters, which would put pressure on the Corporation to change its course. All of these were potentially powerful weapons. But, as we have seen in Chapter 3, before 1984 they were either little used or used ineffectually.

In the mid-80s this all changed. Both the shift in the political atmosphere which led to the establishment of the Peacock Committee and the Peacock Committee itself were accompanied by an increasing willingness on the part of the government to use this full range of non-legislative policy instruments on the BBC. And the use of these instruments had, by the early 90s, produced important changes in the Corporation.

Deliberate financial pressure started at the very time when the Peacock Committee was established. In 1985 Home Secretary Leon Brittan had exerted an initial major financial squeeze on the BBC by granting a much smaller licence fee increase than the Corporation had asked for. After Peacock reported, in December 1987 Brittan's successor, Douglas Hurd, declared his 'double squeeze' on BBC finances by indexing the licence fee to general inflation – less than broadcasting inflation – and by starting that indexation from a base which was lower than the BBC was already budgeting for. And in 1991, following a report for the government on the BBC's finances conducted by consultant accountants, Price Waterhouse (Price Waterhouse, 1990), the government set the increase of licence fee at 3 per cent below the increase of the RPI for a year, followed by two more years indexed to the RPI. So, the question of the 'efficiency' of the BBC, which had been foregrounded by Peacock, had from the mid-80s become a routine part of the government's professed agenda. To some extent, the Corporation was protected from the full effect of any squeeze on the licence fee in the 80s by the rise in the number of households and the continued switch from black and white to colour licences. But as Andrew Graham and Gavin Davies have noted, despite this, there was a significant shift for the worse in the real income of the BBC after 1986: 'From 1986–91 the real licence fee receipts, deflated by the labour cost index, actually *fell* by 0.9 per cent per annum' (Graham and Davies, 1992, pp. 205–6). This fall came even before the extra stringency of the RPI minus three settlement of 1991.

Political flak directed against the Corporation also increased in the mid-80s. In August 1985 Brittan took the unprecedented step of writing to the BBC asking the Corporation not to broadcast an episode in the *Real Lives* series that sympathetically treated a prominent Irish republican and an 'extreme' loyalist. The Governors complied with this request, prompting strike action from BBC staff. In September 1986 there was considerable fuss in the Tory press about the BBC 'factual' drama, *The Monocled Mutineer*. And in October two allegedly right-wing Conservative back-benchers won a libel case against the BBC for their portrayal in an edition of the Corporation's flagship current affairs programme, *Panorama*.

Taken separately, and divorced from their context, these incidents were not necessarily more important than the periodic outbursts of right-wing outrage against particular BBC programmes which have been a regular feature of the Corporation's life under both Tory and Labour administrations. Brittan's intervention over *Real Lives* may have taken a constitutionally unprecedented form, but government intervention in programming on Northern Ireland had also been a feature of previous Labour governments (fully detailed in Curtis, 1984). However, coming on top of one another, and occurring in the shadow of the Peacock Committee, these incidents of government flak against the Corporation had more profound consequences than their predecessors. Chief target of the flak was the BBC's then Director-General, Alasdair Milne. It is at this point that the third non-legislative instrument of government policy – its appointment of BBC Governors – became important.

The Thatcher administration had made two appointments to the chairmanship of the BBC's Board of Governors in the first half of the 80s – George Howard in 1980 and Stuart Young in 1983. Whatever might have been the intention behind these appointments, neither Howard nor Young had, as we have seen, turned out to be obvious instruments of a radical government policy within the BBC. Young – despite being the brother of Thatcher's 'favourite cabinet minister' – was widely perceived as having 'gone native' in his BBC post. But, following Young's premature death in 1986, the Tories had the opportunity to make a third appointment to the BBC Chair. It was made at a high point of Tory political hostility to the BBC and at the high point of the government's expressed desire to reform the Corporation.

The government's candidate for Chair was seen at the time as – and was to turn out to be – quite different from the Tories' earlier appointments. Marmaduke Hussey, appointed by the government as BBC Chair in October 1986, was an outsider to broadcasting. That in itself made him no different to most previous BBC Chairs. His background lay in newspaper publishing and he had a recent record of confrontation with the unions in that industry. Hussey's appointment as BBC Chair was warmly endorsed by the Corporation's former Vice-Chair (and most notably 'radical' of previous Tory appointments to the Governors) William Rees-Mogg. 'Hussey', commented Rees-Mogg, 'will see through the BBC mandarins at a glance' (Milne, 1989, p. 188).

Within a few months of taking up his appointment, in January 1987, Hussey effectively sacked Milne. Michael Checkland, perhaps symptomatically a BBC accountant and not a programme-maker like Milne, was appointed as the new Director-General. At the same time, John Birt was brought in from LWT as Deputy Director-General. Birt was to oversee a new unified News and Current Affairs Directorate.

So, with the appointment of Hussey, the government had instituted a major managerial shake-up at the top of the BBC at the very same time as it was beginning to exert a serious financial squeeze on the Corporation. The shake-up also occurred in the immediate aftermath of the deep questioning of the Corporation's traditional basis by the Peacock Committee and in the wake of some of the heaviest government-generated, or government-supporting, political flak that the BBC had faced for several years. The result was a deep and lasting change in the senior managerial culture in the BBC. The background to the shake-up ensured that the new management team was more sympathetic to government thinking and saw itself as confronted with two major tasks: to diminish the political flak from the government and its supporters, and to order the Corporation's affairs in response to the government's financial squeeze.

The first of these tasks was dealt with by Birt's reorganisation of BBC news and current affairs. His establishment of a unified News and Current Affairs Directorate both heightened the profile of news and current affairs within the Corporation and increased its 'professionalism' – with, for instance, subject specialists on economics and social affairs. Some aspects of Birt's approach to 'professionalism' involved making news and current affairs more 'responsible' and therefore less likely to fall foul of the Tories on political grounds. An early event, at which Birt outlined his criticisms of former BBC practices on news and current affairs, is said to have

> left some participants with the uncomfortable feeling that a straitjacket was about to be imposed which would at best cramp and at worst stifle completely any innovation or creativity in BBC journalism – particularly journalism in awkward political areas. (Barnett and Curry, 1994, p. 85)

In the following years there were a number of incidents which seemed to many observers to confirm these fears. One notable example occurred on the eve of the 1992 general election. An edition of the BBC's flagship current affairs programme, *Panorama*, had been prepared, entitled 'Sliding into Slump'. Presented by the BBC's economics editor, Peter Jay, it analysed where the blame lay for Britain's economic problems. On the Friday before transmission the programme was pulled: 'The consequences were swift and predictable. Those who had long been convinced that Birt was leading the BBC down a path of closet connivance with the government saw this as the final confirmation' (Barnett and Curry, 1994, pp. 169–70).

The second problem, the financial squeeze, prompted two initiatives within the Corporation. If, as the BBC senior management increasingly came to accept, the licence fee was to remain pegged to the RPI or below, the main source of BBC income would fall in real terms. So either the BBC would be forced to diminish the services it provided – not an option seriously contemplated by the new management or ever specifically canvassed by the government – or the financial shortfall had to be made up. There were two possible ways of doing this. There could be 'savings' on costs, through increased efficiency. And extra income could be earned through increased commercial operations. From Hussey's sacking of Milne, through into the 90s, the BBC increasingly vocally pursued both options. Together they entailed an increased commercialisation of the culture of the Corporation. But each had somewhat different consequences in terms of public debate and government policy.

It should not, however, be thought that the drive to commercialism within the

BBC was simply a coldly calculated attempt to make financial ends meet. It was also, to a considerable extent, a directly political initiative by the new management of the Corporation, aimed at courting favour with the government. As one internal BBC strategy discussion document put it in 1991:

> Beyond the needs of the consumer, there is a need to run with the political tide. Entrepreneurialism was a requirement of the 1980s and will still have an important place to play in the public sector in the 1990s. The BBC's involvement in commerce signals that it is part of the market place. (unpublished Charter Review task force party report on 'The BBC: the Entrepreneur' p. 1)

Before the Green Paper the more prominent of the Corporation's two strategies to meet the financial squeeze was 'savings' on costs. In 1989 Checkland set up a committee under Director of Finance, Ian Phillips, to recommend ways of saving money. In January 1990, it presented its report, *Funding the Future*, which proposed measures to save £75 million by 1993 (BBC *Annual Report*, 1989/90, p. 7). At the end of 1990, the government's consultants on the licence fee settlement, claimed that, in addition to these, a further £131 million of cost savings could be made by 1995/6 (Price Waterhouse, 1990, p. 7). By the summer of 1992 the Governors were noting that 'Significant savings in manpower, resources and costs have already been made through rationalisation of our activities and improved productivity. A net reduction of about 2,000 jobs occurred during the year [1991/2] in the Home Services' (BBC *Annual Report*, 1991/2, p. 7).

These cuts were by no means the end of the process. In 1991 the Corporation unveiled what the Governors subsequently described as 'a much more radical initiative'. Under Producer Choice, to become fully operational throughout BBC television in April 1993:

> cash budgets will be allocated to all programme-makers who will be free to use either outside or in-house facilities to get the best value for money. . . . Under Producer Choice resource departments will be funded only by selling their services to programme makers. (BBC *Annual Report*, 1991/2, pp. 7, 21)

Whatever cost savings might eventually be achieved by this new mode of BBC organisation – and there were some sceptical voices from both within and outside the Corporation on this score – Producer Choice was of great political significance in terms of the relationship between the BBC and the government. Well over a year before the government publicly revealed its hand on the future of the Corporation, the BBC management had declared their firm intention to introduce a fully-fledged internal market into BBC television, and an internal market which was open to outside competition. This was precisely the form of organisation that the government was then introducing, as a central part of its strategy, throughout the public sector, most notably (and notoriously) in the National Health Service. In the subsequent debate over charter renewal, Producer Choice was to figure prominently in the positions of both BBC and government.

The change in the managerial culture of the BBC instituted in the late 80s and early 90s by Hussey, Checkland and Birt may have found favour with the government, but it was also increasingly the subject of a series of bitter criticisms from a range of prominent figures in the television industry: for example, Channel Four Chief Executive, Michael Grade, and veteran BBC India correspondent, Mark Tully (Tully, 1993). Grade's attack, made in the keynote MacTaggart Lecture at the Edinburgh International Television Festival in August 1992, was both one of the earliest and one of the most damning of such critiques.

Over the previous five years, argued Grade:

> the BBC Governors have adopted a policy of political appeasement. They have half embraced the free market but in doing so have set the BBC on a course which can only lead to terminal decline. ... The Governors determined to throw themselves at the mercy of a government that had shown the BBC no mercy at all. They decided that the only way to win back Government support, and therefore safeguard future levels of licence fee increases, was to try to catch up with the political mood of the times and be seen to be taking charge. More and more they encroached on the day-to-day management of the place. (EITF, 1993, pp. 96–7)

Grade's comments were made three months before the publication of the government's Green Paper on *The Future of the BBC* and the BBC's *Extending Choice*. Whether or not one agreed with Grade's judgment on the ultimately dire consequences of the BBC's subservience to the government, the two documents show the process that he identified in action – a process of BBC subservience and government 'reward'.

In formal terms, the Green Paper put virtually every aspect of the BBC up to question. The headlines of its 'Key Issues' section asked:

> What should be the aims of public service broadcasting in the future?
> ... What kind of programmes and services should the BBC provide?
> ... What other functions should the BBC carry out in the future?
> ... How should the BBC respond to the challenges of the commercial media world?
> ... How should the BBC services and programmes be paid for?
> ... How can the BBC be made more accountable while keeping its editorial independence? (DNH, 1992, pp. 12–13)

On the face of it no answer was ruled out. In that sense the *Independent* was quite correct to see the Green Paper as 'long on options' and 'short on recommendations'. In practice, this openness carried within it much scarcely veiled direction. Many of the nostrums prescribed for the BBC by the free-market right in the mid-80s, which had then found favour in government circles, were now treated by the government with polite clinical disdain. For example, the Green Paper's section on 'Advertising on BBC Services' (pp. 33–4) could scarcely be read as seriously trying to reopen the debate on the issue which had been officially opened up with the appointment of the Peacock Committee and then closed off by its report. As we have already observed, the only 'radical' proposal apparently seriously canvassed in the Green Paper was the idea of a Public Service Broadcasting Council (p. 39). And even this was canvassed in a distinctly non-committal way.

There was, however, one clear lead given by the Green Paper – on what it called 'Value for Money':

> The Government has urged the BBC to improve its efficiency. The decision to hold licence fee increases below the levels of inflation, as measured by the Retail Price Index,

has encouraged the BBC to look for ways of reducing its costs and diverting funds from administration to programmes. The BBC's initiatives, 'Producer Choice' and 'Re-shaping for the Future', and its scrutiny of overheads, are all steps in this direction. (p. 35)

For its part, the BBC, in *Extending Choice*, made no attempt to argue the case for increased public funding for broadcasting. It appeared to accept the inevitability of a licence fee pegged to less than the rate of inflation and therefore declining in real terms.

And so, the BBC's strategy document echoed the Green Paper in emphasising cost savings. *Extending Choice*, like the Green Paper, included a major section entitled 'Value for Money'. It began with a proud recitation of the cuts the BBC had recently made; outlined the themes of Producer Choice, which it declared to be 'at the heart of the process of change'; and ended with the declaration that: 'The BBC of the future will deliver clear public service purposes which are different from those of the commercial broadcasting market. But it will use the market to help achieve its purposes and test its efficiency' (BBC, 1992, pp. 52–5).

The rest of *Extending Choice* also sat comfortably with government thinking. Three strands of the BBC's strategy for 'the new broadcasting age' are particularly worth noting in this context – the Corporation's emphasis on news and current affairs, its pitch to represent the 'national culture' and its approach to 'popular' programming.

*Extending Choice* was explicit in accepting that public service broadcasting must inevitably narrow in scope in a multi-channel environment:

> The rapid expansion of commercially funded broadcasting services through the 1990s will not invalidate the need for publicly funded broadcasting: but it will serve more clearly to limit and to define the specific role that it should play in pursuit of its public purpose.
> In the past as a dominant provider, the BBC had an obligation to cover all audiences and broadcasting needs: in the future it will have an obligation to focus on performing a set of clearly defined roles that best complement the enlarged commercial sector. (p. 19)

The four roles for a public service broadcaster that *Extending Choice* singled out were:

1. Providing the comprehensive, in-depth and impartial news and information coverage across a range of broadcasting outlets that is needed to support a fair and informed national debate.
2. Supporting and stimulating the development and expression of British culture and entertainment.
3. Guaranteeing the provision of programming and services that create opportunities for education.
4. Stimulating the communication of cultures and ideas between Britain and abroad. (p. 19)

It was probably no accident that news and current affairs came first. The BBC had just put extra resources into this area and reorganised it as a single directorate.

These developments had been associated with John Birt and had, as we have seen, been accompanied by a new 'responsibility' in the treatment of controversial issues. And from July 1991 Birt had been designated by the Governors as Michael Checkland's successor after March (or, as it turned out, January) 1993.

The high priority that *Extending Choice* gave to news and current affairs was further demonstrated by the fact that it was the only area where a completely new service – rolling-news channels on both radio and television – was flagged up as a 'public service priority' for the BBC. This emphasis on news and current affairs was probably at least in part motivated by the fact that it is the one area of television that politicians (including Tory politicians) are actually familiar with. The BBC's emphasis on news and current affairs had already been accompanied by an organisational and ideological tightening up which made it less likely to embarrass the government. *Extending Choice* effectively promised more of the same.

In its preparations for the charter renewal debate the BBC had engaged in considerable internal discussions about how far it should, on the one hand, concentrate on the 'high ground' and, on the other hand, to what degree – if any – it should pull back from its current range of popular programming. Criticism from the press and politicians of the BBC for screening popular entertainment that was more appropriate to ITV has long been a feature of the broadcasting debate. The popular imported mini-series, *The Thorn Birds*, had been a particular target in the run-up to the Peacock Committee (Leapman, 1986, p. 17). Supposedly overly 'highbrow' programming on the BBC has also been, equally traditionally, the object of criticism (often from the same sources). If 'highbrow' programming lost the BBC audiences, then it, as a result, weakened its political case for the licence fee, a dilemma that public broadcasters in all countries have faced (see Achille and Miege, 1994).

One solution *Extending Choice* came up with was to put together all nonfactual programming under the heading, 'Expressing British Culture and Entertainment'. In terms of crude *realpolitik*, the solution was an ingenious one – the most banal soap or light-entertainment show could be justified as expressing 'British culture', and an obvious appeal was made to the Tory desire to reassert the 'national heritage' (expressed outside broadcasting in, for example, the national curriculum).

Circumstantial evidence that exactly this sort of cynical politicking was being engaged in can be found in *Extending Choice*'s examples of the 'national culture' the BBC was expressing. The four examples of 'classic literary adaptions' were 'Dickens, Conrad, Trollope and George Eliot'. How did Trollope get into the big four? Was it entirely accidental that he happened to be John Major's favourite author? *Extending Choice* made a token recognition of the problem of cultural and social pluralism, highlighted by Annan, by promising that the BBC would 'reflect the full cultural diversity of the country'. But that did not sit well with its very conventional middlebrow lists of 'best of British'.

In short, there was good reason to believe that on culture, as on news and current affairs, the implicit bargain that the BBC had made with the Tories was to reemphasise some of the more paternalistic aspects of Reithianism, and to pull the BBC back from potentially subversive pluralism.

*Extending Choice* did not limit its treatment of the 'highbrow versus lowbrow' argument about public service broadcasting to trying to wish the problem away under the banner of national culture. It also signalled a small but significant move towards the 'highbrow' – or at least away from the most 'lowbrow' in the overall mix of BBC programming: 'There should be no room on the BBC's airwaves for derivative, "formula" comedy or entertainment formats; nor for simple and unchallenging game shows and people shows which will be provided in abundance on other channels . . .' (BBC, 1992, p. 33).

For a year and a half following the publication of the Green Paper and *Extending Choice* an extensive debate was conducted about the issues of the future of the BBC. But the debate rarely caught fire; it did not extend much beyond élite circles, and among these there was a remarkable degree of consensus. There was almost unanimous support from official contributors to the debate for maintaining in full the BBC's current range of both television and radio services; for maintaining the licence fee as the BBC's prime source of funding; and in rejecting the idea of a Public Service Broadcasting Council. On each of these issues, overt opponents of the new consensus were in a tiny minority (Goodwin and Stevenson, 1994, pp. 8–18). On all of these questions the new consensus coincided with *Extending Choice*. However, on one other issue the consensus parted company with it. *Extending Choice* had signalled some degree of withdrawal from types of popular programming which would be adequately provided by commercial broadcasters. Scarcely any respondents to the Green Paper agreed with this, while a number specifically criticised it (pp. 55–61).

Substantial controversy centred on other matters. A range of organisations kept up the long-standing criticism (going back into the 70s debates) that the BBC was too 'London-centred' (pp. 29–37). There was both fear, and to a lesser extent, enthusiasm for the BBC's commercial activities and for Producer Choice (pp. 19–28, 50–3). But probably the most widely voiced criticisms of the BBC's current practice fell under the general heading of what might be termed the Corporation's constitutional status. The thrust of the criticisms was that in both formal and practical terms the BBC was to some important degree lacking in accountability. The Governors were a particular target, regarded as both unaccountable and interfering (pp. 70–9).

The consensus we have identified among formal respondents to the Green Paper was also effectively shared by the back-bench cross-party House of Commons National Heritage Committee, which took evidence and produced a report in the year following the publication of the Green Paper. Most importantly, the Committee's report on *The Future of the BBC* 'rejected the idea of making the BBC rely on direct advertising' and stated that 'after considering the various funding opinions the Committee has, with great reluctance, come to the conclusion that the present flat rate licence system has the fewest objections to it' (National Heritage Committee, 1993, Vol. 1, p. xxviii).

# The BBC as world-beater

The formal debate on the renewal of the BBC's charter came to an end in July 1994 with the publication of the government's plans for the Corporation in a White Paper, also called *The Future of the BBC*. There were few surprises. What had been implicit in the 1992 Green Paper had been reinforced by the consensus we have described and was now made explicit in the 1994 White Paper – no advertising on the BBC, the continuation of the licence fee (at least until 2002) and maintenance of the full range of the BBC's existing services. The intervening debate had produced little change. The one 'radical' option seriously canvassed in the Green Paper – a Public Service Broadcasting Council – had found little support and was therefore unceremoniously dropped.

Probably the biggest issue raised in the 1992/3 debate on the Green Paper had been the general question of what might be termed the 'governance' of the BBC, and in particular the question of the Governors. Here, despite the numerous expressions of dissatisfaction, the 1994 White Paper firmly maintained the status quo. The BBC was to continue on the basis of Royal Charter, not Act of Parliament. And the Governors were to remain appointed by the government, without either any sort of democratic accountability or public scrutiny.

The one move on 'accountability' that the White Paper did make was not so much a response to the real concerns that had been raised by critics in the debate as an application to the BBC of the 'Citizen's Charter' initiatives which the Major government was then trying to implement right across the public sector: 'The BBC should operate its public services according to the principles of the Citizen's Charter. It should make clear the standards to which it will aspire in a new statement of promises to its audiences' (DNH, 1994, p. 44).

One significant absence in the White Paper was any comment on the BBC's apparent intention, expressed in *Extending Choice*, to shift its range of programming a significant degree up-market. As we have seen, this proposal had in general been received unfavourably in the debate on the Green Paper. Most outside observers who expressed an opinion firmly believed that the Corporation should remain in the field of all types of popular entertainment, and believed that any attempt to withdraw from that full range would result in the BBC becoming a 'public service ghetto'. Perhaps as a result of this response, perhaps because it became apparent that the government, in its new mood towards the BBC, was indifferent to the issue, between 1992 and 1994 the BBC itself rapidly backtracked on the 'complementary' (to the commercial sector) programming philosophy it had advanced in *Extending Choice*. In July 1993, the new Controller of BBC 1, Alan Yentob, announced that research had shown that the BBC was 'superserving' the middle classes, and that it had to attract viewers from lower socio-economic groups (*Daily Telegraph*, 14 July 1993, p. 2). With that announcement the BBC effectively abandoned the slight, but significant, shift away from the full range of popular programming signalled by *Extending Choice*.

There was only one significant change between the government's position on the BBC suggested in the Green Paper of 1992 and the stance eventually explicitly adopted in the 1994 White Paper. The change could be seen in the White Paper's subtitles. Alongside 'serving the nation' came 'competing worldwide'. Whereas before 1992 cost-cutting had been the most prominent of the BBC's two means of meeting the licence fee deficit, now commercial revenue-earning came to the fore.

The BBC had run commercial operations long before the Thatcher government, mainly domestic print operations like the *Radio Times* and the international sales of BBC programmes to foreign broadcasters. These operations had provided the BBC with a small commercial income to supplement the licence fee. In the early years of the Thatcher government these commercial operations had continued largely without comment. In the years after the Peacock Report they became the object of rather contradictory government concern. On the one hand, the government, and its competition regulators, judged that some aspects of the BBC's domestic commercial activities, particularly in the print field, amounted to 'unfair competition'. So the BBC's monopoly over its programme listings was abolished (thus damaging the position of the *Radio Times*) and its ability to promote on air its specialist consumer magazines (an important and expanding area of BBC commercial activity) was curtailed (MMC, 1985, 1992). On the other hand, the BBC was specifically required by the government to make commercial use of its night-time hours. This requirement was not to prove commercially successful – the attempts to sell night services made a loss.

During the same period, the BBC itself had embarked on three other, more significant, initiatives in the commercial field. Its print and programme sales arm, BBC Enterprises, had embarked on what some observers called a 'dash for growth'. This involved a rather unsuccessful diversification of BBC commercial activities from which the Corporation later withdrew (Davenport, 1993, p. 26). Second, in November 1991 the Corporation launched BBC World Service Television (WSTV). WSTV was first conceived several years before as a logical extension of BBC World Service Radio, an international, government-funded public service that employed the new technology of satellite delivery of television. The BBC World Service lobbied government to provide extra funding to extend its international public service radio services to television. This lobbying was unsuccessful. BBC World Service nevertheless continued with the project on the basis of 'self-funding' public service. However, by the time WSTV was launched in 1991 its rationale was shifting again – towards the straightforwardly commercial. WSTV would exploit the supposed international demand for BBC programmes and the new delivery systems, so as to earn extra money for the BBC. Lastly, in November 1992, the BBC launched a UK-directed satellite channel, UK Gold, using its library material, in partnership with the ousted ITV mainstay, Thames Television, and the US cable-operator, Cox.

These new commercial initiatives by the BBC figured in both the government's Green Paper and in the BBC's *Extending Choice*, albeit in a subordinate place. Less than two years later, in the 1994 White Paper, they figured altogether more prominently:

> The BBC's more recent proposals are designed to provide a strategic purpose for its commercial activities. The BBC has given considerable thought to its plans for these activities in the future, especially the international opportunities. ... The Government welcomes the initiatives which the BBC has undertaken and considers that it should continue to develop its commercial activities. (DNH, 1994, p. 23)

The White Paper maintained that the BBC's 'long-term objectives and values as a public service broadcaster should underpin all its other activities'. It also insisted that 'the BBC's commercial activities should be conducted in ways which are fair to its competitors. That means that they must not be subsidised by the licence fee or the Grant-in-Aid which finances World Service Radio.' But, with those two riders, the White Paper set down, for the first time in the history of British broadcasting policy, a major new role for the Corporation as a player in the global communications market:

> The BBC's commercial activities in the United Kingdom are likely to increase through cable and satellite services and through publishing. However, the Government believes that the BBC's commercial initiatives should aim increasingly at international markets, so helping to create and sustain a United Kingdom presence in an international multi-media world, and increasing the United Kingdom's competitiveness. (p. 24)

This official declaration of the BBC as a potential world-beater in the new media markets was by no means a unilateral imposition of strategy by government. As the White Paper clearly recognised, the initiatives had been made by the BBC itself. Particularly in the early stages of the inception of WSTV, these were no doubt the product of what has sometimes been rather jaundicedly termed 'BBC imperialism' – the desire of the Corporation to participate in any new broadcasting developments. But, more importantly, the BBC's international commercial initiatives were also the result of its new management's eager response to the twin government pressures of financial stringency and conformity to Tory norms for the public sector. The BBC's international commercial initiatives would both help make ends meet, without extra public funding, and also demonstrate the Corporation's participation in the 'Enterprise Culture'.

These international commercial initiatives had also, between the Green Paper of 1992 and the White Paper of 1994, received enthusiastic endorsement and further impetus from the House of Commons National Heritage Committee. This was not simply a case of Conservative back-benchers doing the bidding of their government. The Committee's Labour Chair, Gerald Kaufman, was openly enthusiastic about a commercial international 'multimedia' future for the BBC. Kaufman's views were extreme, by the standards of either the government or his own party colleagues, but what they do indicate is the growing and bi-partisan enthusiasm among politicians for the BBC in its role as a global player – an enthusiasm which extended to the Opposition front benches. A year before he became Prime Minister, Tony Blair declared that 'Britain is fortunate to have potential competitive advantages' in inventing and marketing the information economy. These include 'our leading information companies, from BT to Pearson, from Ionica to Reuters, from Mercury to the BBC' (Blair, 1996, p. 104). As Blair's comments also indicate, support for the BBC's international commercial role was also increasingly linked to a similarly bi-partisan enthusiasm for new developments in information technology. We will chart the further developments along these lines in the next chapter.

The 1994 White Paper effectively sealed the government's new policy on the future of the BBC. The small print remained to be sorted out, and it was on 30 April 1996 that the new BBC Royal Charter and Agreement finally came into effect. They run until the end of 2006. Celebrating the occasion, the then National Heritage Secretary, Virginia Bottomley, observed:

> [The Charter and Agreement] provide a strong and secure framework for the BBC's public service broadcasting and the flexibility necessary to enable it to develop its commercial services to meet the challenges of the next century. The BBC is a unique and valuable national resource and it is important for audiences in the United Kingdom that the BBC can continue to develop its rich tradition of high quality public service broadcasting. (DNH News Release, 1996)

These were official platitudes but they had considerable substance. To crystal-ball-gazers of the mid-80s, this mid-90s settlement of the BBC's future would have come as a considerable surprise. Then, Margaret Thatcher was eagerly trying to foist advertising on the BBC; the Peacock Committee was looking to a subscription-based future for the Corporation; assorted free-market think-tanks and press pundits were centre-stage advocating privatisation of (particularly the popular) chunks of the BBC's programme services; and prophets of the multi-channel revolution were portraying the old public service warhorse as set for rapid and terminal decline.

A decade later the picture looked very different. The options of advertising or subscription funding for the BBC were confined to the margins of domestic public debate and rejected by the UK government. The licence fee as the Corporation's primary source of finance was guaranteed until 2002. Every one of the BBC's two national television channels and five national radio channels (one, Radio 5, established in the mid-80s) remained firmly in public hands, with their full range of programming intact. And on top of that the BBC now had the extra status of being officially proclaimed a national commercial champion in the world market.

There was just one important reduction in the formal scope of the Corporation's activities. In the 1996 Broadcasting Act the government privatised the BBC's transmission (a policy signalled in the 1994 White Paper (DNH, 1994, p. 28)). But this was the only important formal price that the BBC paid for the government's endorsement of its established domestic position and enthusiastic embrace of the BBC's new ambition to be a substantial international commercial player.

The publication of the 1994 White Paper may have finally removed the BBC from any threat of formal government-imposed changes, but it did not remove the basic squeeze on its core revenue base that the government had exerted over the previous decade. Now, the BBC perhaps felt more confident of its position and thus more able to raise the issue in public. So, in 1996, for the first time for a decade, the Corporation publicly canvassed the need for an increase in the real value of the licence fee. Speaking to the Edinburgh International Television Festival in August 1996, BBC Director-General John Birt raised the issue:

> If the BBC is to sustain the existing level of services; if it is to remain as creative and dynamic an institution ...; if it is to innovate with high quality services in the new technologies ..., then at some point in the future – and for the first time since 1985 – we shall need a real increase in the level of the licence fee. (Birt, 1996, p. 18)

This was the opening round of a campaign by the Corporation to increase its public funding through the licence fee. However, despite, or perhaps because of the government's new-found enthusiasm for the BBC as a potential UK world-beater, one of the Tory administration's last major decisions on television was to turn down such pleas. On 18 December 1996, Heritage Secretary, Virginia Bottomley, announced a new five-year licence fee formula, starting with an increase pegged to RPI in 1997/8 and RPI *plus* 3 per cent in 1998/9, but followed by RPI minus a ½ per cent in 1999/2000, RPI *minus* 1 per cent in 2000/1 and RPI *minus* 2.5 per cent in 2001/2 (DNH News Release, 18 December 1996). The net result, over the five years, was slightly below RPI. In other words, the financial squeeze was to continue, despite the BBC's belated pleas. The long-term implications of that squeeze, coupled with the BBC's new international commercial role, are of major importance. They were rendered even more important by a second initiative announced by the Corporation in 1996.

In May of that year – scarcely a week after the new charter came into operation – the BBC took full advantage of its new-found security to mount an ambitious bid for a substantial extension of public service provision using digital technology. In *Extending Choice in the Digital Age* the BBC promised licence payers 'a digital dividend' of extra public services. Using the extra channel capacity provided by digital terrestrial broadcasting, these new public services would include: simulcasting of BBC 1 and 2 in wide-screen format; complementary channels to BBC 1 and 2 providing extra information, follow-up programming, extended live coverage and more; a 24-hour television news channel; and extra educational provision (BBC, 1996, pp. 27–38).

On the face of it *Extending Choice in the Digital Age* marked two bold steps for the BBC. First, the Corporation made an early and apparently wholehearted commitment to exploiting digital terrestrial broadcasting. That put it way ahead of most public service broadcasters (and – as we shall see in the next chapter – the government in 1996 was particularly keen to push digital terrestrial broadcasting). Second, the BBC made it clear that its exploitation of this new distribution technology was intended, in part, to involve the delivery of extra public service provision. This was a radical break from the BBC approach to the new distribution technologies of cable and satellite. Since the mid-80s the BBC had regarded such new distribution technologies only as extra opportunities to sell programming.

The problem that remained was how such extra public service provision would be paid for. *Extending Choice in the Digital Age* put forward two answers. It declared that there would be more 'savings', this time through the use of new technology. (BBC, 1996, pp. 63–4). But this claim sat uneasily with the campaign that the Corporation was mounting at the very same time: namely, an increase in the real value of the licence fee, on the grounds that soon there would be no room for further substantial internal savings on costs.

Second, *Extending Choice in the Digital Age* claimed that there would be a 'virtuous circle' whereby 'commercial earnings will further improve the quality of our service programmes and, therefore, the assets which can be exploited around the world (p. 39). This idea of a 'virtuous circle' between public service and commercial activities applied not simply to the BBC's new digital operations, but was effectively at the centre of the whole 1994 White Paper strategy of combining (public service) 'serving the nation' with 'competing worldwide'.

The BBC's traditional public service role has been twofold. World Service Radio had its own, admittedly ambiguous, international public service role – 'impartial' political news and analysis, publicly funded, by the UK Foreign Office. Alongside that, BBC Home Services provided a public service to the domestic audience, financed by the licence fee. In neither case was there an unqualified 'virtuous circle' linking traditional public service requirements with the new commercial operations. The international public service role was clearly at odds with the political requirements of some of the states within which the BBC hoped to expand its commercial operations. As a result of these WSTV was excluded from Malaysia and China, and the BBC was forced to abandon its Arabic television service (because of political opposition from its commercial partners, who were closely connected with the Saudi regime).

Less obviously but, if anything, more importantly, the tension between public service and commercial operations extended to the domestic front. To take one not unimportant example, much of the BBC's domestic public service remit has traditionally involved providing high-quality drama about contemporary UK working-class life. Such subject matter has very limited export potential. However, costume drama with a 'heritage' orientation, which documents UK middle- or upper-class life in the past, has much more of an international market. A public service broadcaster oriented to a domestic audience would prioritise the former over the latter. A commercial broadcaster oriented to an international audience would prioritise the latter over the former (Sparks, 1995, pp. 336–8).

There was, then, a fundamental question mark over the BBC which the Tories bequeathed to their successors. Ten years of financial squeeze and a new managerial regime had not *formally* altered the BBC's public service role. But together they contributed to a more indirect and long-term, but still substantial, threat to that public service role. That threat was contained in the BBC's new role in the world television market. Despite all the formal safeguards the government and the Corporation had introduced in the new charter and licence, by 1997 there was the real prospect that the (mainly international) commercial tail of the BBC would soon start wagging the (primarily domestic) public service dog.

## Note

1. For example, by *Sunday Times* editor, Andrew Neil, in a presentation to the 1991 Edinburgh International Television Festival (Neil, 1991, p. 6).

# 10   Into the Multimedia Age?

The 1994 White Paper on the *Future of the BBC* foregrounded an expression which had hardly featured in previous government pronouncements on broadcasting policy. The new watchword word was 'multimedia'.

'The next 10 to 15 years will bring rapid and exciting changes in broadcasting,' proclaimed the second paragraph of the White Paper:

> New technologies are emerging and the boundaries between broadcasting, telecommunications and other media are becoming blurred. New services are being created, which combine aspects of different media, and which have become known as multi-media services. There will be new opportunities for United Kingdom businesses in providing such multi-media services in an expanding global market. (DNH, 1994, p. 1)

So far as the substance of *The Future of the BBC* was concerned, the prominence given to the term 'multimedia' was somewhat misleading. When the White Paper went on to say that the BBC should 'evolve into an international multimedia enterprise, building on its present commercial services for audiences in this country and overseas', what it in practice meant was that the Corporation should market internationally, by now quite conventional, cable- and satellite-delivered television services. But the use of the term was nevertheless significant. From roughly 1993 onwards, debate on media policy in Britain had undergone a profound change in emphasis. Terms like 'multimedia', 'digital revolution' 'information superhighway' and 'convergence' had begun to dominate discussion on all media policy – and that included, quite centrally, television policy. From one point of view this new focus of discussion was simply the result of molecular changes in the technology, economics and politics of the media which had begun at least as far back as the 70s. Nevertheless, there was a real sense in which, by 1994, a gradual accumulation of quantitative changes had produced a qualitative transformation in the framework of British media policy debate.

A variety of factors accelerated this transformation. In the USA, Bill Clinton's 1992 election campaign and his new administration had popularised the notion of the 'information superhighway'. In Europe, 1994 saw the publication of the Bangemann Report on *Europe and the Global Information Society* (Bangemann et al., 1994). And in Britain, in 1993, leaks appeared in the press that British Telecom was now technically able to provide video-on-demand (VOD) of acceptable standard to a majority of customers over existing twisted copper pairs by the use of ADSL compression technology. The precise provenance of the leaks was much debated. But whatever the exact motives and substance of the BT VOD leaks, it is undeniable that from roughly that time British media policy debate began to be taken up by 'multimedia' and associated buzz-words to an extent qualitatively different from the previous decade.

This shift in the climate of debate brought in turn a crucial, but largely unacknowledged, shift in Tory television policy. Between 1981 and 1984 there had been a firm link between Conservative broadcasting and telecommunications policies, much influenced by the then current concerns about the 'information society'. As we have seen in Chapters 4 and 5, much of the innovatory broadcasting policy of the early Thatcher years on satellite and broadband cable was made from a perspective which considered broadcasting and telecommunications together as one aspect of a growing information technology sector.

But throughout the twists and turns of the very considerable debate on the terrestrial channels that followed, from 1984 right through into 1993, this attempt to link broadcasting policy to telecommunications policy largely disappeared from government thinking (Peacock's vision of a broadband multi-channel future being the one major – but, as we have seen, rapidly rejected – exception). The telecommunications or general information technology implications of broadcasting policy went largely undiscussed by the government after 1984. The Tories simply steered telecommunications along a parallel, but effectively quite separate, deregulatory course. (For a perceptive contemporary view of these developments, see Negrine, 1988).) From both pro- and anti-government sides, telecommunications, or more general information technology considerations, figured only marginally in the debates on the 1988 Broadcasting White Paper, the 1990 Broadcasting Act or surrounding BBC charter renewal.

So the shift in the mind-set of Tory television policy, symbolised by the language of the opening of the 1994 BBC White Paper, was not a shift into totally new terrain. It was also, to a significant degree, a shift back to the concerns and priorities of the early 80s. But in the debates of the mid-90s that followed this shift, very little general consideration was paid by the government – or indeed by many other participants – to the lessons that might be learnt from the Tories' first, distinctly disappointing dry run towards the brave new world of new communications technologies that we have outlined in Chapters 4 and 5.

The new mode of thinking that crystallised in 1993/4 extended to far more substantial issues than the rather empty use of the term 'multimedia' coined in the 1994 BBC White Paper. In the same year as *The Future of the BBC* was published two new issues of television policy came to the forefront of public debate, apparently more firmly grounded in the development of the new converging communication technologies. One was the question of who would build the UK 'information superhighway', or, more mundanely, what balance should be struck between BT and the cable industry in the provision of television entertainment to promote that building. The second issue concerned the question of cross-media ownership. To these was added in the following year a third issue – what to do about developing the new distribution technology of digital terrestrial television. These three issues, which had figured very little in debate on either the 1990 Broadcasting Act or BBC charter renewal, came to dominate Tory television policy from 1994 onwards. Some of them, and some of the problems that had arisen from the implementation of the 1990 Act, would be tackled by the government in a new Broadcasting Act in 1996.

# Who will build the superhighway?

As we have seen, Tory media policy of the early 80s had regarded broadband cable as part of both broadcasting and telecommunications. Cable policy was, as the 1983 Cable White Paper had put it, 'in a sense the crossroads at which broadcasting and telecommunications issues meet' (Home Office and Department of Industry, 1983, p. 5).

The regulatory regime laid down in 1984 had allowed cable operators to provide all telecommunications services apart from voice telephony. This last area, for the moment, had been restricted to the duopoly of BT and its fledgling government-encouraged competitor, Mercury (although cable companies could, and some soon did begin to, provide voice telephony services in partnership with one of the two public telephone operators). In return BT (and Mercury) were prevented from either carrying or providing broadcast video.

These arrangements were central to the government's strategy of fostering infrastructure competition in telecommunications. Cable operators were to be encouraged by having a clear run on television services, and Mercury was given a clear run to compete with BT on voice telephony. Even before the arrangements were modified in 1991 they provided one of the world's most 'liberal' regulatory environments for cable – one which was surely a significant factor in the mushrooming North American cable *and* telephone companies' investment in UK cable from the late 80s onwards.

In the government's 1991 review of its telecommunications duopoly policy (DTI, 1991), cable operators were allowed to interconnect and to provide voice telephony in their own right. This modification in telecommunications competition policy enabled a rapid growth in cable voice telephony subscribers. In 1994 telephone lines provided by cable operators more than doubled from 314,000 to 717,000 (ITC Press Release, 27 January 1995). Cable operators in Britain, exploiting this second important revenue stream, thus began to present themselves as significant competitors to BT in the provision of 'plain old telephone services', and consequently as potential competitors in more advanced telecommunications services.

The exact boundaries of competence between BT and the cable operators had long been a source of conflict between the two parties and an issue of debate in telecommunications policy. But they only became an issue of more general concern with the new focus of media debate on the 'superhighway' and the leaked claim that BT was now able to deliver VOD over its existing network by means of ADSL. One indicator of this extension of formerly specifically telecommunications concerns into more general media debate was the inclusion of the question of whether BT should be allowed to broadcast entertainment in a debate on the new Broadcasting Act at the Edinburgh International Television Festival in August 1994. It was the first time for many years that a question of *telecommunications* policy had become a point of issue among the *television* community.

It was in this new climate that in March 1994 the House of Commons Trade and Industry Committee began hearings on *Optical Fibre Networks*. The Committee's report, published in July 1994, began with the now popular premise that

The potential now exists for an enormous range of new services, which are likely to have profound consequences for economic performance and for the ways in which people organise their business and social lives. ... There is concern that government policies could be hindering or not sufficiently encouraging the development of the most advanced infrastructures and services, and that this could result in the UK falling behind other countries, with damaging consequences. (HoC, 1994, p. 9)

Here was a key instance of the mid-90s return of British media policy to the industrial and information technology concerns of the early 80s.

Despite the grandiose premise of 'an enormous range of new services', the Select Committee's investigations essentially boiled down to reconciling the competing claims of cable and BT over their part in building the broadband infrastructure for the new services. BT maintained that if the ban on its broadcasting television was lifted early, then it was ready to invest £15 billion in providing optic fibre to the home (pp. 25, 33). The cable industry countered with the claim that it was already building the superhighway (p. 28). Both claims looked dubious. BT was careful to avoid a specific commitment that if the ban were lifted it would immediately and fully embark on its putative investment. On the other hand, the cable industry was still to build many of its franchises, and a third of the country remained unfranchised. Also, the lack of interactive services, or even effective technical provision for such services, raised questions of whether the precise sort of infrastructure the cable industry was actually building was quite the 'super-highway' the industry now claimed (p. 28).

The competing claims of BT and the cable industry raised some serious problems for the government's continued objective of developing competition in telecommunications. If BT's claims were conceded to, then the cable industry would be left stranded, deprived of its monopoly in providing television services which had enabled it to compete effectively against its still far bigger and far more established rival. But if the cable industry's case were conceded to, then that seemed likely to remove a key incentive from the player most powerfully placed to build the superhighway – BT.

The Tory-dominated House of Commons Select Committee (with Labour support) argued that this dilemma should be resolved in favour of BT. It proposed that unfranchised areas should be offered for franchising to operators including BT; the government should make clear its aim to allow any company to provide any service to any customer; and restrictions on BT carrying entertainment should be ended on a franchise-by-franchise basis, with a general declared aim of ending all restrictions on BT by 2002 (p. 48). The Committee's proposals were endorsed by the Labour front bench.

But within a few months, the government responded to these proposals by resolving the dilemma in quite a different direction – in favour of the cable industry. It accepted that BT should be allowed to compete for franchises in previously unfranchised areas and thus supply entertainment services in those areas where they gained a franchise. In these (but only these) areas BT would be allowed to 'test new technologies alongside their existing services, making use of the same technologies where possible'; and so not be forced to compete with itself (DTI, 1994, p. 14). But so far as existing franchised areas were concerned (two-thirds of the country), and new franchises won by cable operators, the restrictions on BT carrying broadcast video services would continue. The government's key reasoning behind this stance was as follows:

> The stable regulatory regime which has been created by the Government has enabled substantial investments to be made. This investment of billions of pounds by the cable franchises is not free from risk. . . . To seek to foreshadow later changes in the regulatory regime [by announcing a firm early date for lifting the restrictions on BT] would not, in the Government's view, assist the development of broadband communications in the UK as it would be likely to have a devastating impact on the plans for future investment by many of the major companies currently involved. (p. 28)

In other words, the government's policy priority from 1984 onwards of fostering infrastructure competition was to remain sacrosanct. And, as key agents in this policy, the investments of the cable companies would continue to be protected, even if that inhibited the development of a multimedia infrastructure by BT.

## Cross-media ownership

The 1990 Broadcasting Act had codified long-standing concerns to limit cross-media ownership, by imposing a statutory 20 per cent ceiling on national newspaper ownership of an ITV licence. As we saw in Chaper 8, after the start of broadcasting by the new licensees at the beginning of 1993 the government rapidly came under pressure from within ITV to liberalise the parallel restrictions on ownership of one regional ITV licence by another, resulting in Peter Brooke's announcement, at the end of 1993, that large ITV regional companies would henceforth be allowed to own one other large licence. The rationale for this change had not involved 'multimedia'. Rather the loosening of ownership restrictions was justified on the grounds that unless bigger ITV companies were allowed to consolidate they would be taken over by European media companies.

But at the same time as the lobby was growing for relaxing the restrictions on concentration of ownership *within* ITV, a campaign started to liberalise the restrictions on ownership of ITV from *outside*. And here the 'multimedia' future was, at least on paper, a central concern.

In July 1993 the British Media Industry Group (BMIG) was formed by four major UK newspaper groups – Associated Newspapers, Pearson, the *Guardian* Media Group and the *Telegraph*. Its aim was to campaign for relaxation of restrictions on *cross-media* ownership, most notably the 20 per cent restriction on newspapers.

As a result of pressure on this score, particularly, but not only, from the newspaper industry, in January 1994 the Secretary of State for National Heritage, Peter Brooke, announced a review of cross-media ownership rules. He based his rationale for the review squarely on the multimedia revolution:

> The Berlin Walls which separated communication, entertainment and information are crumbling. . . . Traditionally, the sectors which are now being brought closer together by technology have been separated by legislation restricting ownership stakes. . . . The drive is for alliances which bring all sectors under one roof. (DNH News Release, 17 January 1994)

The first BMIG submission to Brooke's review also based its argument squarely on the multimedia revolution:

> Multi-media developments (convergence, digital compression and globalisation) are set to blur and obliterate distinctions between the different media. Print, television and electronic databases will be perceived as simply different formats for exploitation – not separate industries. . . . These developments point to the need for new and creative strategic alternatives where existing media companies can join forces with new firms . . . to provide new services to consumers via new delivery systems. Existing media companies, particularly newspaper publishers, must therefore be permitted either to join these new alliances or to compete with these non-media based companies to safeguard their future. This is currently being hampered by the UK regulatory framework. . . . British laws on cross media ownership in particular are bringing disproportionate disadvantages to UK companies within Europe and are hampering their ability to compete in the global market. . . . The British Media Industry Group and similar organisations are willing to undertake the risks and investments involved in diversifying into the new multinational and multi-media market. Regulators must act now to allow them this opportunity. (BMIG, 1994, p. 2)

Thanks, among other things, to relatively uncritical reporting in its members' newspapers, the general thrust of the BMIG's case rapidly gained the status of something approaching conventional wisdom in the mid-90s debate on cross-media ownership in the UK (for a critique, see Goodwin, 1995a). But, rather like the cable industry's claim to be building the superhighway, closer examination raised some rather awkward questions.

The first problem was that the newspaper industry had wanted to get into television ever since the birth of the new medium – many years before the multimedia revolution. In 1954, when the ITA first carved up the commercial television map, newspapers had substantial shareholdings in two of the four groups initially offered contracts. Since then, both local and national newspaper groups had exhibited a hefty presence in every extension of the ITV network and in every new ITV franchise round. So, if, from 1993, newspaper proprietors wanted to get more involved in television, it was more out of ambition to be associated with a glamorous industry, or, more likely, the desire to be part of another profitable business – not because of a, as yet non-existent, multimedia revolution.

Second, the BMIG based their case on the premise that current developments were

> pointing media companies in the direction of multi-media activities; only in this way can they hope to use software (essentially information and programming) efficiently, supplying to what would historically have been regarded as a number of different media markets. (BMIG, 1994, p. 7)

But many years of experience of newspaper involvement in television showed remarkably little in the way of technical synergies, or circulation of software between the print and the audiovisual media.

Third, the BMIG was remarkably silent on what the new multimedia services were would enable its members to contribute to. No doubt it was possible to fill in this gap. But whatever services might be envisaged, it is hard to see how their provision would be qualitatively enhanced by newspaper companies possessing a conventional terrestrial television broadcasting licence. Yet relaxing restrictions on the holding of these conventional terrestrial licences was precisely what the BMIG campaign was all about, and it was also the main question which the government's cross-media ownership review was designed to address.

## The Labour Party changes course

Although by 1994 the government strongly claimed to embrace the multimedia revolution, it was still relatively cautious about some of the new policies being urged upon it in the name of multimedia. We have just seen how the government turned down BT's cross-party-supported superhighway overtures, as to do so would have meant upsetting the Tories' long-established policy of telecommunications infrastructure competition. The cross-media ownership campaign at first appeared to elicit a similarly luke-warm government response. Indeed, the Department of National Heritage (dubbed the 'Department of Nothing Happening' by some of the newspapers whose proprietors were involved in the campaign) delayed producing its conclusions for more than a year.

The various reasons for Tory caution can be debated. Simple political exhaustion of the administration was undoubtedly one factor. Another reason may have been that, at the time, the government was experiencing a distinctly uncomfortable relationship with the press, including its own traditional political supporters. But whatever the reasons, politics abhors a vacuum and the gap was rapidly filled by the unlikely candidate of the Labour Party.

For nearly a decade and a half, Labour had been opponents of the Tories' efforts at the commercially oriented restructuring of British television, and in general focused their arguments on support for the public service tradition in British broadcasting. They had also traditionally been opponents of the concentration of media power, particularly in the guise of Rupert Murdoch's News International. Lastly, they had not, before the early 90s, been in any way noted for a desire to subsume broadcasting policy under the banner of a more general information technology policy or to re-link it with telecommunications policy. So, from 1979 right through to the early 90s, inasmuch as it had influence on the outcome of government broadcasting policy, the Labour Party had consistently exerted that influence to restrain the Tories' more deregulatory ambitions.

From 1993 the Opposition's stance rapidly changed. In part this was a result of the rightward move of the Labour Party, which had been under way since 1983 and which had rapidly accelerated since the party's unprecedented fourth consecutive general election defeat in 1992. Under its new leader from 1994, Tony Blair, the party projected itself as the centre-left 'New Labour', now accepting as accomplished facts much of the market-oriented economic and social restructuring of the Thatcher and Major years, and determined not to make any commitments involving increases in public expenditure.

At the same time, Labour was riding high in the opinion polls and therefore clear favourite to win the next general election, due at the latest in 1997. In these circumstances, the party became the object of particular attention by communications industry lobbyists, often disenchanted with what they believed to be the caution of the current government approach, and eager to make their mark on what they increasingly regarded as the likely next administration.

Labour appears to have welcomed these advances with some enthusiasm, not least because it was keen to secure more favourable press coverage of its own general politics. Early evidence of this new coming together of the Labour Party and big media companies can be found in the party's 21st Century Media Conference held in July 1994. The conference was sponsored by the Cable Television Association (now the Cable Communications Association – the trade association of the cable industry), speakers included Peter Smith from News International and the conference organiser happened, among his other roles, to be a paid lobbyist for the BMIG (Goodwin, 1994).

Labour's Shadow Secretary of State for National Heritage at the time, Marjorie Mowlam, began her discussion paper for the conference with premises that will now be familiar: 'An ongoing technological revolution could radically change our working lives and our leisure opportunities. ... The entertainment, information and communications media hold the key to unlocking this future.' Mowlam went on to call for a 'fresh approach' to communications regulation in the UK: 'a new competition policy and a rationalised regulatory structure to meet the challenges of the new market place'. She did not spell out what that structure might be. But the overall drift of Labour's new approach was already clear in Mowlam's paper.

She clearly indicated that Labour had to a considerable degree accepted the case of both BT and the newspaper industry lobbies:

> The printed product will reduce in importance when, for instance, a personal selection of the daily news can be delivered down a cable and printed in the home or office. UK telephone companies are eager to use their new cable networks to deliver programme services and reap the financial benefits that these will bring. The present regulatory structure in the UK restricts both of these developments. Newspapers are largely kept out of ownership of terrestrial television and British telecommunications companies are prevented from broadcasting on their own cable networks. (Mowlam, 1994)

The new Labour Party was now apparently happy to be seen in some respects as *more* deregulatory than the government on media matters. Speaking to a conference organised by the left-wing Campaign for Press and Broadcasting Freedom in March 1995, Mowlam's successor as Shadow Heritage Secretary (and after May 1997 Labour's National Heritage Secretary), Chris Smith, described the government's delay in reporting on cross-media ownership as 'a seriously lost opportunity'. Asked directly whether Labour was more deregulatory than the Conservatives over cross-media ownership (as had been publicly suggested the previous week by Associated Newspapers boss, David English), Smith replied 'no'. But he then added: 'What I am in favour of is the right sort of regulation. That does not mean I am in favour of less, nor necessarily of more.'

On cross-media regulation, Smith appeared to be attracted by some form of the 'share of voice' formula, which had been advocated by the BMIG (see next section). In practice, given that the Labour Party was by now scrupulously avoiding making any challenge to Rupert Murdoch's current stake in UK media (see Brown, 1995), any version of such a formula would allow each of the BMIG members to reach at least the same level of 'share of voice' as Murdoch. That would have given them precisely the entry into controlling interests in ITV licences which they desired. In that respect, at least, the drift of Labour media policy had already, by 1995, begun to adopt a clearly more deregulatory tone than current Conservative policy. This fundamental shift in Labour media policy in the mid-90s plainly meant that Tory policy on the subject would, from then on, develop within significantly different political constraints than it had done between the Peacock Committee and the 1990 Broadcasting Act.

## The 1995 White Paper on Media Ownership

After well over a year of consultation, the new Heritage Secretary, Stephen Dorrell, finally published a White Paper, *Media Ownership: The Government's Proposals*, in May 1995 (DNH,1995a). In the preceding few months the concept of 'share of voice' had rapidly gained attention in public debate as the method for resolving the issue of cross-media ownership. It had been introduced into the UK debate by News International (Arthur Anderson Consulting, 1994), canvassed by the BMIG in its second submission (BMIG, 1995) and had by now, as we have seen, gained the support of the Labour Party.

The basic premise of 'share of voice' was that the shares of audience in a particular area of each of the various major forms of media (television, radio and newspapers) should somehow be added up so as to determine the overall share of a particular company in *all* media in the area. So, for example, a company that had a third of the television audience in an area, a third of the radio audience and a third of the newspaper readership might be considered to have a ninth of the total 'share of voice' in the area. Consequently, ownership limits could be set on a cross-media basis, without setting particular limits on the ownership of one medium by another. One could, for example, say that no company should be allowed to own more than 25 per cent of all media in the area, even if that 25 per cent included television, radio and newspapers.

But, however attractive 'share of voice' might seem to prophets of convergence and partisans of the liberalisation of cross-ownership rules, it was fraught by a variety of technical problems highlighted by some of the consultants' reports which the government itself had commissioned (e.g. NERA, 1995). The example we have given is not unproblematic. How were audiences for different media to be measured? Should public service media – with an obligation to be politically impartial – be counted in the same way as private media which could be politically partisan? How were markets to be defined, and was national media to be counted in local markets or vice versa? And, above all, how were the audiences for different media to be added up?

Different solutions to these technical problems produced radically different assessments of 'share of voice', and therefore radically different political conclusions. One method of answering the technical questions might produce a measure which showed News International dwarfed by the BBC. In another, the BBC might not even figure, while News International would stand awkwardly far ahead of the rest of the media pack.

Dorrell's 1995 White Paper presented a technically ingenious and politically pragmatic response to the considerable pressures that the government now faced to 'do something' about the cross-media ownership issue. Failure to act would mean appearing to bury their heads in the sand in the face of the now much proclaimed 'multimedia revolution', and would risk further antagonising their former friends in the press and being outflanked by Labour.

*Media Ownership* proposed a two-stage approach to the issue. At the 'earliest legislative opportunity', the government would enact primary legislation to, most crucially:

> allow newspaper groups with less than 20% of national newspaper circulation to apply to control television broadcasters constituting up to 15% of the total television market (defined by audience share including public sector broadcasters) subject to a limit of two Channel 3/5 licences. (DNH, 1995a, p. 1)

The technical ingenuity of these proposals lay in combining the fashionable 'share of voice' formula with old style absolute limits on newspaper groups above a certain size. So newspaper proprietors with over 20 per cent share of *newspaper audiences* would still be prohibited from benefiting from the new 'share of voice' provisions and thus remain excluded from controlling interests in terrestrial television.

The political pragmatism of the White Paper lay in the fact that its proposals allowed each of the four BMIG lobbyists to control chunks of terrestrial television (and between them, in theory, virtually the whole of it), but at the same time, the 20 per cent of national newspaper circulation threshold prevented News International (with over 30 per cent of the national newspaper market) from doing likewise. In all previous debates on cross-media ownership over the past decade it was Murdoch who had been the main bogeyman. And in many circles he remained so. However, an important, but perhaps incidental, corollary of the 20 per cent ceiling on newspaper ownership, proposed by the White Paper as the cut-off point for the operation of 'share of voice', was that Mirror Group Newspapers (with a quarter of national newspaper circulation) would also remain excluded from controlling interests in terrestrial television.

There was a second stage to the government's proposals. 'In the longer term,' *Media Ownership* continued, 'as the number of broadcasters increases and increasing technological convergence occurs a more integrated system of ownership control may be desirable.' The government therefore set out more farreaching but vaguer plans for a system which would:

> – define the total media market;
> – reflect the different levels of influence of different media;
> – set thresholds beyond which it would be for an independent regulator to determine whether acquisitions or holdings were in the public interest; ... [and]
> – set out the public interest criteria against which the regulator would act. (p. 2)

But this second stage was put off until the indefinite future. It was also subject to the same technical pitfalls which we have already described for the 'share of voice' approach. So these longer-term proposals in *Media Ownership* were the subject of far less public debate than the government's shorter-term proposals. But the immediate measures proposed by the White Paper were greeted with considerable support by the BMIG lobbyists, and with scarcely concealed pique by Murdoch (Murdoch, 1995, p. 20).

## Digital Terrestrial Television

Three months after *Media Ownership* the government published their second 1995 White Paper on broadcasting, this time on the subject of a new distribution technology. *Digital Terrestrial Broadcasting: The Government's Proposals* (DNH, 1995b) was unveiled by Dorrell's successor as National Heritage Secretary, Virginia Bottomley, in August 1995.

The central importance of digital technology to broadcasting policy is that it enables several times the number of channels to be broadcast on the same spectrum than would be possible with analogue format. So whereas the analogue format had limited UK terrestrial television to four or five national channels, a digital format might increase that number to twenty. How was this new increase in channel capacity to be managed? And how were these new channels to be allocated and run?

Technically, digital terrestrial broadcasting had been possible for a long time, and indeed a few contributors to the broadcasting debates of the late 80s and early 90s had bemoaned the fact that the government had not seriously considered it then. So, in first publishing a White Paper on the subject in 1995, the government was scarcely engaging in far-sighted planning. But the plans which it did announce, and which it then proceded to implement with the 1996 Broadcasting Act, suddenly put the UK at the international forefront of digital *terrestrial* television development.

Two other basic technical features of digital broadcasting are also worth mentioning at this stage. First, digital reception – whether of terrestrial, satellite or cable broadcast – requires a new, and not inexpensive, decoder or set-top box. So new channels on digital terrestrial television would not have the immediate audiences that Channel Four had, or Channel 5 would soon enjoy. Instead, they would have to compete from scratch for the sale of new reception equipment in a market in which cable and satellite were already established. That presented a fundamental question mark over the future of digital terrestrial television. To put the problem crudely, why should the viewer pay out to get twenty channels of digital terrestrial television, when, for a similar outlay, he or she could already get fifty channels from cable or satellite?

Second, digital format does not just increase the number of channels available to terrestrial television. It also multiplies the number of channels available to cable and satellite. So whereas terrestrial television channels might increase from a handful to a score, cable and satellite channels could at the same time grow from dozens to hundreds. So any policy for digital terrestrial television also raised fundamental questions about digital cable and satellite.

The 1995 White Paper on *Digital Terrestrial Broadcasting* began with the proposition that the new technology 'could mean many more television channels and radio stations'. This was uncontentious if it applied to digital broadcasting as a whole – terrestrial, cable and satellite. But whether digital *terrestrial* broadcasting, and particularly television, would play a significant part in that expansion of channels was to a very large degree dependent on whether government policy positively fostered the rapid development of digital terrestrial television. Unless it did so, digital *terrestrial* television might simply be bypassed by digital satellite and cable. And indeed, probably the majority of contemporary commentators on the White Paper expressed considerable scepticism about the prospects of digital terrestrial television in the UK, in the face of the likely imminent launch by BSkyB of a digital satellite service.

The White Paper continued with two fashionable but altogether more debatable claims. 'For many people, it [digital broadcasting] will provide their first experience of the full potential of the information superhighways. It will provide significant opportunities for the British manufacturing and programme production industries' (p. 1). Both these themes closely echoed the claims made in justification of early Tory cable and satellite policy. Such claims might well turn out to be just as empty in their 90s version as they had in the 80s. If digital terrestrial broadcasting was to be outflanked by digital cable and satellite, new technology might again end up by largely delivering non-UK programming over a non-UK infrastructure. And even if digital terrestrial broadcasting did get going, the links between it and the fully fledged information superhighway were tenuous. There was a sense, then, in which the bold claims made by the government for digital terrestrial television concealed, and perhaps were even intended to conceal, a lack of boldness in the government's overall strategy towards the general development of new interactive communications technologies.

The specific arrangements for digital terrestrial broadcasting which the White Paper proposed were complex. But their central elements can be quickly summarised. The ITC was to be responsible for licensing and regulating digital terrestrial television. The Commission would allocate each of the frequencies available for digital terrestrial broadcasting (initially six), not to broadcasters, but to providers of 'muliplexes'. The White Paper explained this centrepiece of the government's proposals as follows:

> Digital technology [allows] several television channels to be broadcast on the same frequency channel. The television channels are combined using computer technology known as 'multiplexing'. If a frequency channel for digital broadcasting were allocated to a single broadcaster, that would mean allocating each broadcaster the equivalent of at least three television channels and potentially many more. The spectrum would in effect be in the control of perhaps six broadcasters, so limiting the opportunities for new broadcasters and for competition, and constraining the variety of programmes on offer to the viewer. Frequency channels for digital terrestrial television will therefore be allocated to the providers of the multiplexes which will bring together, prior to transmission, the batch of programme services on each frequency channel. Although imperceptible to viewers, the multiplex provider will be an intermediary between them and the broadcasters. To apply for the right to use a frequency channel, a multiplex provider will therefore need to have in place contracts with a number of broadcasters, each supplying one or more channels to be broadcast through the multiplex. (DNH, 1995b)

The ITC would have discretion as to whom it allocated the multiplex licences, subject to three criteria:

(a) investment in infrastructure over time in order to provide services as quickly and as widely as possible across the UK;

(b) investment … to promote the early take-up of digital television, including investment to encourage take-up of receivers; and

(c) the variety of services to be transmitted. (p. 9)

This was a quite fundamental departure from the principle of licence allocation which the government had stuck to throughout the debate on terrestrial commercial television from the 1988 White Paper to the 1990 Broadcasting Act. Then the government had insisted on a cash-bid element as essential in the allocation of television licences. In 1995, so far as digital terrestrial television was concerned, the principle of the cash bid was quietly abandoned.

Parallel to this was another change in government principle from the late 80s and 90s. The 1990 Broadcasting Act had authorised the ITC to license cable and satellite channels – but these licences could effectively be obtained on demand and did not involve any positive programme requirements. The 1995 White Paper proposed that the ITC should license not only multiplexes but also digital terrestrial *channels*. These licences would be along the same lines as those for cable and satellite channels, but 'with the addition of key programming proposals made in the application which the relevant multiplex provider made to the ITC' (p. 11). In 1990 the 'additional' channels that would be carried by cable and satellite were not considered by the government to need any positive programming requirements – their programming make-up would simply be a matter for the consumer and the market. But by 1995 the 'additional' services provided by digital terrestrial television were to be allocated, at least in part, on the basis of programming, and what they had proposed was then to be made a positive programming requirement of their licence.

*Digital Terrestrial Broadcasting* contained a third element which also indicated a rather different approach to new broadcasting developments than might have been expected from the government a few years before. The 1995 White Paper maintained that it was 'essential to give public service broadcasters the opportunity of a place in the new [digital terrestrial] technology'. So BBC 1, BBC 2, ITV, Channel Four and Channel 5 would have a place on a multiplex (about a third of the capacity) reserved for them (p. 12). This was in sharp contrast to government policy on cable and satellite (at least since the demise of BSB). In these new technologies there had been, and continued to be, no 'essential place' for public service broadcasters.

## The 1996 Broadcasting Act

In December 1995 Heritage Secretary, Virginia Bottomley, published a new Broadcasting Bill. During the first half of 1996 the bill was debated and amended, first in the House of Lords and then in the Commons, and finally passed onto the statute book in July as the 1996 Broadcasting Act. It was the last major piece of broadcasting legislation passed by the Conservative administration.

Bottomley's bill had three distinct elements. First, it endeavoured to address some, but by no means all, of the problems that had been perceived to arise from the workings of the 1990 Act. Among the most notable of these were ownership rules, Channel Four funding and the plethora of regulatory bodies for television. Second, the bill provided the legislative framework for the privatisation of BBC transmission – a move which the government had tentatively signalled in its 1994 White Paper on *The Future of the BBC* and had subsequently decided to proceed with. Third, and most important, the bill put into place the framework for the 'digital revolution' in broadcasting which the government had set down in its two 1995 White Papers on *Media Ownership* and *Digital Terrestrial Broadcasting*. Overall, claimed Bottomley, 'The Broadcasting Bill gives all media organisations a chance to expand, develop new services and exploit new opportunities' (*Broadcast*, 19 July 1996, p. 21).

Debate on the 1996 Broadcasting Act was at times as heated as the debate on the 1990 Act, and in 1996, as in 1990, the government made a number of significant concessions to its critics during the passage of the bill through Parliament. But there was an important difference between the debates on the two Acts. In 1990, the lines of controversy and amendment had largely fallen into a single overall pattern, as both the parliamentary opposition and much of the television industry sought to mitigate the government's deregulatory thrust. In 1996 the lines of controversy were much less consistently drawn.

The key reason for this was the about-turn in Labour broadcasting policy in the mid-90s which we have already outlined. In contrast to 1990, the Labour Party accepted the the central thrust of the 1996 Act. As *Broadcast's* parliamentary correspondent observed in January 1996:

> Labour appears to have accepted that the present climate of deregulation is necessary for the UK broadcasting industry to move into the digital era. Lord Donoghue, Labour's Heritage spokesman, commented on the 'courage and ingenuity' of the Broadcasting Bill, which received its second reading this week. It attempted to grasp the nettle of digital television, he said, and he welcomed the guarantee of access for existing terrestrial broadcasters. (*Broadcast*, 19 January 1996, p. 5)

This new Labour approach was demonstrated most dramatically over cross-media ownership. The bill incorporated almost unchanged the government's proposals outlined in the 1995 White Paper on *Media Ownership*. These, it will be remembered, allowed newspaper groups to control ITV licences, so long as they had less than 20 per cent of national newspaper circulation. Labour supported the government's relaxation of restrictions on cross-media ownership, but it now wanted to take them further. So, when the bill came to the Commons, Labour's Shadow Heritage Secretary, Jack Cunningham, attacked the 20 per cent ceiling on the grounds that it presented a regulatory obstacle to the development of strong media companies. In effect, Labour was arguing that Mirror Group Newspapers and News International should also be allowed into terrestrial television. Bottomley faced similar pressure to remove the ceiling from within her own Cabinet. Nevertheless, the Cabinet as a whole decided to maintain the block on the two biggest newspaper groups, and Bottomley accused Labour of 'lurching from paranoid terror of large media groups to sycophantic devotion to them' (*Financial Times*, 17 April 1996, p. 9). Labour persisted, and in the Commons committee stage of the bill supported a move by two Tory members to remove the

20 per cent limit. The government, however, carried the vote with the support of the smaller opposition parties.

So, on one major issue of debate on the new bill, the government found itself heavily pressured by the Opposition to be even more deregulatory than it intended. It resisted the pressure.

The two other major controversies surrounding the bill had a very different thrust. In each of these, the government found itself pressured to *strengthen* regulation – on the listing of major sporting events and on controls over conditional-access systems.

These two issues were on the face of it very different: the first looking back to an age of 'national' events on free television as of right; the second looking forward to the new technological future. But the large amount of concern expressed about both stemmed from the same source – worry about Rupert Murdoch's dominance of satellite television. Murdoch, it was alleged, would take away from 'free' television more sporting events of traditional importance, and he was close to controlling the 'digital gateway'. The government made concessions to this mood on both issues, largely token in the case of listed events, detailed and substantial in the case of conditional access (for government thinking on these two issues, see DNH, 1996, and DTI, 1996).

The centrepiece of the 1996 Broadcasting Act was digital terrestrial broadcasting. The Act put into legislation the proposals outlined in the 1995 White Paper substantially unchanged. It would, claimed Virginia Bottomley, 'help British companies exploit digital technology to create new jobs. . . . It will allow us to be a major player in the emerging world market' (DNH News Release, 25 July 1996). 'If digital is going anywhere in Europe, it will be here,' echoed her colleague, Heritage Minister, Lord Inglewood. The UK would 'lead the digital broadcasting revolution' (DNH News Release, 4 July 1996). The big question mark over this enthusiasm was, as we have seen, whether digital *terrestrial* television (in which the UK government was undoubtedly now ahead of other countries) had any sort of viable future against digital *cable* and, perhaps of more immediate importance in the UK, digital *satellite*.

This widespread scepticism about digital terrestrial television diminished when the ITC received applications for the digital multiplexes in January 1997. One of the two major applicants, British Digital Broadcasting (BDB), was a consortium of Carlton Communications, Granada and BSkyB. The alliance of the owners of four of the biggest ITV licences with the dominant force in the UK satellite television market was seen by many observers as a force – and perhaps the only force – which could make a reality of digital terrestrial television in Britain. That might be correct. But it hardly amounted to putting Britain at the heart of the digital revolution. BDB offered simply an alternative means of distributing existing satellite channels, of which the most attractive would probably be BSkyB's leading sport and movie channels. In contrast to the other major applicant, Digital Television Network (DTN), it offered no new or interactive services.

The Tories ended their long period in office trying to sound upbeat about having set the framework for a multimedia revolution. Whether that framework was a solid one was altogether more dubious. 'Building the superhighway' had foundered on their longstanding commitment to the cable industry. Digital terrestrial television was a poor substitute, and even its future seemed largely dependent on the business calculations of Rupert Murdoch.

# 11   The Balance Sheet

It will be several years before we can even begin to draw up a complete balance sheet of the full effects of Tory television policy between 1979 and 1997. The 1996 Broadcasting Act was only just coming into operation by the time the Tories lost office in May 1997. One of its most important creations, the digital terrestrial multiplexes, had not even been allocated in May 1997, never mind commenced broadcasting. What the likely consumer demand for digital terrestrial broadcasting would be, and, indeed, whether or not digital terrestrial television would even effectively take off in the UK, were still very open questions in 1997. The answers will only begin to become apparent several years into a Labour administration. The same can be said for the consequences of many other, and much earlier, aspects of Tory television policy – the effect of Channel 5 on the ITV and Channel Four regime laid down in 1990, being one obvious example.

But, by the time they lost the general election of May 1997, the Conservatives had been in office for eighteen years, and had been trying to implement various changes in television from practically the first day of that period. Some of the institutional changes they had effected were already long established. Channel Four had been broadcasting for nearly fifteen years, UK-directed satellite television for eight. The new managerial regime at the BBC was over ten years old, and the new ITV regime well into its fifth year.

So a preliminary balance sheet of Tory television policy is surely both possible and desirable. Such a balance sheet – assessing the changes in television which had already taken place by the time the Tories left office – must form the starting point for any overall assessment of the television policy of the Thatcher and Major governments. By May 1997, in what ways had UK television changed since Thatcher's election victory of May 1979? How much were these changes a consequence of Tory policies during those eighteen years? And what do they tell us about those policies?

## UK Television 1997

Figures on different aspects of the industry indicate the complexities of the answers to those questions. First, audience share. As we saw in Chapter 1, in 1979 British television had effectively consisted of just three – all terrestrial – channels. Their proportion of viewing in 1980 had been:

| | |
|---|---|
| BBC 1 | 39% |
| BBC 2 | 12% |

ITV          49%
(AGB, 1996a, p. 46)

By May 1997 just two other terrestrial channels had been added – and one of these, Channel 5, had only started broadcasting at the very end of this period, in late March 1997. On the other hand, more than fifty nationally available cable and satellite channels had come into existence. In the first few weeks of May 1997 the share of viewing of these various channels was as follows:

BBC 1                    31.9%
BBC 2                    12.1%
ITV                      31.5%
C4                       10.7%
C5                        2.4%
All cable and satellite  11.4%
Viewing 28 April to 18 May 1997
(William Phillips, in *Broadcast*, 6 June 1997, p. 31)

These figures present us with one crude but important preliminary verdict on the initial results of sixteen years of Tory television policy – how much of the old and new elements of television the audience watched. In May 1997 more than three-quarters of viewing was still of the same three channels that the viewers had been limited to when the Tories took office. And, of the other quarter, more than half was from the terrestrial Channels Four and 5 (the great bulk from Channel Four). In 1997 all fifty cable and satellite channels together still took about the same share as either Channel Four or BBC 2 did individually. These figures suggest two simple conclusions.

First, after eighteen years of Tory policy-making, when it came to what the average viewer watched, the broadcasting duopoly identified by both Annan and Peacock was still very much alive. Second – again, from the viewers' point of view – easily the biggest single quantitative change achieved by the Tory government was still its very first broadcasting reform – Channel Four. The sum total of viewing of all the cable and satellite channels had only just overtaken it.

It could no doubt be objected that such a picture freezes the statistical frame too early. From 1989, when Sky began broadcasting a specifically UK-directed service, the number of households in the UK with multi-channel television (through either satellite or cable) has grown steadily and impressively. From virtually nothing in 1989, by the time of the BARB Establishment Survey of June 1996, it had risen to 5.126 million – 21.8 per cent of television households – and was still growing steadily. Because those households tended to be bigger than average, that meant that by June 1996 27 per cent of individual UK viewers had access in their home to multi-channel television (BARB, 1996, p. 91–2). When the Tories left office nearly a year later, that figure must have been approaching 30 per cent. Cable and satellite in the UK had most definitely come of age.

But they had done so considerably more slowly than most observers, and particularly most observers who shared the government's 80s vision of broadcasting developments, had anticipated. For example, in 1987, well after the delays and problems in the attempts to implement early Tory cable and satellite policy had become apparent, Saatchi and Saatchi had forecast that in 1995 combined cable and satellite penetration would be 45.4 per cent of UK homes – two and a half times what it in fact turned out to be in that year (Saatchi & Saatchi, 1987).

Nearly 30 per cent of British television viewers with home access to multi-channel television in 1997 was nevertheless a major change in British broadcasting from 1979, but it still left more than 70 per cent who were still totally reliant – or still chose to rely – on the terrestrial channels. Those who already had access to cable and satellite were still devoting the considerable majority of their viewing to the terrestrial channels even as the number of cable and satellite channels proliferated. Within multi-channel homes, the proportion of viewing going to cable and satellite channels in 1996 was 36.6 per cent (a rise from 30.8 per cent in 1992) (*Screen Digest*, February 1997, p. 48). In other words, even in multi-channel homes, between 60 and 70 per cent of viewing was of the terrestrial channels. For the average viewer, the dominance of the terrestrial channels – and in effect the continued dominance of the old television duopoly – seems likely to outlive the Conservative administration for many years.

A second set of figures presents a rather more dramatic picture of change. In 1979 revenue for television came from just two sources – the licence fee and advertising. By 1995 these had long been joined by a third new major revenue stream – subscription. In 1995/6 the licence fee raised £1,820 million, of which £1,130 million went to BBC television (BBC *Annual Report and Accounts*, 1996, pp. 78–9). In 1996 the total revenue of commercial television broadcasters (terrestrial, cable and satellite) was £4,164 million. Of this, £1,045 million was from subscription, the vast majority of the rest came from advertising. Subscription was the most rapidly growing of the three major television revenue streams. In 1994 it had constituted just 17 per cent of commercial television revenues; by 1996 that had risen to 25 per cent (ITC *Annual Report*, 1996, p. 11).

This growth of subscription in the years since the launch of Sky's UK-directed service demonstrated that Booz Allen's 1987 report for the Home Office (see Chapter 6) was correct in its belief that there was a significant and, then, as yet untapped market in the UK for premium television services which could be directly financed by the viewer. But the largest single chunks of this subscription revenue, and still, in the mid-90s, the ones most immediately likely to grow, came from just two genres – sport and feature films. Neither fed much back into the UK programme production industry. Revenue from movie channels flowed to what had predictably turned out to be their overwhelmingly dominant suppliers – the Hollywood studios. Subscription revenue from sports programming fed back into higher wages for the sports stars, and higher profits, and perhaps better facilities, for the increasingly commercially driven sports clubs.

Both of these developments had been foreseen in early official considerations of what were likely in theory to be the consequences of pay-TV (see Chapters 3 and 4). It had been anticipated that pay-TV would start with movies, and that unless there was some form of quota or levy the British film industry was too weak to profit from this. Early reports had also warned that development of pay-TV could lead to a 'siphoning off' of programming from free TV. This was precisely what happened with regard to sport. Murdoch's sports channels massively bid up sports rights and took sporting event after sporting event out of the hands of the 'free' television broadcasters of the duopoly. It was precisely this development that led to 'reserved' sporting events featuring as such a prominent issue in the debate surrounding the 1996 Broadcasting Act.

The rise of subscription funding for television brought with it a significant corollary. Satellite and cable had not simply brought into being a third major type of revenue stream for television in the UK, they were also overwhelmingly dependent on that stream. In its 1996 Annual Report, for example, BSkyB revealed that 84 per cent of its turnover came from subscription and just 11 per cent from advertising. That meant that satellite and cable as yet presented very little direct threat to the traditional revenue stream of commercial terrestrial television. In 1996 cable and satellite advertising revenue leapt by 37 per cent over the previous year. But it still constituted only 8 per cent of total television advertising revenue, compared with 20 per cent for Channel Four and 72 per cent for ITV and GMTV (ITC *Annual Report*, 1996, p. 11). Again, the actual performance in the mid-90s differed markedly from many mid-80s predictions. In 1987 Saatchi and Saatchi had forecast that cable and satellite would be taking 13.4 per cent of television advertising revenue by 1995 (Saatchi and Saatchi, 1987). As events turned out in that year, they took less than half this figure.

So, by the time the Tories left office, the two traditional secure television revenue streams of UK television – licence fee for the BBC and monopoly sale of television advertising for ITV – had become fragile, but still remained intact. In 1997 ITV's advertising revenue was challenged more by the dampened competition presented (post-1990 Broadcasting Act) by Channel Four than by the potentially unfettered competition of satellite and cable. It was this division of television finance into separate and secure revenue streams, each funding a different broadcaster, that formed the financial underpinning of the traditional television duopoly. As of the mid-90s, cable and satellite were only just beginning to threaten it at the edges, because their growth had largely been financed by a new third revenue stream. So, in financial as well as in viewing terms, by May 1997 the British television duopoly was still a force to be reckoned with.

A third aspect of change in UK television between the late 70s and the mid-90s, is the shift in patterns of employment in the television industry. Incomplete, undetailed and sometimes inconsistent statistics make exact comparisons impossible. But certain general trends are clear.

In 1979, as we have seen, employment in UK television was (apart from the, even then, largely casually employed 'talent') confined to permanent employment in the vertically integrated BBC and ITV companies. From then, until the mid-80s, both the ITV companies and the BBC added to their permanently employed payroll. But from the mid-80s the trend reversed, as the old broadcasters cut back their numbers.

The reversal occurred slightly earlier in the BBC. In 1979/80 BBC Home Services (both television and radio) reported an establishment of 23,182 authorised posts. This crept up to a high point of 25,412 in 1985/6, and then started falling (Goodwin, 1991, p. 33). By March 1996 BBC Home Services employed 19,882 staff (BBC Annual Report and Accounts, 1996, p. 46). In ten years the BBC had shed perhaps 5,000 'permanent' jobs in television.

The reversal came perhaps a year later in ITV, but was more dramatic. Numbers employed by the fifteen regional ITV companies, commercial breakfast television and ITN peaked at 16,937 in their financial years ending between July 1987 and June 1988 (Goodwin, 1991, p. 21). By 1993/4 the companies covering these same franchises were down to 9,018 (including subsidiaries, London News Network and TSMS) (Phillips, 1995, p. 21). From a slightly smaller base than the BBC, by 1994 the ITV companies had shed nearly 7,000 jobs. And, with further concentration in the commercial terrestrial television, and the consequent opportunities for reduction in staffing these entailed, the job losses in ITV continued in subsequent years.

So, taken together, the television duopoly shed perhaps 12,000 jobs after the mid-80s. Not all of this was the simple result of the same work being done by fewer people. Other general trends were at work, three of which each made an important contribution to the decline in numbers directly employed in the duopoly. Some of the job losses were the result of the contracting out by both BBC and ITV of 'non-core business' like security and catering. Some were a consequence of the greatly increased use that BBC and ITV made of independent production. In the mid-80s, before the government announced its 25 per cent quota, both the BBC and ITV still made only tiny use of independents. By 1995/6 the BBC estimated that 29 per cent of its television programme output came from independents, while in 1996 33 per cent of ITV hours (excluding sport and repeats) were produced by independent producers (BBC *Annual Report*, 1995/6, p. 65; ITC *Annual Report*, 1996, p. 121). A third chunk of the reduction in staff numbers 'on the books' came from a shift by both sides of the duopoly towards making more use of freelance employment.

Against these reductions in permanent employment in the television duopoly should be set the growth from virtually nothing in 1979 of three other sectors of television employment – the cable and satellite broadcasters, independent television producers and independent television facilities providers. We simply do not know how many people these sectors employed in 1979, but together it can hardly have numbered more than hundreds.

In the mid-90s overall statistics on employment in each of these sectors is still shady. But the following figures suggest how significant they had become.

In 1995, the overwhelmingly dominant player in satellite and cable broadcasting, BSkyB, employed an average of 3,054 people. This was about three times the number of the largest ITV company in the same year. But it should be noted that the great majority (1,884) of these BSkyB employees were in subscriber management (BSkyB *Annual Report*, 1995, p. 10).

With large numbers of often small companies, and no equivalent giants to BSkyB, numbers employed in independent facilities and independent production have always been particularly difficult to pin down. But two surveys suggest how important they had become by the mid-90s. Coopers & Lybrand estimated that in 1995 'independent' (including ones linked to broadcasters) facilities employed 6,500–7,000 staff. Not all of these people spent all their time working on television – they also worked on advertisements, corporate videos, feature films and music videos. But the majority of the work of the whole facilities sector was for broadcast television.

In 1995 Price Waterhouse estimated that the six hundred or so independent television production companies operating in the UK in 1995 together employed 12,000 'person equivalents'. That rather clumsy expression was an attempt to sum up the reality of employment in independent production, where less than a quarter of that 12,000 were 'core' staff of the companies, working for them regardless of particular commissions. The rest were essentially freelances, working for particular companies on particular commissions for months, or, more often, weeks at a time (Price Waterhouse, 1995, pp. 13, 26).

Freelancing had from the start been the norm in independent production. But by the mid-90s it was also becoming significant in most other fields of television employment. A major survey of the core specialised occupations of the UK television, video and film industries, conducted in 1993/4, concluded that of the 28,000 specialised workers in production, technical and post-production areas, 15,000 were working on a freelance or short- (less than one year) contract basis. This figure, of 54 per cent freelance, showed a marked growth in freelancing from the 39 per cent found in a similar survey done in 1989 (Woolf and Holly, 1994, 'Selected Main Points').

So probably the biggest statistical change to the British television industry between 1979 and 1995 occurred in the field of employment. In 1979 practically all of British television employees (again, with the exception of 'talent') were directly employed by the two poles of the duopoly; in 1995 perhaps half of them were employed by cable or satellite broadcasters, independent producers, independent facilities companies or were freelance.

But, even here, the change needs to be put into perspective. About half of the British television workforce in 1995 was still directly employed by the BBC or ITV. And much of the work of the rest of them was still carried out for these two sectors. In 1995, for example, Price Waterhouse found that 52.4 per cent of the income of the independent producers they surveyed came from BBC and ITV as opposed to just 1.5 per cent from cable and satellite (Price Waterhouse, 1995, p. 6). Even in employment terms, in 1995 the duopoly was still by no means dead.

Changes in the structure of employment in television are bound up with changes in the structure of the industry. And here, at various times, the Tories set themselves a number of (not necessarily consistent) goals: to make the industry less vertically integrated; to make the industry more 'competitive' and therefore more 'efficient' in terms of what it delivered to the domestic viewer; and to develop opportunities for the UK industry on the world market. Between the late 70s and the early 90s, how far did the structure of the British television industry make any clear shifts in these directions?

There were clear changes on the degree of vertical integration. In 1979 the industry had been effectively 100 per cent vertically integrated. By 1997 the growth of the independent production sector had ensured a significant erosion of that situation. One new major broadcaster (Channel Four) either acquired or commissioned from independent producers virtually all of its programming. The BBC, as we have seen, got 29 per cent of its commissioned programmes from independents; for ITV this figure was 33 per cent. The great majority of cable and satellite programme spending was on acquisitions. So, eighteen years on, major inroads had been made in splitting away programme-making from broadcasting in what had started as a totally vertically integrated industry.

It should not, however, be assumed that this meant the break-up of the entire vertically integrated structure. To make what by now is a familiar point, the figures for independent production we have given still leave 71 per cent of the BBC's commissioned programmes, and 67 per cent of ITV's, being made in-house. Equally important, at the very same time as the 25 per cent independent quota became firmly established, there were signs of a move back to vertical integration between production and broadcasting in commercial television. This began with the 1991 franchise race when a number of larger independent producers took stakes in consortia bidding for ITV licences. It developed in subsequent years, as large media companies like Carlton and Pearson, with a stake in broadcasters, took over several of the larger independents. So, for example, by 1996, Pearson owned major independent producers like Thames and Grundy, but was also a major partner in the soon-to-be-broadcast Channel 5.

The same went for cable and satellite broadcasters. Most of their programming was acquired, but the sources of acquisition were very often controlled by the same international media companies which owned the channels. Indeed, ownership of a satellite channel, as a vehicle through which to recycle a programme-makers' own programme library, had, in the mid-90s, become the standard pattern for satellite and cable channels in Britain. It would, therefore, be unwise to conclude that the partial diminution of vertical integration in British television that had occurred by the mid-90s will necessarily continue in future years.

Changes in the degree of competition in the industry are even less susceptible to statistical measure. In 1979 British television had essentially not been organised on a competitive basis – aside from a not unimportant competition for audiences (and prestige) between the BBC and ITV. By the mid-90s a number of institutional frameworks for increasing competition were in operation: there was the internal market and market-testing of Producer Choice in the BBC; the ITV Network Centre with its conscious divorce between ITV companies as producers and as broadcasters, which ensured that network production could no longer be simply carved up between the 'big five' as it had been in 1979; Channel Four competed with ITV for the sale of advertising, albeit within important limits; independent producers competed to pitch programmes to the terrestrial broadcasters; and satellite and cable competed with the terrestrial broadcasters, more for certain types of programming than for advertising. We have, however, already seen the limits, in terms of competition, of some of these new structures.

Three other points need to be added about the competitive environment of British television in the mid-90s. First, whatever the limits of the institutional changes, there can be little doubt that by the mid-90s the culture of commercial competition permeated the industry to a qualitatively higher degree than it had in the late 70s. Second, there was no necessary overall equation in the domestic market between competitiveness and 'efficiency' in terms of the domestic viewer getting more programmes for less cost. The relative efficiency of independent, as opposed to in-house, production, in either the BBC or ITV, remained unproven during this period. And one of the consequences of increased competition in television, particularly from the satellite broadcasters, was a several-fold increase in the price of certain important programme inputs, particularly sports rights and talent. So here there was a clear increase in broadcasting costs that was directly attributable to competition. Third, though overall competition in television may have increased, cable and satellite broadcasting in Britain in the mid-90s was, contrary to many earlier expectations, dominated by one company, BSkyB, under the control of one international media giant, Rupert Murdoch's News Corporation. That raised quite new issues about competition in television from those that the Tories had earlier attempted to address. These showed up in concerns as varied as programme pricing to cable companies and control of conditional-access systems.

The last aspect of our snapshot of British television in the mid-90s is the position of the British industry in the world market. In 1979 British television had been almost wholly contained in the domestic market, with one exception. Britain was in 1979 the largest exporter of television programming after the USA. From that base, growth in British television's place in the world market was not dramatic. ITV took no part in the growth of commercial television in Europe in the early 80s or, indeed, thereafter. Two ITV companies, TVS and Thames, did acquire important US producers in the late 80s and early 90s, but achieved disappointing results with them, and soon sold out. The exercise has not been repeated. Cable and satellite failed to fulfil the hopes expressed for them for the British hardware and programme industries. Indeed, events turned out quite the reverse.

So by the mid-90s British television's position in the world market was not qualitatively different from what it had been in the late 70s. It sold rather more of its originally home-commissioned programmes overseas. But Britain still remained a net importer of television programming – in 1995 UK television programme exports were worth $394 million, while imports cost $644 million (*Screen Digest*, April 1997, p. 84). And both imports and exports were still dwarfed in money terms by domestic expenditure on domestically consumed programming. In the mid-90s Britain's big independent producers rarely produced commissions for foreign broadcasters (the one major exception, Grundy, was significantly an Australian producer whose international production activities were established well before it was acquired by Pearson). Britain's big domestic terrestrial broadcasters, most notably the BBC, had begun to develop international cable and satellite outlets, but, as of 1997, with little or no net return.

So, by the time the Tories left office, the often heralded transformation of British television from a high-quality domestic provider into a significant player in a significant world market was still an aspiration rather than an already achieved reality.

A balance sheet of British television in the mid-90s has, therefore, to record both significant change from the late 70s and significant continuity. There were real and substantial changes: the once all-embracing duopoly now sat side by side with important new broadcasters and important new producers; a third major revenue stream – subscription – had been created; a new culture of economic competition existed throughout the industry, supported by some important new institutions; and a new pattern of employment had developed. But alongside these changes, battered but by no means totally bowed, the old duopoly still survived.

# Intentions and Outcomes in Tory Television Policy

How much were these changes in the British television industry between 1979 and 1997 direct consequences of Tory policy during that same period? Or how much were they the products of other factors? And, inasmuch as the changes were the consequences of Tory policies, how much were they *intended* consequences of those policies? To ask these questions is to return to the general debate about the nature of 'Thatcherism' that we raised in the introduction to this book. We suggested that behind the apparently sharp polarities of this debate there lay a spectrum of possibilities, ranging from coherent projects to opportunistic reaction to events, where just the two extreme poles of a complete blueprint and complete opportunism were ruled out.

Our survey of Tory television policy from 1979 to 1997 prompts one crucial observation about where television lay on this spectrum. In this area, at least, there was quite simply no over-arching 'Thatcherite project' for institutional reform. There was no single, even remotely coherent plan of action which guided Tory policy from the beginning of Margaret Thatcher's administration to the end of John Major's. Quite the opposite. Over these eighteen years Tory television policy lurched from one 'project' of reform to another.

In opposition, before 1979, the Tories had effectively accepted the existing television duopoly and made their own pragmatic response to the 70s critics and the Annan Report. They had shown little interest in the new broadcasting technologies. During Margaret Thatcher's first term, between 1979 and 1983, the Tories stuck firmly to the first two of these perspectives. They made no attempt to change either the BBC or ITV, and they carried through their previous commitment to establish a fourth terrestrial channel, along the lines they had mapped out in opposition. That channel did to a considerable extent succeed in fulfilling the aspirations of the Annan Report. There was, however, during those first four years of government, a sharp break from pre-1979 Tory thinking on new broadcasting technologies. Between 1979 and 1983 these were taken very seriously, and the government made ambitious plans for both cable and satellite television. These plans linked the new television distribution technologies both to the broader 'information revolution' and to industrial policy – the first time in Britain that industrial policy had played an important part in policy on television.

After 1983 the Tories radically changed course, on both the main structures of terrestrial television and, in practice, the new distribution technologies. Between roughly 1984 and 1990, far from accepting the terrestrial television duopoly, the government focused its attentions precisely on trying to significantly reform it. At the same time, the ambitious plans for cable and satellite foundered, and were left either to stagnate or to face the (unanticipated) play of market forces. The more general 'information revolution' effectively disappeared from the cutting-edge of government television policy during this period.

Within this second phase of Tory television policy there was a further, but equally important, lurch. The post-1983 Tory endeavour to reform the terrestrial television duopoly started quite explicitly with the BBC. ITV was not a significant issue in government thinking before the Peacock Committee got down to business. It was only after the Committee had rejected Margaret Thatcher's preferred option of putting advertising on the BBC, and made its more general recommendations, that the Tories shifted their attention away from the BBC and towards the 'commercial' side of terrestrial broadcasting. The result was the 1988 Broadcasting White Paper and the 1990 Broadcasting Act.

As we have seen, the Tories' attempts to fundamentally reform 'commercial' terrestrial television between 1988 and 1990 were not well received, and as a result were considerably modified in both letter and, even more, substance.

So the Tories emerged distinctly bruised from their efforts to reform the 'commercial' side of the duopoly. Douglas Hurd, who, as Home Secretary, had been the Cabinet Minister who unveiled the 1988 White Paper, which formed the blueprint for the reform, later observed with dry understatement that the 1990 Broadcasting Act was one of the 'least successful' of Margaret Thatcher's reforms (*Spectator*, 6 November 1993). The consequence of the poor reception of the 1990 Act was yet another lurch in policy when the Tories returned to the question of the future of the BBC after the 1992 election. As we have seen, during the process of BBC charter renewal there was no attempt to put the Corporation on a fundamentally different regulatory or financial footing. Instead, the government encouraged the BBC to maintain its pre-eminent place in the British broadcasting system, subject to two (not unimportant) conditions. The Corporation was required to be seen to be undertaking substantial internal restructuring in the interests of efficiency, and it was also encouraged to be a significant national player on the world television market.

Finally, from about 1994, Tory television policy lurched yet again. For most of the previous decade it had focused on a narrow conception of broadcasting, centred above all on the main terrestrial channels and largely unconnected with the broader issues of the 'information revolution'. After 1994 the supposed 'information revolution' returned to the centre of Tory television policy.

One indicator of this series of lurches in policy was that some of the priorities of one period were undone in a later one. So, for example, Tory satellite and cable policy in the early years was centred on the promotion of 'national' industry. In later years the government rationale for cable and satellite policy was quite different – the promotion of 'inward investment'. To take another example, the 1990 Broadcasting Act codified strict restrictions on the concentration of television ownership and on cross-ownership. Yet scarcely had these restrictions been put in place than the Tories began systematically to undo them.

What caused these lurches in television policy? One important factor was undoubtedly the more general changes in the government approach to policy which took place during those eighteen years. Andrew Gamble identifies three phases of the Thatcher years: 'Thatcherism mark I, 1979–83; Thatcherism mark II, 1983–87; Thatcherism mark III, 1987–90' (Gamble, 1994, p. 106). To these we can add a fourth – the period of John Major's premiership, 1990–7.

Some of the major shifts in specifically television policy can be mapped onto this more general period of the Thatcher/Major years. The government's acceptance of the terrestrial duopoly before 1983 coincided with the continued influence of Tory 'wets' in Thatcher's first administration. Specifically, it coincided with the influential 'wet' (and notably pro-public service broadcasting) William Whitelaw's period as Home Secretary, and the Cabinet Minister with responsibility for television. The move to reform the duopoly after 1983 can therefore be seen as a particular instance of the growing 'radicalisation' of the Thatcher administration, which Gamble (1994, p. 130) and others have identified, and of the marginalisation of the 'wets' in the Cabinet after her first term.

Similarly, the shift away from further attempts at structural reform of the terrestrial duopoly after 1990 was not simply a result of the poor reception of the 1988 White Paper and the 1990 Act. It also coincided with Thatcher's fall from the premiership and its aftermath. One important factor in Thatcher's forced exit was the unpopularity of some of the more 'radical' of her third-term policies, most notably the poll tax. Given that background, her successor's administration was likely to be initially generally more cautious and more 'consolidationist'. This was precisely what happened with television, in both the implementation of the 1990 Act and in the conduct of BBC charter renewal.

However, the shifts in Tory television policy over these eighteen years were not simply the reflection of more general shifts in government policy. They were also, to a significant extent, the result of particular features of the industry itself and of events within it. Two aspects of this are worth noting.

First, a number of developments in the politics of the industry prompted opportunistic reactions by the government. One notable example was the conclusions of the Peacock Committee. The Committee was set up with the specific intention of supporting advertising on the BBC. When it reported against this, but also added a number of important recommendations about the organisation of commercial terrestrial television, the government responded by radically changing course. It shelved its attempt to enforce fundamental changes in the BBC's finances, and, in place of this, adopted some of the Committee's proposals on the reform of ITV. So this particular shift in direction came not out of the government's general politics, but out of a pragmatic response to very specific developments within the politics of the television industry. Had the Peacock Committee done as the government, or at least Margaret Thatcher, intended, and endorsed advertising on the BBC, then the Tories would almost certainly have pushed that through – with major consequences for subsequent television policy – and might never have embarked on the attempted reform of ITV.

Second, several major developments occurred in the television industry which, at the very least, were not the original intentions or expectations of previous government policy. Tory television policy then opportunistically adapted itself to these developments, *post hoc.* Satellite policy is an important example of this. Tory policy in the early 80s had been directed towards fostering a nationally based satellite television system. A foreign-based, but UK-directed, satellite service was seen as a potential threat to this. However, when such a service started, in the form of Sky and then BSkyB, the government both encouraged it (by turning a blind eye to its regulatory infringements) and then reformulated the rationale of its satellite policy as being designed precisely to foster such a development.

Another example of an opportunistic response to developments within the industry was evident in the Tories' approach to independent production. The Tories originally brought the independent production sector into existence for 'cultural' rather than economic reasons, as part of the creation of Channel Four, following on from the lead given by Annan and the 70s critics. It was only after the independent production sector was established, and began to formulate its own demands for expansion, that the government seized on these as a way of fostering competition and efficiency within the television system as a whole.

So, in its specific institutional proposals, Tory television policy over its eighteen years in office was characterised by both major zigzags and a good deal of opportunistic reaction to events. But there was, nevertheless, one underlying theme to it, a feature that Andrew Gamble identifies as one of the 'three overriding objectives' of Thatcherism: 'reviv(ing) market liberalism as the dominant public philosophy' (Gamble, 1994, p. 4). Throughout all the zigzags and opportunism, between 1979 and 1997 Tory television policy did maintain one, and only one, consistent thrust – to make television more a matter of the marketplace, and less a matter of public service. The early emphasis on the possible 'industrial benefits' of cable and satellite to be promoted by private capital; the attempt to put advertising on the BBC; the post-Peacock attempt to reform ITV; the restructuring of the BBC, with Producer Choice and 'competing worldwide'; and the post-1994 concerns with the 'digital revolution' – all these shared the unifying drive of 'the market' as against 'public service'.

This underlying theme of 'marketisation' is not one specific to television policy. In practically all aspects of life the replacement of 'public service' by the 'disciplines of the market' was a key feature of government rhetoric during the whole of the Thatcher and the Major years. It was also one of the central features of real economic, social and cultural change during this period.

Some of the major changes that took place in British television during these eighteen years were the result, not of a specific television policy by the Tories, but of their more general policies to 'revive market liberalism as the dominant public philosophy'. One example of this was the weakening of vertical integration in the television industry. Independent production and franchise auctions no doubt played a significant part in this. But the promotion of 'competitive tendering' and 'market-testing' were a general feature of Tory policy in the 80s and 90s. Another example of general policy having its effects on television is the decline of trade union influence in the television industry. Again, some specifically television initiatives, particularly the encouragement of independent production and (both the prospect and the reality of) the ITV franchise auction undoubtedly played a significant role in this weakening of trade unionism in the industry. But the massive decline of union power within the television industry was as much, if not more, the result of general Tory anti-union policy. General measures on picketing and secondary action contributed to decisive union defeats in the television industry (witness the events at TV-am).[1]

So the replacement of the 'public service' by the 'market' ethos in television was real enough, but it was not specific to television. It was the result, in approximately equal measures, of both specifically television policy and Tory policy in general. (The question of how much it was also the result of deeper economic, social and technological forces we will address in the next section of this chapter.)

Tory television policy from 1979 to 1997 therefore displayed two central but apparently contradictory features – zigzags and opportunism in specifics, alongside a continual drive towards 'marketisation' in practical consequence. How are we to explain this contradiction?

Part of the explanation is that 'Thatcherism' was not simply about the market. It was also about state control. As the title of Gamble's book neatly expresses it, Thatcherism was for 'The Free Economy *and* the Strong State'. From Reith onwards, one central element of the British public service broadcasting tradition has been about state-directed social control over morals, culture and politics. One might expect Tories, and particularly Thatcherite Tories, to have a good deal of sympathy for this element in the public service broadcasting tradition, and for it to play a perhaps equal part to 'fostering the market' in their television policy.

There was plenty of room for these two strands of policy to come into conflict. The government's rejection of the free-market Peacock Committee's desire to end censorious controls is a particularly notable example. So how important was this conflict between the desire for a free market in television and the equally deeply felt desire for television to act as an instrument of state-directed moral education? Was this contradiction the prime cause of the policy zigzags we have identified?

At the formal level, there was, from the beginning of the Thatcher administration to the end of Major's, a good deal of state paternalism mixed in with the free-market liberalism of Tory television policy. The Conservative government early on established the Broadcasting Complaints Commission. Under the influence of the 'taste and decency' lobby it later added to this the Broadcasting Standards Council. The 1988 White Paper stressed the continuation and strengthening of 'consumer protection' regulation of all television services. The government banned foreign-based satellite pornography channels and, particularly in its later years, regularly berated the industry over violence. On top of this, as we have seen, the government exerted particular pressure on the political tone of the BBC.

This censorious strain in Tory television policy was not unimportant, but its effects should not be exaggerated. During the Thatcher and Major years, there was no significant rolling back of the liberal 60s and 70s in the general tone of what appeared on British television. Portrayals of sex and sexuality on television were, if anything, more, not less, uninhibited in the mid-90s than they had been in the late 70s. The bounds of 'taste and decency' permitted on British television screens widened over these years, despite the Tories' overt efforts. And, not withstanding the government's more covert efforts to make political coverage 'safer', anti-government and anti-Establishment investigative journalism continued to enjoy a prominent position in British television – a position, many would argue, more prominent than it had in the British press.

The state paternalist strand in Tory television policy was not only relatively ineffective it also rarely clashed with the practical results of freeing up the market. The new commercial or commercialised television which Tory policy enabled in the UK was hardly a hotbed of pornography or political subversion. So the lurches in Tory television policy were not primarily the result of the conflict between the two Conservative goals of reviving market liberalism and promoting moral paternalism. They resulted, rather, from problems inherent in the one goal of reviving market liberalism. And they were exacerbated by some of the specific features of the established UK television system. Our survey points to three basic problems.

The first was the strength, adaptability and interdependence of the institutions of the UK television duopoly which the Tories inherited. Those institutions produced, and continued to produce, throughout this period, large quantities of massively popular programming. That meant, as we noted in our introduction, little active direct popular political pressure for change. It also limited the gaps which new commercial players could exploit. In addition, the range and mix of programming produced by the established television institutions commanded, and continued to command, widespread support among the élite circles within which debate on television policy largely took place. Most Tory efforts at pro-market reform of the television system thus encountered a powerful counter-thrust of 'if it ain't broke, don't fix it'. In this respect the debate on television policy in the UK during the 80s and 90s stands in contrast to that in many other European countries where the established television systems were both weaker and more brittle.

The established regulatory bodies of the British television system also showed considerable strength and adaptability during the Tory years. Indeed, on a number of occasions it was they, rather than the government, who were effectively making policy, albeit within formal parameters laid down by government. So, in the early 80s, the IBA filled in the structural details of the new Channel Four. The 1990 Broadcasting Act formally replaced the IBA with the ITC, but much of the approach, authority and personnel of the old IBA survived into the new commission. As we have seen, from the end of 1990 onwards it was the ITC which effectively made policy on the new commercial terrestrial television, and in doing so drew much of the sting from the Tories' efforts to increase the importance of the market, as against public service, in this side of the system.

The management of the BBC is a rather different case, but here too we can note important elements of persistence, adaptability and policy initiative. The difference with the IBA/ITC is that, as we described in Chapter 9, the government instituted a new regime in the BBC which effectively operated in the pro-market direction. So, much of the authority and adaptability of the BBC central management was, from the mid-80s onwards, deployed to further the market mechanisms in television generally favoured by the Tories. When the BBC actually came to make policy, as it increasingly did in the 90s, with initiatives like Producer Choice and BBC Worldwide (which were BBC initiatives, not direct government suggestions), these were along lines in keeping with the Tories' pro-market drive.

But there was an important limit to this. However much the BBC's management might endorse and promote aspects of the market after 1986, the Corporation was still firmly involved in adaption for its own institutional survival. And, during the whole of this period, that institutional survival still meant survival as a public corporation, with substantial public funding. In adapting to protect its institutional base, the BBC was considerably more successful than many of its Continental cousins, not least because it started from an altogether more resilient base.

Lastly, the main institutions of British television which the Tories endeavoured to change were highly interdependent. The basic division of revenue streams into two, each of which underpinned one side of the system, was a formula supported by both sides. To upset it by privatising or putting advertising on the BBC was to risk destabilising not merely programming but also the business activities of the established commercial operators. Unlike the situation in most of Europe in the late 70s, in the UK, powerful commercial interests were already in television, co-existing quite happily with public service, and wary of new commercial rivals.

There were, it is true, significant outsiders in the UK who wanted to get into television and supported market liberalism in order to do so. Notable among these were the independent producers, Carlton and Murdoch. All of these were at various times important allies of Tory television policy. But they did not constitute a unified and all-encompassing commercial block united to destroy the public service system so as to gain their own commercial place. The established ITV companies already occupied that place, while the independent producers' pro-market enthusiasm was tempered by their continued desire to support public funding (a growing part of which would flow to them).

These strengths of the established British television system were an important element in the twists and turns of Tory television policy. Each attempt the Tories made to fundamentally change the system encountered powerful institutional resistance – a resistance which often forced the Tories to change course and try another approach. Two other factors reinforced this strength of the established television system to exacerbate the swings in Tory television policy.

First, the general goal of reviving market liberalism concealed within it several different and often conflicting policy goals. There were different reasons why one could favour the market, and fundamental policy dilemmas still remained whichever course was chosen. On the one hand, the market could be regarded as the most efficient means of delivering a particular provision which was itself publicly set and funded. This was the rationale for compulsory competitive tendering in local government and the internal market in the health service. Here, the Tories did not, on the face of it, deny the need for publicly determined (and often still publicly funded) public service. What they argued for was that this publicly determined service was most efficiently provided for by the use of market mechanisms. The government essentially took the same approach to ITV in the 1988 White Paper and the 1990 Broadcasting Act, and to the BBC in the first half of the 90s. Whatever further consequences might be feared or hoped for from them, reform of ITV and Producer Choice in the BBC were promoted primarily as attempts to increase the efficiency of publicly determined provision, by means of the market, not as attempts to do away with the publicly determined provision altogether.

But market liberalism could also involve the replacement of public service goals by the operation of the market. The Tories' promotion of private health insurance might be seen as an example of this. An aspect of need which had previously required public provision could now be provided directly by the market. Here, public service was not simply better provided by the use of market mechanisms, it was (wholly or partly) *replaced* by the market. Some important aspects of Tory television policy involved precisely this distinctly stronger version of promoting market liberalism. So, for example, Tory cable and satellite policy was centrally concerned not with the more efficient provision of a public service, but with the fostering of industry *per se*. Television no doubt had its particular features, as had any other industry, but, at least so far as the new distribution technologies were concerned, there was no longer perceived to be a public service which needed to be provided. Instead, policy could proceed along 'industrial' lines.

There was therefore a basic tension in Tory television policy, between market liberalism as a new and more efficient means of providing public service and market liberalism as a replacement for public service. In both the ITV reforms and the new BBC, they opted for the former. On cable and satellite, the Tories opted for the latter. Treating cable and satellite just like any other industry was itself a radical break from the pre-Thatcher tradition of British television policy. But it still left major dilemmas, both general and specific to the industry, about what the goals of this industrial policy should be.

One such dilemma was whether policy should be directed towards promoting domestically owned industry, exporting and investing abroad, or whether it should be aimed at the promotion of inward investment. We have already noted the U-turn that the Tories performed on this in respect of cable and satellite. It was a reversal of industrial policy that was paralleled in much of manufacturing industry.

But there were also industrial policy dilemmas that were more specific to the television industry. One was the problematic relationship of television programming or 'software' to television 'hardware'. Equally problematic was the relationship of television broadcasting to the more general information industry. Was television being promoted as an industry in its own right (with sales of programming or the export of broadcasting expertise as the primary goal)? Was it being promoted primarily in the expectation that it would in turn promote the electronic hardware industry? Or was it being promoted as a lever to foster the 'information revolution'? As we have seen, Tory television policy displayed changing and uncertain answers to these questions.

Lastly, there was the problematic relationship of the organisation of the domestic television industry to its position in the world market. Viewed from a domestic perspective, market liberalism suggested the promotion of internal competition and the break-up of vertical integration. But the successful performance of domestic champions on the world market required large vertically integrated players relatively untrammelled by domestic competitive restrictions. Tory policy on ITV, the BBC and on cable television shifted uncomfortably and uncertainly between these objectives.

If the very goal of market liberalism in television contained fundamental contradictions, so too did the overall means of achieving it. There were different possible strategies available that market liberals could use to unravel the established public service system. In Chapter 6 we noted two implicitly different approaches contained in the publications of the free-market think-tanks which preceded the establishment of the Peacock Committee. One advocated privatising and/or putting advertising on the BBC, another emphasised the possibilities of direct consumer payment for television. A further possibility might have been to start with the more or less complete deregulation of ITV. The Peacock Committee itself came up with yet another strategy.

These approaches were not fundamentally different in their long-term aim – a largely consumer and advertising-funded, multi-channel television market, with vestigial elements of public provision. But they each involved very different consequences and problems in the short and medium term. Tory television policy adopted none of them wholeheartedly. Instead, the government flirted with one and then moved on to another.

# Technology, the market and the future

The picture of Tory television policy we have painted is that of, on the one hand, a series of zigzags, reversals and unanticipated consequences, and on the other hand, a number of important (if often exaggerated) long-term changes in the UK television industry over the eighteen years of Tory office. This combination might tempt one to conclude that the changes in the industry are not so much the consequence of Tory policy, but rather the inevitable result of some more fundamental processes, in which case it mattered little what policy initiatives the Tories pursued on television – things would have turned out much the same anyway.

Such a view takes us firmly back to the argument of the first chapter of this book. Our case there was that each of the supposedly fundamental processes going on behind changes in the television industry in the 80s and 90s – social and cultural, economic and technological – was rather less able to directly produce changes in the pre-existing structures of television than is often supposed. From this we tentatively concluded that government policy was the key to determining what changes actually happened.

To see whether that case stands up in relation to the record of Tory television policy and the changes in the industry we have outlined in the rest of this book, we need to pose a series of historical 'what ifs'. What if this or that policy had been otherwise? Would the changes in the industry have been that much different?

We can crudely, but usefully, distinguish two types of 'what ifs'. The first type would include the possible alternative policies which the Tories might have pursued at particular times within the overall political parameters covered by their administration. The second would include possible alternative policies which were disallowed by the underlying ethos of the administration. The first group includes a multitude of intriguing possibilities. It will be sufficient for our general argument – that government policy was the decisive factor – to briefly examine just five of the most important of these. We will take them in roughly chronological order.

Tory television policy after 1979 began by establishing the fourth terrestrial channel as an 'alternative' channel, advertising-funded but protected from competition. This was not the only option open to the government. Both in terms of the previous debate on the fourth channel and the subsequent ethos of the administration, there were obvious alternative scenarios. The fourth channel could have been established as 'ITV 2', a strictly commercial channel, either controlled by, or in competition with, ITV. Either possibility, particularly the first, would have had major consequences for subsequent developments. Both options would have involved considerably more 'lowest common denominator' and less 'alternative' programming. They might also have involved a different type of independent production sector, or no such sector at all. The fourth channel could also have been given over to commercial pay-TV (like Canal-plus in France, established at much the same time as Channel Four). There is little reason to believe that such an operation would not have been commercially successful. Had it been tried, and had it been successful, then Rupert Murdoch's subsequent satellite-based domination of the UK pay-TV market would have, at the least, been altogether more problematic. The fourth channel that was established – Channel Four – has been widely seen as important, innovative and successful. Its distinctive characteristics, which have gained it these plaudits, were, however, the result of government action, not technological or economic inevitability. The Tories could have acted otherwise – with very different results.

Channel Four might, of course, be considered something of an exception so far as an overall assessment of Tory television policy is concerned. It was, after all, the last terrestrial channel to be allocated before cable and satellite channels had come on the scene. Tory policy on cable and satellite therefore provides a more general test of how much government policy actually counted.

In the early 80s the Tories tried – and, as events turned out, failed – to launch a national DBS system, initially run by the BBC, and a national cable television network as a precursor to a range of interactive services. But, suppose the Tories had tried slightly harder to implement these goals. Suppose, in particular, that they had been willing to inject some public money into these declared projects or to promote BT as the monopoly provider of cable television. On the satellite side that would almost certainly have resulted in the BBC launching a national DBS service, as NHK did in Japan. Of course a successful DBS launch by the BBC would not have guaranteed that the BBC would have been able to maintain its initial advantage in the satellite field. Foreign-based competitors would have eventually emerged. But given what we now know about the considerable advantages accruing to the pioneers in the multi-channel field, we can say with some confidence that a successful BBC DBS launch would have meant that Murdoch's Sky and BSkyB would have faced a far less easy ride to dominance in the UK multi-channel market.

Cable is a more problematic issue. It might be argued, with some justice, that the Tory government's early hopes for cable were, quite simply, illusory: that given the amount of investment involved, and the lack of immediate consumer interest in interactive services, nothing the Tories could have done would have achieved any substantially different result from what in fact happened. But this is to ignore the considerably greater pace of broadband cabling achieved in the same period in other European countries, most notably Germany. Perhaps a different government policy in the early 80s – for instance one which prioritised BT in cabling – would have achieved more impressive results. If it had, then a number of other things would have followed – again less room for Murdoch, but also more and earlier opportunities for interactive services.

In the second half of the 80s the Tories concentrated their attention on reform of the terrestrial television duopoly. Here again there is plenty of room for 'what ifs'. Supposing, for instance, the Peacock Committee had proved more responsive to Margaret Thatcher's wishes and had supported advertising in the BBC. The government would then have almost certainly implemented its recommendations in that regard. And if it had done so, there can be little doubt that, ten years on, the BBC would have been a very different institution from what it in fact turned out to be in the mid-90s – almost certainly, far more like its weaker, advertising-dependent European cousins.

The Tories' subsequent turn towards reforming the commercial side of the duopoly raises similar questions. Suppose, as they apparently at least half desired in the 1988 White Paper, the Tories had really deregulated UK commercial television, removing from it most of the positive programme requirements, and from its regulators their discretion to enforce substantial requirements. The consequences might not have been as dire as some of the more alarmist critics predicted, but they would have been real enough. If deregulation had been pursued to such an extent, both ITV and Channel Four would have been altogether more fundamentally changed by the 1991 franchise auction.

We could continue. But even from the limited number of key policy decisions we have just examined, one conclusion is inescapable. *Government policy counted.* Different policies would have produced substantially different outcomes. UK television in 1997 was by no means a simple result of technological or economic inevitability. For good or ill, its actual shape in that year was to a very large extent the result of the vagaries of Tory policy over the previous eighteen years.

As we have already remarked, these vagaries of policy occurred within certain overall political parameters which remained fixed throughout the Thatcher and Major administrations. Perhaps the most powerful of these, and certainly the most consistently adhered to, was that no substantial extra public funding should be devoted to broadcasting. This principle was in keeping with the more general politics of the Thatcher and Major administrations. But this does not mean that it was in any way technologically determined. There was nothing intrinsic to the new technologies of television distribution that required they only be utilised for commercial purposes. True, satellite delivery would eventually have led to some form of foreign-based commercial television competition. But had extra public funding created attractive extra public channels early on, then such competition would have been altogether more marginal. So in this bigger sense, too, Tory policy decisively shaped the form of British television in 1997.

But in this bigger sense it also did something more. 'No extra public spending' is perhaps the central governing policy principle which the New Labour administration of Tony Blair has openly inherited from its Tory predecessors. And, like the Tories, New Labour sees this general principle as an automatic constraint on broadcasting policy. So, to ask the question 'what if' broadcasting policy had not been governed by this overriding principle is not just to pose historical questions about the development of UK television in the eighteen years between 1979 and 1997. It is also to pose some crucial questions about the future development of UK television in the years that follow.

## Note

1. This decline was already well under way even before the passage and implementation of the 1990 Broadcasting Act. In 1987 Margaret Thatcher accused the television industry of being the 'last bastion of restrictive practices' (Davidson, 1992, p. 10). But when these supposed 'restrictive practices' were subsequently referred to the Monopolies and Mergers Commission, the MMC concluded that:

   'changes in employment and working practices were very evident during the course of our inquiry, so much so that we were conscious, as was put to us, that we were "shooting at a moving target" ...

   'In areas of work involving ACTT, BETA and EEPTU, we found either that reference [restrictive] practices did not exist at 31 December 1988, or ... could be realistically expected to disappear as a result of current or intended negotiations, or management decisions.' (MMC, 1989, p. 1)

# Further Reading

The starting point for post-1979 television policy in the UK is the public service television duopoly which the Tories inherited and the framework of policy debate that went with it. These are best approached through the reports of the last two major inquiries on broadcasting which were held before Margaret Thatcher took office. The first of these, chaired by Sir Harry Pilkington, reported in 1962 and effectively established the public service duopoly; the second, chaired by Lord Annan, reported in 1977 and described the duopoly at its high point (Pilkington, 1962; Annan, 1977). Detailed institutional histories of ITV and BBC in the years preceding the Thatcher administration can be found respectively in Potter (1989, 1990) and Briggs (1995), although Briggs only takes the story to 1974. Useful, if partial, accounts of the '70s critics' of the duopoly can be found in Annan (1977) and Lambert (1982). Some background detail on pre-1979 approaches to one of the new broadcasting technologies (cable) is contained in Hollins (1984).

The background to the foundation of Channel Four is chronicled in Lambert (1982). Early Tory approaches to satellite and cable respectively are outlined in two government reports, Home Office (1981) and ITAP (1982). With the benefit of hindsight, both reports repay close reading. The ramifications of the ITAP report on cable for both television and telecommunications, as seen by the government at the time, are amplified in two further reports: Hunt (1982) and Home Office and Department of Industry (1983).

Important independent early-80s free-market views on television can be found in Veljanovski and Bishop (1983) and Adam Smith Institute (1984). But, in many respects the centrepiece of free-market thinking on television during these years, and the fulcrum around which much of Tory television policy revolved, is the Peacock Report (1986). Again, with hindsight, it repays detailed reading.

The Tory government's considered response to Peacock and its blueprint for the reform of the advertising-funded sector of television are crisply, if not entirely precisely, outlined in the 1988 White Paper, *Broadcasting in the 90s: Competition, Choice and Quality* (Home Office, 1988). Contemporary reactions to the 1988 White Paper are recorded in Stevenson and Smedley (1989). Two useful critical accounts of Tory television policy in the 80s, from a viewpoint that closely reflects this book, are Hood and O'Leary (1990) and O'Malley (1994).

The 1991 ITV franchise race is journalistically, but ably, described in Davidson (1992). One crucial element in the race, the ITC's *Invitations to Apply* (1991a and b), are well worth detailed consideration.

The Tories early-90s approach to the BBC is outlined in its Green and White Papers on *The Future of the BBC* (DNH, 1992, 1994), while contemporary reactions to government policy on the BBC are recorded in Goodwin and Stevenson (1994). The BBC's own strategy for the future at the time is set out in *Extending Choice* (BBC, 1992). A useful account of developments in the BBC between the Peacock Report and the 1994 White Paper can be found in Barnett and Curry (1994).

Discussion on broadcasting and telecommunications policy and the information superhighway can be found in HoC (1994). The government's response to this discussion is set out in DTI (1994). Government thinking, in the latter stages of the Major administration, on two other problems raised for television by the digital revolution is set out in two 1995 White Papers – *Media Ownership* and *Digital Broadcasting* (DNH, 1995a and b). The BBC's own strategy for the digital revolution is advanced in BBC (1996).

# Works Cited

Achille, Yves and Miege, Bernard, 'The Limits to the Adaption Strategies of European Public Service Television', *Media, Culture and Society* vol. 16, pp. 31–46, 1994.

Adam Smith Institute, *Communications Policy* (Omega Report) (London: Adam Smith Institute, 1984).

AGB, *The AGB Television Yearbook 1996* (produced in association with BARB), 2 vols. (London: Taylor Nelson AGB Publications, 1996).

AGB, *The AGB Cable and Satellite Yearbook 1996* (produced in association with BARB) (London: Taylor Nelson AGB Publications, 1996).

Altman, Wilfred, Thomas, Denis and Sawers, David, *TV: From Monopoly to Competition – and Back?* (London: Institute of Economic Affairs, 1962).

Annan, Lord (Chair), *Report of the Committee on The Future of Broadcasting* (London: HMSO, Cmnd. 6753, 1977).

Armstrong, Philip, Glyn, Andrew and Harrison, John, *Capitalism Since World War II* (London: Fontana, 1984).

Arthur Anderson Consulting, *UK Media Concentration* (Report prepared for News International plc., 1994).

Bangemann, Martin et al, *Europe and the Global Information Society: Recommendations to the European Council* (Brussels: European Council, 1994).

BARB (Broadcasters' Audience Research Board), *Establishment Survey of TV Homes: ITV and Channel Four Area Report June 1996 Volume 1* (London: BARB, 1996).

Barnett, Steven and Curry, Andrew, *The Battle for the BBC* (London: Aurum Press, 1994).

BBC, *Extending Choice: The BBC's Role in the New Broadcasting Age* (London: BBC, 1992).

BBC, *People and Programmes: BBC Radio and Television for an Age of Choice* (London: BBC, 1995).

BBC, *Extending Choice in the Digital Age* (London: BBC, 1996).

Birt, John, *A Glorious Future: Quality Broadcasting in the Digital Age* (James MacTaggart Memorial Lecture 1996) (London: BBC Press Service, 1996).

Blair, Tony, *New Britain: My Vision of a Young Country* (London: Fourth Estate, 1996).

Blumler, Jay, 'The New Television Marketplace: Imperatives, Implications, Issues', in James Curran and Michael Gurevitch (eds), *Mass, Media and Society*, first edition (London: Edward Arnold, 1991), pp. 194–215.

BMIG (British Media Industry Group), *The Future of the British Media Industry* (London: BMIG, 1994).

BMIG (British Media Industry Group), *A New Approach to Cross-Media Ownership* (London: BMIG, 1995).

Booz Allen (and Hamilton), *Subscription Television: A Study for the Home Office* (London: HMSO, 1987).

Briggs, Asa, *Competition 1955–74: Volume 5 of The History of Broadcasting in the United Kingdom* (Oxford: Oxford University Press, 1995).

Brittan, Samuel, 'The Case for the Consumer Market', in Cento Veljanovski (ed.), *Freedom in Broadcasting* (London: Institute of Economic Affairs, 1989).

Brittan, Samuel, 'Towards a Broadcasting Market: Recommendations of the British Peacock Committee', in Jay Blumler and T. J. Nossiter (eds), *Broadcasting Finance in Transition* (Oxford: Oxford University Press, 1991).

Brown, Kevin, 'Labour Backs Off Threat to Murdoch', *Financial Times*, 24 March 1995, p. 7.

Butler, E., Pirie, M. and Young, P. *The Omega File: A Comprehensive Review of Government Functions* (London: Adam Smith Institute, 1985).

Cable Authority, *Annual Report and Accounts*, 1984/6 (covers period 1 December 1984–31 March 1986); 1986/7 to 1989/90; and *Final Report and Accounts* (covers period 1 April–31 December 1990) (London: Cable Authority).

Cable Television Association, *The Cable TV and Telecom Yearbook 1993* (Dunstable: WOAC Communications Company, 1993).

Caine, Sir Sydney, *Paying for TV?* (London: Institute of Economic Affairs, 1968).

Channel Four, *Annual Report and Accounts*, 1982/3 to 1989/90, nine months to December 31 1990, 1991–5 (London: Channel Four).

Channel Four, *The Channel 4 Funding Formula – The Case for Abolition* (London: Channel Four, 1994).

Cheong, Ken and Foster, Robin, 'Auctioning the ITV Franchises', in Gordon Hughes and David Vines (eds), *Deregulation and the Future of Commercial Television* (Aberdeen: Aberdeen University Press, 1989), pp. 91–125.

Collins, Richard, *Television: Policy and Culture* (London: Unwin Hyman, 1990).

Collins, Richard, *Satellite Television in Western Europe*, Revised Edition (London: John Libbey, 1992).

Collins, Richard, Garnham, Nicholas and Locksley, Gareth, *The Economics of Television: The UK Case* (London: Sage, 1988).

Coopers & Lybrand, 'All Around the Houses: Facilities Survey 1996', *Broadcast in Production* (Supplement to *Broadcast* 5 July 1996), pp. 4–8.

CQT (Campaign for Quality Television), *The Broadcasting Bill: Takeovers and Quality* (London: CQT, 1990).

Craig, F.W.S., *British General Election Manifestos 1959–1987* (Aldershot: Parliamentary Research Services, 1990).

Curran, James and Seaton, Jean, *Power without Responsibility: The Press and Broadcasting in Britain*, third edition (London: Routledge, 1988).

Curtis, Liz, *Ireland: The Propaganda War* (London: Pluto, 1984).

Davenport, James, 'Starship Enterprises', *Fact* (PACT members monthly), May 1993, pp. 26–9.

Davidson, Andrew, *Under the Hammer – the ITV Franchise Battle* (London: Heinemann, 1992).

Davis, Jonathan, *TV, UK: A Special Report* (Peterborough, Cambridgeshire: Knowledge Research, 1991).

DNH (Department of National Heritage), *The Future of the BBC: A Consultation Document* (Green Paper) (London: HMSO, Cm. 2098, 1992).

DNH (Department of National Heritage), *The Future of the BBC: Serving the Nation, Competing World-wide* (White Paper) (London: HMSO, Cm. 2621, 1994).

DNH (Department of National Heritage), *Media Ownership: The Government's Proposals* (London: DNH, Cm. 2872, 1995a).

DNH (Department of National Heritage), *Digital Terrestrial Broadcasting* (London: DNH, Cm. 2946, 1995b).

DNH (Department of National Heritage), *Broadcasting Sports Rights: Informing the Debate* (London: DNH, 1996).

DTI (Department of Trade and Industry), *Competition and Choice: Telecommunications Policy for the 1990s* (London: HMSO, Cm. 1461, 1991).

DTI (Department of Trade and Industry), *Creating the Superhighways of the Future: Developing Broadband Communications in the UK* (London: HMSO, Cm. 2734, 1994).

DTI (Department of Trade and Industry), *The Regulation of Conditional Access Systems for Digital Television: Final Consultation Paper on Detailed Implementation Proposals* (London: DTI, 1996).

Dyas, Pamela, *How Not to Allocate TV4* (London: Bow Group, 1973).

Dyson, Kenneth and Humphreys, Peter (eds), *The Political Economy of Communications: International and European Dimensions* (London: Routledge, 1990).

EITF (Edinburgh International Television Festival) *The Television Book 1993*, edited by David Housham (London: Edinburgh International Television Festival, 1993).

Gamble, Andrew, *The Free Economy and the Strong State: The Politics of Thatcherism*, second edition (London: Macmillan, 1994).

Garnham, Nicholas, *Structures of Television*, revised edition (London: BFI, 1978).

GHS (General Household Survey), *Living in Britain: Results from the 1994 General Household Survey* (London: HMSO, 1996).

Goodfriend, Andre, 'Satellite Broadcasting in the UK', in Ralph Negrine (ed.), *Satellite Broadcasting: The Politics and Implications of the New Media* (London: Routledge, 1988).

Goodwin, Peter, 'Unemployment Trends', *Broadcast*, 15 March 1996, pp. 31–3.

Goodwin, Peter, 'Labouring under a Misapprehension', *Broadcast*, 8 July 1994.

Goodwin, Peter, 'A Green Light for the Moguls' Charter?', *British Journalism Review*, vol. 6 no. 1, 1995a.

Goodwin, Peter, 'Not Worth the Paper . . .', *Broadcast*, 24 March 1995, 1995b.

Goodwin, Peter and Stevenson, Wilf, *Responses to the Green Paper* (London: BFI, 1994).

Graham, Andrew and Davies, Gavyn, 'The Public Funding of Broadcasting', in Tim Congdon et al, *Paying for Broadcasting: The Handbook* (London: Routledge, 1992), pp. 167–221.

Green, David G., *The New Right: The Counter-Revolution in Political, Economic and Social Thought* (Brighton: Wheatsheaf, 1987).

Harvey, Sylvia, 'Channel 4 Television: From Annan to Grade', in Stuart Hood (ed.), *Behind the Screens: The Structure of British Television in the Nineties* (London: Lawrence & Wishart, 1994), pp. 102–32.

Henley Centre, *Media Futures 1993* (London: Henley Centre, 1993).

Herzel, Leo, 'Public Interest and the Market in Color Television', *University of Chicago Law Review*, vol. 18, Summer, 1951, pp. 802–16.

Hobsbawm, Eric, *Age of Extremes: The Short Twentieth Century 1914-1991* (London: Michael Joseph, 1994).

HoC (House of Commons Trade and Industry Committee), *Optical Fibre Networks* (London: HMSO, 1994).

Hollins, Timothy, *Beyond Broadcasting: Into the Cable Age* (London: BFI for the Broadcasting Research Unit, 1984).

Home Affairs Committee (House of Commons), *The Future of Broadcasting*, vol. I (Report together with the Proceedings of the Committee) (London: HMSO, 1988).

Home Affairs Committee (House of Commons), *The Future of Broadcasting*, vol. II (Minutes of Evidence and Appendices) (London: HMSO, 1988).

Home Office, *Broadcasting* (London: HMSO, Cmnd. 7294, 1978).

Home Office, *Direct Broadcasting by Satellite* (London: HMSO, 1981).

Home Office, *Broadcasting in the '90s: Competition, Choice and Quality* (London: HMSO, Cm. 517, 1988).

Home Office and Department of Industry, *The Development of Cable Systems and Services* (London: HMSO, 1983).

Hood, Stuart and O'Leary, Garret, *Questions of Broadcasting* (London: Methuen, 1990).

Hunt, Lord (of Tamworth), *Report of the Inquiry into Cable Expansion and Broadcasting Policy* (London: Home Office, 1982).

Hutton, Will, *The State We're In* (London: Jonathan Cape, 1995).

IBA (Independent Broadcasting Authority) *Annual Reports* (London: IBA).

IBA (Independent Broadcasting Authority), *The IBA's Response to the Government's White Paper on Broadcasting* (London: IBA, 1989).

Isaacs, Jeremy, *Storm Over 4: A Personal Account* (London: Weidenfeld & Nicolson, 1989).

ITAP (Cabinet Office Information Technology Advisory Panel), *Cable Systems* (London: Cabinet Office, 1982).

ITC (Independent Television Commission), *Invitation to Apply for Channel 3 Regional Licence (Draft for Consultation)* (London: ITC, 1990a).

ITC (Independent Television Commission), *Invitation to Apply for Channel 3 National Licences (Draft for Consultation)* (London: ITC, 1990b).

ITC (Independent Television Commission), *Invitation to Apply for Channel 3 Regional Licences* (London: ITC, 1991a).

ITC (Independent Television Commission), *Invitation to Apply for the Channel 3 Breakfast-Time Licence* (London: ITC, 1991b).

ITC (Independent Television Commission), *Trends in Viewing in Cable TV Homes 1990–1995* (London: ITC, 1996).

ITC (Independent Television Commission), *Annual Report and Accounts*, 1991–6 (London: ITC).

ITVA (Independent Television Association), *A Response to the Government's White Paper* (London: ITVA, 1989).

Jakubowicz, Karol, 'Begin with the BBC', *Fact* (PACT members monthly), May 1993, p. 23.

Lambert, Stephen, *Channel Four: Television with a Difference?* (London: BFI, 1982).

Lawson, Nigel, *The View fom No. 11: Memoirs of a Tory Radical* (London: Bantam Press, 1992).

Leapman, Michael, *The Last Days of the Beeb* (London: Allen & Unwin, 1986).

Littleboy, P., Street, S. and Isard, P., *The Prospects for Cable TV in the UK* (London: Williams de Broe Hill Chaplin & Co., 1982).

Miller, Nod and Allen, Rod, *And Now for the BBC .. : Proceedings of the 22nd University of Manchester Broadcasting Symposium* (London: John Libbey, 1991).

Milne, Alasdair, *DG: The Memoirs of a British Broadcaster* (London: Coronet, 1989).

MMC (Monopolies and Mergers Commission), *The British Broadcasting Corporation and Independent Television Publications Limited* (London: HMSO, Cmnd. 9614, 1985).

MMC (Monopolies and Mergers Commission), *Labour Practices in TV and Film-Making* (London: HMSO, Cm. 666, 1989).

MMC (Monopolies and Mergers Commission), *Television Broadcasting Services* (London: HMSO, Cm. 2035, 1992).

Mowlam, Marjorie, '21st Century Media: A Discussion Paper', in *21st Century Media* conference brochure (London: 1994).

Murdoch, Rupert, 'Delivering Investment and Innovation', *House Magazine*, 29 May 1995, p. 20.

National Heritage Committee (House of Commons), *The Future of the BBC*, vols. 1 and 2 (London: HMSO, 1993).

Negrine, Ralph, 'New Media in Britain: Is There a Policy?', in Kenneth Dyson and Peter Humphreys (eds), *Broadcasting and New Media Policies in Western Europe* (London: Routledge, 1988).

Neil, Andrew, Speech to 1991 Edinburgh International Television Festival (transcript from News International Press Office, 1991).

NERA (National Economic Research Associates), *Methods of Media Market Measurement: A study for the Department of National Heritage* (London: NERA, 1995).

Neuman, W. Russell, *The Future of the Mass Audience* (Cambridge: Cambridge University Press, 1991).

Noam, Eli, *Television in Europe* (New York: Oxford University Press, 1991).

Nossiter, T.J., 'British Television: A Mixed Economy', in Home Office, *Research on the Range and Quality of Broadcasting Services: A Report for the Committee on the Financing of the BBC* (London: HMSO, 1986).

O'Malley, Tom, *Closedown? The BBC and Government Broadcasting Policy, 1979–92* (London: Pluto Press, 1994).

Paulu, Burton, *Television and Radio in the United Kingdom* (London: Macmillan, 1981).

Peacock, Professor Alan (Chair), *Report of the Committee on the Financing of the BBC* (London: HMSO, Cmnd. 9824, 1986).

Phillips, William, 'Casual Affairs', *Broadcast*, 3 February 1995, pp. 20–1.

Phillips, William, 'In Space, You're Not Alone', *Broadcast*, 22 February 1996, p. 21.

Pilkington, Harry (Chair), *Report of the Committee on Broadcasting* (London: HMSO, Cmnd. 1753, 1962).

Potter, Jeremy, *Independent Television in Britain Volume 3: Politics and Control 1968–80* (London: Macmillan, 1989).

Potter, Jeremy, *Independent Television in Britain Volume 4: Companies and Programmes 1968–80* (London: Macmillan, 1990).

Price Waterhouse, *Television Licence Fee: A Study for the Home Office* (Management Summary) (London: HMSO, 1990).

Price Waterhouse, *Production '95: The Results of the 1995 Price Waterhouse/PACT Survey of UK Independent Production Companies* (London: PACT, 1995).

Riddell, Peter, *The Thatcher Era: And its Legacy* (Oxford: Basil Blackwell, 1991).

Saatchi & Saatchi, *The Media Landscape: Now to 1995* (London: Saatchi & Saatchi Compton Ltd, 1987).

Scannell, Paddy, 'Britain: Public Service Broadcasting, from National Culture to Multiculturalism', in Marc Raboy (ed.), *Public Broadcasting for the 21st Century* (Luton: University of Luton Press, 1996), pp. 23–41.

Scannell, Paddy and Cardiff, David, *A Social History of British Broadcasting Volume One 1922–1939: Serving the Nation* (Oxford: Basil Blackwell, 1991).

Schumpeter, Joseph. *Capitalism, Socialism and Democracy* (New York Harper, 1942).

Sendall, Bernard, *Independent Television in Britain Volume 1: Origin and Foundation 1966–62* (London: Macmillan, 1982).

Shawcross, William, *Rupert Murdoch* (London: Chatto & Windus, 1993).

Smith, Anthony, *The Shadow in the Cave* (London: Quartet, 1976).

Sparks, Colin, 'Independent Production: Unions and Casualization', in Stuart Hood (ed.), *Behind the Screens: The Structure of British Television in the Nineties* (London: Lawrence & Wishart, 1994), pp. 133–54.

Sparks, Colin, 'The Future of Public Service Broadcasting in Britain', *Critical Studies in Mass Communication*, 12, 1995, pp. 325–41.

Stevenson, Wilf and Smedley, Nick, *Responses to the White Paper: Broadcasting Debate 3* (London: BFI, 1989).

Syfret, Toby, 'Paved with Gold', *Cable and Satellite Europe*, October 1996, pp. 45–50.

Thatcher, Margaret, *The Downing Street Years* (London: Harper Collins, 1993).

Tomos, Angharad, 'Realising a Dream', in Simon Blanchard and David Morley (eds), *What's this Channel Four?* (London: Comedia, 1982).

Trethowan, Ian, *Split Screen* (London: Hamish Hamilton, 1984).

Tully, Mark, 'An Ill Wind of Change on the Airwaves' (edited transcript of address to the Radio Academy Festival in Birmingham), *Guardian*, 14 July 1993, p. 6.

UNESCO, *Statistical Yearbook 1989* (Paris: UNESCO, 1989)

Veljanovski, C. G. and Bishop, W. D., *Choice by Cable: The Economics of a New Era in Television*, Hobart Paper 96 (London: Institute of Economic Affairs, 1983).

Whitelaw, William, *The Whitelaw Memoirs* (London: Aurum Press, 1989).

Williams, Raymond, *Television: Technology and Cultural Form* (London: Fontana/Collins, 1974).

Woolf, Myra and Holly, Sara, *Employment Patterns and Training Needs* (London: Skillset, 1994).

# INDEX